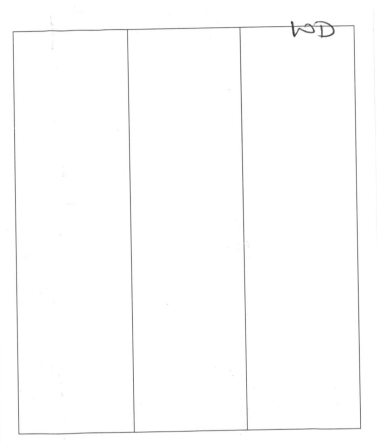

Down MEMORY LANE

This edition first published in the UK in 2009
By Green Umbrella Publishing

www.gupublishing.co.uk

Publishers Jules Gammond and Vanessa Gardner

Creative Director: Kevin Gardner

Picture Credits: Getty Images, Leonie Schwarz and Harry Harris

Printed and bound by J. H. Haynes & Co. Ltd., Sparkford

ISBN: 978-1-906635-64-0

Harry Harris is a Double winner of the prestigious British Sports Journalist of the Year award, and he is the only football writer to win the coveted British Variety Club of Great Britain Silver Heart for Contribution to Sports Journalism. Harry is also a Double winner of the Sports Story of the Year award, the only journalist ever to win this accolade twice.

Harry appears regularly as an analyst on football related matters on all major TV news and sports programmes and channels, including *Richard & Judy* and *Newsnight*, *BBC News*, *ITV News at Ten*, *Channel 5 News*, plus Sky and Setanta. He is also a regular on Radio 5 Live, Radio 4, and talkSPORT. He has been interviewed on *Football Focus*, appeared on the original *Hold The Back Page* and Jimmy Hill's *Sunday Supplement* on Sky.

Harry is arguably the most prolific writer of best selling football books of his generation. Among his 60 books are the highly acclaimed best seller *Pelé – His Life and Times*, plus *All The Way Jose*, *Chelsea Century*, and *Wayne Rooney – The Story of Football's Wonder Kid*, a series of autobiographies for Ruud Gullit, Paul Merson, Glenn Hoddle, Gary Mabbutt, Steve McMahon, Terry Neill, and of course, Bill Nicholson's *Glory, Glory – My Life With Spurs*. Plus biographies on Jurgen Klinsmann, Sir Alex Ferguson, Jose Mourinho, Terry Venables, Zola and Vialli. He also wrote George Best's last book, and best seller, *Hard Tackles and Dirty Baths*.

Harry has written one of the most influential football columns in the country for three decades. He has worked for the *Daily Mail*, *Daily Mirror*, *Daily Express*, *Daily Star*, *Sunday Express* and *Star on Sunday*, nearly 30 years as the No 1 football writer on a succession of top newspapers.

Harry is now head of communications, PR and media for an exciting new entertainment and icons/events company Football Nights, with John Hollins as consultant which has already had highly successful charitable events at Stamford Bridge and the David Beckham Academy.

Down MEMORY LANE

A Spurs Fan's View Of The Last Fifty Years

Written By Harry **Harris**

To my (not so) mad Mum Sara.

With special thanks

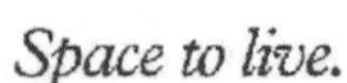

David Wilson Homes

Contents

Acknowledgments.

Top of my list is the FA's first independent chairman, Lord David Triesman of Tottenham and my deepest appreciation for his kind words in his preface.

Same applies to Steve Perryman, whose fierce tackle in his prime is only matched by some of the acidic words he had to say about me, together with any back handed praise. Stevie P hasn't changed.

Thanks also to another Spurs legend, Glenn Hoddle for also penning a foreword for this book.

My thanks too goes to my publisher Vanessa Gardner, Spurs supporting Carl Edwards for his encouragement, my editor Rebecca Ellis and designer Kevin Gardner, all at Green Umbrella.

To Paul Barber, the Spurs commercial manager, Donna Cullen, director of communications at Tottenham Hotspur plc, for all her help and encouragement, Press Officer John Fennelly and to Victoria Howarth heading up the club's retail department.

To Brian Reade, former *Daily Mirror* colleague, who suggested I wrote a book about Spurs when I congratulated him on his brilliant account of a lifetime supporting Liverpool.

And of course, my lovely wife and best friend, Linda for all her invaluable support (although lots of her support goes to Chelsea!)

Foreword By Glenn Hoddle.

The one thing I have had in common with Harry, is that we are both Spurs fans, who coincidently first went to watch the team at the same age of eight.

My first game was a reserve match at the Lane against Leicester, when I went with a friend and his dad, and then my dad took me to my first big game, Spurs v Forest. I was hooked.

I don't know why I was hooked, it was just the whole experience, the smell of the grass, the whole event of such a big stadium packed with fans, the noise, the atmosphere, and watching such talents as Jimmy Greaves.

I lived in Harlow and that was a huge catchment area for Spurs supporters, even more so then than it is now. I remember turning up at Harlow Town station to catch the train with my dad to White Hart Lane station, and Harlow was just as packed as White Hart Lane, the trains were full and it was a journey I was soon to take every Tuesday and Thursday evening once I signed schoolboy forms for the club at the age of 11.

In those days the schoolboys and apprentices were given tickets for the game, and we sat on these little benches in the front of the stand, where we had the most incredible pitch side view watching some immense talents such as Martin Chivers, Alan Mullery, Martin Peters, Phil Beal and Mike England.

We sat so close to the action, no more than a couple of yards from the white line, that you could almost touch the players, and you could even smell the liniment oils on their muscles. You could hear the players' verbal exchanges with each other, and feel the crunching tackles, aspects of the game you never appreciated in the stands.

I was a skilful player who wanted to do the right things, but I was also quite small as a 10 and 11 year old, very thin, and one game watching Mike England and Peter Osgood kicking lumps out of each other gave me quite a different perspective of a profession I was determined to follow. The centre-forward and centre-half were giants who were elbowing and kicking to such an extent I could hear and virtually feel the thumps against each player's shin pads. It made me appreciate that this game was not just all about scoring goals and making goals, but also about the physical pain that you would need to experience. For a creative player, this made an enormous impact on me at such an early age. It was a rude awakening.

My favourite player? Funnily enough, even though I was and I am still a huge Spurs fan my favourite player was George Best. He was the greatest individual I saw as a kid. It was such a great pleasure when Manchester United came to town and I could see Best. I loved to watch Best, Law and Charlton. I remember sitting behind the goal at the Lane when all three played against Spurs, it was a wonderful experience.

Bill Nicholson signed me as a youth player, and he even picked me once to sit on the bench for a European Cup tie in Belgrade against Red Star and I can remember Harry when he was on the local paper, the *Weekly Herald* writing about me when I scored a hat-trick in the youth team.

Terry Neill was the manager when I first got selected for the first team, and Harry wrote an article about my emergence into the senior side coming through the ranks. When I made my debut coming on against Norwich, the headline in the *Herald* was one I shall never forget...

"And You Ain't Seen Nothing Yet..."

There was a smash hit record in the charts at the time, from Bachman Turner Overdrive and that was the catch line in it. It was typical of Harry's kind of journalism to try to jazz things up. I loved it, but my mum loved it even more and cut it out and stuck it in a scrap book.

I felt I had a lot in common with Harry at the time as his writing emphasised the Spurs tradition of playing stylish football and that is why he pushed for me to be in the team. I've no idea how much he influenced Terry Neill's decision to pick me, but he keeps telling me it was his idea!

Foreword By Steve Perryman.

Whatever I might think of Harry, and I have some very strong opinions, there is no doubt that he changed the face of local and national journalism.

When he arrived on the local *North London Weekly Herald*, my first impression was this was a guy who livened up the match reports. As a player, you are always protective of your own professional performance, and as captain of the side I felt a responsibility towards the entire team. So, I did not like the way he sometimes reported our games, there was a sharp edge we had not been used to from the local paper before.

But Harry did make the local paper more professional, and you would have to say, why not? However, we didn't sometimes like the way he stirred the waters, and of course, it didn't do him any harm as he made his reputation and moved onto the bigger stage with national newspapers.

On the national press, with papers such as the *Daily Mail*, the *Daily Mirror* for many years, and the *Daily Express*, I have read his columns with interest, as he does produce some thought provoking articles.

However, I cannot be honest with him unless I also state my opinion that I felt he wielded far too much influence with certain Spurs chairmen, namely Irving Scholar and Sir Alan Sugar.

I always felt he was in Scholar's camp when I was a player at the club, and I know they had a very close relationship so Harry had the inside track. I accept that Irving and Harry had the best interests of the club at heart as they are both Spurs fans but Irving was the first of the new breed of chairmen, and while his heart was in the right place as far as his love for Spurs, I did have my run ins with him over the 1984 UEFA Cup bonuses. Irving also drove his first manager Keith Burkinshaw potty with the amount of phone calls! That's not to say I didn't have my own dispute with the manager over a new contract!

As for Sugar, I felt, from working on the inside as Ossie's assistant, that Harry was a tool for Sugar, and for that reason I took a dislike to the way Harry operated as an ally of Sugar's which no doubt suited his career. In fairness I did have, and probably still do, have a jaundiced view of anything to do with Sugar, and I am not going to elaborate why. Perhaps Harry is a touch unfortunate that he has been dragged into it, from my view point of Sugar.

Harry used him as much as Sugar thought he was using Harry. The result was that Harry had exclusive stories and an incredible in with one of the most powerful men in the country. But this was MY club they were playing with, and so at times it all made me very angry.

I wouldn't describe Harry as one of the "suits" who were infiltrating the board rooms and having far too much influence on the management of the clubs, because he was a journalist doing his job and getting some damn good stories in his papers.

The reason I took an exception is that Harry never saw the real inside story of the Sugar regime with Sugar's appointed chief executive Claude Littner and the way he operated. The finer details of what really went on behind closed doors is for another day, when my book is published!

I was hopeful somewhere along the line someone would stand up and disagree with Sugar when it needed disagreement. Sugar had surrounded himself with too many yes men, like Littner.

Equally, I am not saying I am pro Terry Venables or anti him, nor am I saying I am pro or anti Sugar in their personal fight about what they got up to inside the club. So, perhaps it is harsh to blame Harry for doing his job and finding out as much as he could. Sugar though, I am sure, used Harry to gain information about the wider game. Sugar loves the press when it suits him but hates things in the press when they are critical of him. If it doesn't suit Sugar than there can be big trouble. Also, I felt the way he ran the club put extra pressure on his manager, and it became intolerable for Ossie and myself at times. Contrast that to the way Sir Alex Ferguson runs Manchester United, there are no directors interfering, nobody telling him who to buy or sell. Last season, he had five draws in as many games at the start of the season and it might have looked like a crisis time, but it wasn't. There was no panic and he went on to win the Premier League and the Champions League.

I had my run ins with Sugar when I was Ossie's assistant to the extent that I fell out of love with football and even Tottenham – that's how bad it got for me, anyway.

I am sure Harry will give his own unique insight into what he feels went on between Venables and Sugar in this book. And, if he's writing about 50 years as a Spurs fan, I am convinced it will be something no Spurs fan would want to miss. Equally, his take on the broader aspects of the game would be of immense interest to every fan of football. Even though I am sure it will be more subjective than objective!

Preface By Lord Triesman Of Tottenham.

The first time I went to Spurs was in 1952. My father, uncle and I could go when they could afford it, a consideration made rather more complex for my uncle by his deep interest in greyhounds and their unpredictable impact on his budget.

We would walk briskly up White Hart Lane from my parents' prefab, the adults full of earnest opinions about Ron Burgess and the extent of his greatness. I could follow none of it. But I did already have my own hero in Ted Ditchburn. A very small boy could at least imitate him by diving into the available muddy puddles on the rugby pitch at Tottenham Grammar School which could be reached through a hole in the fence on White Hart Lane.

Inside the ground at White Hart Lane, which is not in the Lane but off Tottenham High Road, of course, the greatest excitement was to be passed hand-to-hand over the heads of the men in the crowd until finally perched on a crash barrier at the front. This was a high octane journey almost like flying and it always seemed an improbable miracle that when passed back at the end I always ended up with my father. A huge family of people, completely unrelated by blood, looked after all the kids as their own. They later did the same for my stepsons as they made the same journey.

These rituals, before the all-seater stadia, will have been repeated the length and breadth of England. And so would be the ritual discussions on the walk to and from the ground, the painstaking analysis, the inevitable clashes of opinion. I well remember years later walking home with my father and uncle when my father would engage in his unrelenting gloom (a feat he even managed coming home from Wembley after Ricky Villa's stunning FA Cup goal). "That Jimmy Greaves. Why did we buy him? He's bone idle. He hung around the centre circle most of the game. He doesn't give a monkeys. No movement. Shameful". My uncle Norman quietly reminded my father, Mick, that Greaves had in fact scored twice in another very decent win. "Yes", said Mick, "but apart from that he was bone idle".

Every football fan will have similar memories and will probably reflect on how different things are now. Of course, Tottenham have never repeated the Greaves years in the stunning Blanchflower team. Nobody stands on the hard concrete of the East or any other stand. The Taylor Report rightly ended the occasional catastrophes with the welcome consequence that the crowd is also no longer so exclusively male.

No one, I suspect, would now pass their kids through the hands of so many strangers. Your responsibilities as parents would not withstand the scrutiny.

And a high proportion of the matches no longer take place on Saturdays let alone at 3pm. Sunday is the new Saturday. Or Monday. Or whenever the TV schedules demand.

These changes reflect on the surface the deeper and rather more difficult changes just below. In North Tottenham people had opinions about Bill Nicholson and the team formed in part because they saw them around the place. Many footballers lived in the same community. You knew whether they smoked or were fond of a drink. If a player or former player opened a tobacconist, managed a pub or had a small shop selling sports ties and medals, everyone knew it and most had been through the door. It was up-close and personal.

That did not mean that every story around North Tottenham was accurate or rumour substantiated. Whatever the ratio of fact and fiction, it was all part of life in our own community. Football and the life of Spurs as a club were community concerns; they were issues for our neighbourhood. Even those who moved from the housing estates in North Tottenham to Enfield, Hertfordshire or Chigwell still had their finger on the pulse through relatives who hadn't moved or from dropping into familiar shops on match days.

I run the risk that these observations will be dismissed as sentimental. I don't think so and in any case football is always a little sentimental. The FA Premier League is a huge and massively successful product for at least some of its clubs and it reaches way beyond those old communities because it is so exciting and full of international quality. Those clubs that have lifted their competitive standards beyond the mainstream of the FA Premier League do reach fans around the world. Some clubs will always be on the end of the joke that if you are a supporter the odds are you come from somewhere hundreds of miles away.

Now this is a remarkable development yet it has in many places increased the physical and emotional distance between club and community. Indeed, people living near many top clubs no longer expect to see a boy from their town in the team, no "Harmer the Charmer" for example. In some clubs they may see no more than a couple of players from the UK. Clubs are increasingly "international brands" whose product as a live experience just happens to be on offer in England.

It is always a relief at Tottenham that till now the core of the team has come from the British Isles.

Nonetheless, a child in Tottenham today would not see a modern manager on the local bus as I quite often saw Bill Nicholson and the increased distance, not least financial distance, between players, managers and supporters has changed the community feel and tradition.

The tradition is carried by a flood of memories. I still have the front page of the London evening papers when Spurs took on Benfica in 1962. Smith is compared with Eusebio and it is the front not the back page. I can close my eyes and still see John White's goal at Forest in the Double year in a 4-0 win, the first time I had seen a ball bent into an impossible parabola. And the second leg of the UEFA Cup final against Wolves (after we had brushed past Milan) when Mullery knocked himself out scoring a goal he didn't know he had scored. Ricky Villa weaving a spell of a goal when days before he had left the Wembley pitch looking like a man bound for the gallows. Steve Perryman's last epic season, an avenging angel, dealing one-by-one with anyone who had kicked Glenn Hoddle because they couldn't deal with him.

It all floods back right up to the present. Unravelling the Arsenal 5-1 in the second leg of the Carling Cup semi-final, and having become chairman of the FA, having to clap politely throughout.

I have always enjoyed Harry Harris' books because he reaches so well back through time to recapture the feelings of the moment, the emotion that goes alongside the facts. It is as true of his Spurs books as his major biographies of players like Pelé.

It must come from the raw, face-to-face experience of a football writer who came through local Tottenham journalism to top level national journalism and authorship. His readers can almost taste the words. I can only speculate but I think it is because he writes out of the heart of the community we are in danger of losing.

Of course, football is also about money, wages, agents, owners, triumphs and scandals because all of them populate football. No account would be complete without them. Yet, in another sense, it is not really about them at all. It is about passion, experience, devotion and memory among people who struggle these days to pay for a season ticket but simply must be at the Lane.

That is where their heart beats fastest. It is them, like all supporters in all clubs, that count.

David Triesman
Lord Triesman of Tottenham
Chairman
The Football Association

Introduction.

The first club to win a major European trophy, the first club to win the Double in the 20th century, a club synonymous with The Beautiful Game; it's tough to be proud and optimistic when your club are rock bottom with only two wins in the first eight league games, but Spurs are different and now they have recruited Harry Redknapp who will attempt a Houdini act to save the club from relegation.

So, there is no shame in rejoicing in Spurs' glorious past. It is a rich heritage of all that is good in football, the style, the attacking ethos, the philosophy of Danny Blanchflower, the grace of Alan Gilzean, the goalscoring phenomenon of Jimmy Greaves, the genius of Paul Gascoigne, the perfect passes of Glenn Hoddle, the start of the foreign revolution with Ossie Ardiles and Ricky Villa, and how Ossie's knees went all trembley on the way to a wonderful exhilarating FA Cup win with The Wembley Goal of All Time from Ricky, to Walking in a Jurgen Wonderland. Yes, even a German could become a hero in a club steeped in Jewish traditions.

For me, it's coming up to 50 years of supporting Spurs. Nearly half a century of loving a team through thick and thin, more recently through thin. But that makes the tears of joy at winning trophies, and winning in style, all the more pleasurable. It's time to relive some wonderful memories of Spurs' glorious past going back to the 1960s.

Juande Ramos won the League Cup after only a handful of games when taking over from the likable and passionate Martin Jol. But an isolated League Cup proved little more than a mirage. While it seemed such a bright idea at the time to lure the Spaniard to Spurs, after all he appeared to have the right CV with back to back UEFA Cups with Seville, it turned out to be a nightmare despite the deceptive euphoria of landing the Carling Cup. Even the arrival of Harry Redknapp might only bring temporary relief, and no Spurs fan can accept that mere survival is the most one can hope for from the season. The reality is that the best time to be a Spurs fan was during the glory days, when it was a blur of black and white memories on television, and the big named "foreign stars" came from Scotland, Ireland and Wales! And what great Jocks they were, with players such as Dave Mackay, and the Welsh epitomised by flying winger Cliff Jones and the Irish in the form of the captain of that famous Double team of 1961, Danny Blanchflower.

But the glory, glory days and European nights of real consequence will come again. Believe me. My dream for the future is to see Spurs in the Champions League. Yes, it can happen, it's not all Fantasy Football. Spurs were not so long ago labelled one of the Big Five. Now there is a Big Four; Manchester United, Chelsea, Arsenal and Liverpool.

However, there is a mini league of clubs aspiring to break the mould. It looked like it might be Spurs under Martin Jol with back to back fifth place finishes and the close, oh the so painfully close call to pip Arsenal.

It can happen, however much it is hard to believe right now!

Spurs have massive support, and their past glories still make them a big name in European football. Spurs' time will come again. Meanwhile, for me, it is time to reflect on those past glories, those legends that made the club so great, and to tell the most revealing stories.

As a fan I have been so fortunate that my job as a football reporter has given me enviable access to the team I love. There has been so much to marvel at on the pitch through the decades but it is the action off the field that I, unlike so many other fans, have been part of.

As a boy growing up kicking a ball around the streets of East London trying desperately to emulate my heroes I never thought for a second that one day I would be sitting in a famous Fleet Street haunt discussing death threats with Irving Scholar and trying to talk him out of selling the club, or being invited to Sir Alan Sugar's home when he first took over to get advise on dealing with Terry Venables. I have been in the thick of it and been privy to some amazing stuff. Not many fans get that close to the heart of their clubs.

I have gone from a youngster getting in through the Boys Entrance to watching from the press box where I got to meet, know and befriend chairmen, managers, players and staff inside the club, and even being invited into the director's box. There can't be many accounts of following football where the fan has been catapulted inside the club to discover the truths other fans never see.

So where did it all begin?

There is a public bench outside of the library opposite the famous Cockerel Clock in Tottenham High Road where my mad mum would wait patiently throughout the match before collecting me for the long bus journey back home.

Together we would make the pilgrimage to White Hart Lane from our home in East London, where the two of us lived at No 13 Pauline House, the third floor of a 17th storey block of basic facility council flats which housed the overflow from the already packed Jewish community in Brick Lane.

It was a short walk to the bus stop, but it was imperative to set off several hours before kick off, to allow for the hour ride to Tottenham High Road onboard the crowded No 149 old Routemaster. It was essential to arrive by around 1pm to join the queues at the time the gates were about to open. The queues were pretty long, quite quickly. This had become a popular venue.

I loved every minute of that bus ride; I became familiar with virtually every inch of road, each landmark, every building. The closer we got to the Tottenham ground the more excited I became.

There was a spring in my step when I leapt off the bus right outside of the ground. You were straight into the ambience of the whole football-spectator experience, nothing like it is today. There was a profusion of stalls selling collections of small, tin badges representing all the clubs. There were programme sellers on every corner, the air was alive with the raucous sound of rattles, graggers my old mum called them, that made such a din at home, but could hardly be heard above the noise of all the other rattles.

Attire was simple enough, a coveted Spurs scarf. No replica shirts with names of the stars and their numbers on the back. I did collect shirts, but they were purchased back in shops, without even the club's badge, let alone a name or number, and who would have thought of shirt sponsorship or billboard advertising? My dear old mum had to buy the badge separately and sow it on by hand or with the Singer sowing machine she used for the fur remnants. But no one thought of wearing those shirts to a game – it was far too cold.

One of my greatest pleasures was to visit the Spurs Supporters Club whose head offices were an old terraced house adjacent to the ground. The club sold all sorts of basic memorabilia, but my favourite was the upstairs section which sold photographs of action pictures of the matches, mostly around a month for the most up-to-date games before they were available. I spent all of my pocket money on those pictures, and as a special treat my mum would often buy one extra one. They took pride of place on my bedroom wall, with a Spurs rug by the side of the bed as a Christmas present. The really dedicated Spurs fans manned the shop and got to know my mum quite well and even gave her some discount on any extra pictures she purchased for me. They knew she couldn't really afford them.

A Spurs pencil or pen was a treasure in those days, compared to the lavish items on sale now.

After the thrill of the game, came the enjoyment of getting back home, waiting outside the corner shop for the Pink editions of the evening paper, a football special with the first match reports and pictures. They would be immediately cut out on returning home and stuck in the scrap book. I had dozens of scrap books, filled with the match reports of journalists such as Steve Curry and Nigel Clarke with whom I ended up working.

By far the biggest thrill was soaking up the atmosphere for the two hours before kick off. Taking in the smell of fried onions to accompany the hot dogs from the multitude of unofficial stands. Now of course it's smoked salmon bagels. Not that my mum ever thought about wasting money on those hot dogs; she packed sandwiches for me instead. I don't think the fact that they weren't Kosher put her off; it was the fact that it was far more cost effective to bring your own food.

At first I would pay the minimum entrance fee at the Boys Enclosure, and kept on going through that turnstile even when I was a year, maybe even two years too old. But it reached the stage, particularly as I was quite tall for my age, when there was no more fooling the gateman, or no longer could my mum persuade him to let me in for the cut price entrance fee. So my mum then came up with seats for the games. Sometimes, as I recall, she even managed to get herself into the ground without a ticket to keep a wary eye on me.

I was hooked and wanted to go to every game so it seemed a season ticket was more cost effective. However, there was a waiting list and it was highly unlikely that I would be able to get my hands on one of those coveted tickets so how my widowed mum managed to acquire one despite a 10-year long waiting list, let alone afford it, I shall never know. But she often performed acts bordering on miraculous to ensure her one and only son got what he wanted, which was a ticket to watch Spurs.

When she failed to beg, borrow or steal a Cup final ticket in 1962 when Spurs returned to Wembley after their formidable Double triumph the year before, I could tell she was never going to let me experience such disappointment again. She could tell how much it meant to me even though she knew that I was perhaps too young to be going off to join such a crush on my own, or be alone inside the stadium.

She made sure she got her hands on a Cup final ticket in 1967 for the all-London final between Spurs and Chelsea; it might have been on the cheap old benches at the front without the best view in the world, but it was a ticket for my first final nonetheless. Heaven. Thankfully Spurs won with Joe Kinnear and Terry Venables in their side, a couple of players with whom I would cross swords in later life when they became managers. While I got on well enough with Venables when I first got to know him as manager of Crystal Palace, our relationship was cemented when he worked for Irving Scholar, but deteriorated during his bitter conflict with Sir Alan Sugar. By contrast, Kinnear and I enjoyed a very sound working relationship, once or twice even meeting at social events and hitting it off.

So, it was as a fan that I idolised the likes of Kinnear, as the young glamour boy of that team, and yes, even Venables, despite the fact that he had a torrid time from most Spurs supporters who took an instant dislike to him as a player.

That was back in the early 1960s, and I've continued a journey as a fan and a journalist that has mostly centred around Spurs for all of my working life. I've not missed a Cup final since, mostly in the Wembley press box, and more lately in the privilege seats, none more so than the Carling Cup final when Spurs beat Chelsea, the first League Cup final in the new lavish £800m stadium where my wife, Linda and I were guests of the Football League and sponsors Carling. My thanks for that marvellous experience goes to Steve Bradley of Hill and Knowlton the public relations company charged with organising our five star lunch and prime location seats in the corporate sector.

So, from childhood beginnings standing for hours waiting to go into the cut price sector to the league's own hospitality section.

I have never forgotten how my love of Spurs began. Yet, sipping champagne with the movers and shakers who fashion the game always gives me a thrill and reminds me of how far one can go with sufficient will power, and no doubt some degree of aptitude for the profession. Most of all a passion for the sport.

It's been a long and tough journey, supporting Spurs, with many bizarre experiences along the way. Throughout that journey my mad mum has never been far behind, perhaps not in body, but in spirit. Even when I hit the dizzy heights of travelling around the world covering matches for the *Daily Mirror* and winning numerous awards along the way, my mum never thought I was being indulged enough so she sent me small food parcels by post! The jiffy bags that arrived at the office with cooked chicken in them became a source of much amusement to my *Mirror* colleagues. Never mind the fact that, at the peak of the *Mirror*'s powers, the expenses were virtually limitless, and the opportunities for fine dining immense, I knew it meant an awful lot to her to think her son was being well fed. For a good Jewish mother this was her lifelong duty.

It is now coming up to almost 50 years of supporting Spurs and I felt the time was right to celebrate my personal half century with some tales, many of them unexpected. The Carling Cup was a sound start, but the start of the 2008-09 season brought renewed misery for supporters who have been deprived for far too long of meaningful success.

The enforced sale of strikers Berbatov, Keane and Defoe in such a short space of time left Ramos struggling to fill the void. In the summer the club sold for as much as they bought. With one of their worst starts in 53 years, they stared up from the foot of the table. How embarrassing then, that while Spurs were propping up the entire Premier League, that Jol's new Hamburg team were top of the Bundesliga.

Out went Ramos and in came Harry Redknapp; from a succession of foreign bosses to one as English as pie and mash and as East End as jellied eels.

To analyse where it has all gone wrong is one issue which I will address in this book. More importantly for me, it's time to look back with pride at a club that has all the right credentials to be successful once more in the future.

It's been too long without a league title and another crack at the elusive European Cup. But still we dream on. I hope you enjoy reading the inside track on Spurs' glorious past as much as I have enjoyed writing it!

Harry Harris
January 2009

CHAPTER ONE

Spurs – An Early Love Affair…

I owe my mad mother an eternal apology. I am sure she was not mad. Obsessed. Most definitely. A typical Jewish mother? Yes. But she was even beyond that archetypal figure, beyond obsessed, she gave obsession a bad name. After the premature death of my father, Jack, at the age of 45, a painful and surprisingly rapid decline riddled with lung cancer, my mother became more than just a mum, she assumed the dual roles of both parents and as I am an only child she filled the void any siblings would have taken up. Sara was a one-off, believe me. She gave up the chance to re-marry even though she became engaged to the lead violinist in the Dorchester Hotel orchestra. When she found out that he had clipped me around the ear for being a pest in his West London flat, she refused to have anything to do with him. Considering we were banned from a Brighton hotel after I smashed a glass table top – by accident – it was clear she had a boisterous boy on her hands, but she coped alone.

She was an overbearing burden at times, but it's been almost 10 years since she died and I do miss her eccentricities now she's gone. She was far from being a likable character in her old age, but into their 80s such Jewish mothers can become more than a bit quirky. Yet, she was doggedly determined that her son should succeed, irrespective of her many personal sacrifices. Sara was passionate about my success, equally as interfering.

My passion was Spurs and football, and that kicked in from a very early age. The East End was the traditional catchment area for West Ham United support, and even more centrally, Leyton Orient. Heroes such as Bobby Moore were the lure for the Hammers, but there had been a sudden shift in the early 1960s towards North London and Spurs. The Double winning side of Bill Nicholson was my inspiration as the beautiful game played the way it should be, and a year later the arrival of Jimmy Greaves cemented my commitment to the cause. Jimmy Greaves was my hero. His goals were works of art, with grace and speed around the penalty area, as master of the goalscoring trade, a true match winner.

My hero-worshipping innocence heightened the sense of theatre and whenever I went to the Lane it was intensified. Having experienced that as a kid, it is imperative that the modern day footballer appreciates his responsibilities both on and off the field. Regrettably a minority still persist in abusing their status. The football authorities have a duty to clamp down, especially the FA whom I believe should stand up for the morals of the sport far more than they have done in the past. Having met Lord Triesman of Tottenham a few times now, and having spoken to the new independent chairman of the FA at great length about certain issues, I am encouraged that he will, indeed, shake up the FA, and stand up for these sort of important issues for his organisation.

There is no doubt that the actions of those who are idolised by the new generation of football fans have a huge influence over their young minds.

I can recall how I collected First Division team shirts, the old fashioned V-neck plain versions with no numbers or names on the back, and the badge had to be sown on by hand – or in Sara's case by her old Singer.

That black original Singer was the only source of income after my dad passed away when I was five. Jack was a gentle, kind hearted East End furrier, whose love of local boxing often had him splashing out on ring side tickets. In the few pictures I have of him, he is either sporting a dickie bow tie or is immaculate in tie and cuff links. With his other passion being poker, he managed to blow all the healthy weekly profits he made by each Monday.

I remember chasing up to the third floor workshop where he expertly stretched the leather backs of the animal skins onto boards, the wet skins allowed to dry to increase their size and accordingly their value. A handful of machinists put together the range of fur coats, shawls and accessories, and I am sure they made a small fortune. It all disappeared in the dark, heavy smoke filled poker rooms to which Jack was lured for the entire weekend, never sleeping, only losing whatever cash he had left after paying off his workers.

We lived in what seemed to someone small, a very big house, with a coal cellar that fascinated and scared me at the same time. An outside loo in the tiniest of back yards, and a football soon to become the most valued possession among the fort and toy racing cars.

I had pictures of my heroes on the wall, would use up my pocket money buying photographs they would sell in the Spurs Supporters Club, and my mum's presents usually had a Spurs flavour, such as a Spurs deep blue rug for the foot of my bed.

When I moved from Old Monteque Street just off Brick Lane to just off the Whitechapel Road, it coincided with having just scraped through the 11-plus and moving on to senior school, Davenant Foundation, an independent grammar.

There were precious few pieces of green areas in the vicinity but the streets were our football pitch, and so too was the school playground. Less than a quarter of a mile away lived Barry Silkman and his family. "Silky" went on to play for Orient, QPR and Manchester City, as well as moving abroad to Israel to play professionally. I got to know him well and enjoyed kicking a football around with him. While I dreamed about being a footballer, Barry made it, starring for Crystal Palace under Malcolm Allison, who took him onto Manchester City. Barry is now a football agent who has worked with Pini Zahavi, the world's No 1 super agent, on some deals.

My first choice career was to be a professional footballer. Regrettably I wasn't quite good enough. In fact "quite" kind of sounds as if I had a chance, half a chance. I had no chance. Yet my mad mum had somehow wangled me a trial with Spurs. She actually wrote to Bill Nicholson and got a reply!

When she showed me the forms, I was shocked. I filled them in, and sent them off. They requested dates of up and coming games, and I provided the club with the forthcoming Davenant Foundation grammar school's senior fixtures.

I was a goalkeeper who had made the senior side a year early, and played alongside Terry Brisley and Dennis Rolfe. I am convinced a scout watched me in a game against an England grammar school XI which Davenant lost 6-1, although I did save a late penalty (which was struck straight at me). After that "trial", the gossip was that Orient were keen on Brisley and Rolfe, and the East End club signed both of them as juniors.

I tried my luck with top amateur club, Enfield, which had a reputation of being not far short of being as professional as the actual Football League clubs. Myself and school chum (a boy by the name of Brown) travelled by bus. We were greeted by their manager, the team's former goalkeeper Tommy Lawrence, in a towel, fresh from the showers, who suggested we should join in the training and "enjoy ourselves". The training was so tough that I was sick after about half an hour, but managed to recover to continue and even play in a practice match. I was put out to left-back, and didn't do too badly but Brown played in his usual advanced midfield role and looked pretty good to me. But neither of us returned. It was far too far for us and the training put us off.

I thought the next best thing to playing would be reporting on football but the careers officer at school, who doubled in the role along with teaching History, suggested it would be just as hard to make it in journalism, as being a footballer, and I should think of a more practical career solution. I tried but I couldn't.

I set out to hone my journalistic skills, while still at school, by working on the school magazine, and taking school reports to the local paper, which they started to publish.

My school report dated July 24th 1968, had this to say from the headmaster, "Gave most useful help in preparing the school magazine." I became a well known face at the local paper, bombarding them with visits, and with reports of school events from sports days to open days, and organising photographers. I managed to wangle some work experience during the summer holidays. The school report, dated July 16th 1969, gave this assessment from the headmaster, "I appreciate his enthusiastic reporting of school events for local newspapers and I hope that his holiday job will help him."

I managed to get a job as the most junior of junior reporters in the smallest of branch offices in Loughton High Road for *The Independent* Group of newspapers. At first, it was the weekly round of local police station, fire brigade, local church and funeral parlour for any bits and pieces that might make some kind of interesting article. On a quiet week, I was told to take a ladder, place it outside of the offices and conduct a survey of how superstitious the local population might be, by seeing who walked round the ladder, rather than under it.

Naturally when the chance cropped up to cover local football teams, such as Harlow Town, I jumped at it. I liked the assignment so much that I ended up training with the club occasionally, and even dreamed of playing for the team. But a five a side game was about as close as I came. I still fancied myself as a goalkeeper, and took part in a five a side tournament at Haringey Sports Centre.

One of my boyhood idols as part of that wonderful Spurs Double team in 1961 was Cliff Jones. I was in awe of his courage and enthusiasm, his incredible ability to climb at the far post and score spectacular goals with his head for such a small man. That enthusiasm for the game continued to shine through when I met him when he was working as a fitness instructor and coach at the Haringey Sports Centre, and he actually played against me as part of that local five a side tournament. His feet were still lightning fast, and when he attacked my goal, it was impossible for me to judge which direction the ball was going. He scored fives times past me; he would chip it over me if I came flying out, or take the ball round me if I hesitated, or simply slot the ball into the corner with uncanny precision. Yes, it was time to give up the dream.

The best part was getting the opportunity to chat with him and to discover such an endearing guy, totally unassuming, anything but the superstar one would associate with such a high profile and hugely successful international. Maybe it was the era? The player still had some sort of affinity with the fans. Although they were highly paid, the differential was far less than it is now. Cliff was a modest man, of modest means, and a truly nice guy.

I am sure many of the modern day players are the same, nice guys. But if Cliff Jones was playing today he would be worth £20m in the transfer market and command £100,000 a week in wages. He would be a multi millionaire who wouldn't need to be a fitness instructor in the local sports centre to supplement his income after finishing an illustrious career laden with medals and plaudits.

I have had the pleasure of chatting to Cliff on the numerous occasions our paths have crossed, mainly at games at the Lane. Cliff is such a well-mannered individual, he suppresses a burst of laughter whenever I remind him of that time I tried to prevent him scoring a bag full of goals in that tournament.

I started out early with an unpaid, charitable weekly radio show on hospital radio at Whips Cross in Leytonstone. My co-host was the football writer from the rival local paper *The Guardian*, Steve Tongue, who went on to become one of the country's most respected football correspondent's of *The Independent on Sunday*.

(Thats him, in the picture on colour page 5, holding the pen and pretending to make notes!) I'm the guy with the head phones draped, professionally looking, over my shoulders, next to Jimmy Neighbour, the young Spurs winger of the time.

Jimmy was one of the nicest people I have ever had the pleasure to meet in football in all these years. The Chingford born footballer broke into the Spurs team at an early age, and had enormous talent, but never seemed to be able to produce enough of it consistently to tie down a regular place, which at times he deserved, but maybe not all the time. His talent was worth persevering with and Bill Nicholson encouraged him a lot. As he developed as a player, he always had time for the young journalist making his way at the *North London Weekly Herald*, and it was a pleasure to have known him.

The changing face of the media and how they operated is capsulated in the picture of me (colour page 6, A), sitting on a grass verge alongside a couple of players, watching the training at the club's old headquarters at Cheshunt. I am next to centre-forward Ian Moores.

Those were the days when the media had access to the Cheshunt facilities, invited usually to watch one session of pre-season training before an interview with Bill Nicholson. The next time such an invite might be forthcoming would be on the eve of a Cup final.

The media would also travel with the squad and stay in the same hotel, although the press would travel to the games in their own coach. A separate coach would also be provided for the excursions to and from the airport. But there were numerous opportunities to meet up with the players for private chats, at the airport waiting to check in, at the other end waiting to collect the luggage, and also bumping into them at the hotel.

Now it's vastly different. The media invariably travel independently. The media never share a team hotel, apart from in exceptional circumstances.

CHAPTER TWO

The Nicholson Years.

David Leggett was the outgoing Spurs specialist full-time reporter for the *North London Weekly Herald* group of newspapers. His primary task was to follow Spurs home and away as well as in Europe. He would then research the reserves and youth team. The pages of the broadsheet newspaper also carried the Arsenal match reports and news. He had been enticed away from the local paper with a good offer to cover football in Scotland for a national and I was the only one left with the small local paper group with any kind of football knowledge, but more importantly with a burning ambition to cover Spurs. This wasn't a job, it was like winning the lottery (not that the lottery had been invented yet). Wow, I couldn't wait.

It was the summer closed season break and manager Bill Nicholson hadn't been away for much of a holiday, he was the first back eager to prepare for the new season. David had made arrangements to say his farewells to Bill and to introduce me as his successor.

Just the thought of meeting the great "Billy Nick", manager of the first Double winning side of the 20th century, filled me with apprehension and excitement all at the same time.

I took my usual route to the main *Herald* offices in Tottenham High Road, from Gants Hill, via the Green Line bus that stopped at the top of my long road of terraced houses.

Gants Hill is the posh annex to the East End, the first over spill from that Brick Lane Jewish community that wanted to better themselves, and had got a decent job and could raise their first mortgage. My mum helped finance that first mortgage and my newly promoted position of sports editor underpinned the mortgage repayments. My mum though, was reluctant to move away from the East End, and that's an understatement. Sara blocked it out of her mind completely that I had gone ahead and purchased my first property in Gants Hill, and that the removal day had finally arrived.

I had packed all my worldly belongings into two suitcases. But she just sat in her favourite armchair and remained there when the door bell rang and the removal men were invited in and had taken out what little furniture we possessed, (including her sowing machine from which she scraped a meagre living with bits of fur scraps she meticulously sowed into, at first fur coats, but as the material ran out, into fur hats and shawls). Sara's argument was that it would become even tougher to beg for more fur scraps from her old contacts and friends if she moved out of the East End where she was also top of the list for charitable hand outs of food and clothing. In desperation I put down a bed sheet (I can recall to this day, that it was a hideous yellow, white and red striped effect) in the middle of the living room floor and just shoved her clothes and bits and pieces into it, tied it in a knot and loaded it and her on to the removal van.

My daily routine had been to catch the bus from Gants Hill to Tottenham, then to walk down the three quarters of a mile to the offices just a few hundred yards from the Spurs ground. But this journey was vastly different. It seemed to take three times as long, even though I wanted it to take half the time. I wanted to be there to meet Bill Nicholson, and yet it was the most frightening prospect of my entire life.

It was a relief to be finally there, outside of Billy Nick's office waiting to go in. Once through that door, David did the customary "handing over" and left me alone with Bill for a quick chat and brief starting of the process of "getting to know you".

"Now then", enquired Bill, trying, no doubt, to be kind to the local boy who must have looked nervous, because I was so nervous, it was hard to prevent myself from trembling. But Bill's tone was kind and considerate. Suddenly I grew in confidence. He could sense here was a boy starting out in his career, and he genuinely wanted to help. I could sense it. "When would you like to see me?" he continued.

I replied, "As I have to write about the team each week with a Wednesday deadline and early Thursday morning for any midweek game, could I see you every Monday morning?" There was a few seconds silence. Just enough to add the rider... "I feel it is vitally important to get your perspective, to find out what the club is thinking, which means what you are thinking and for the local paper to reflect that, and to support the club where ever possible." Do you know, I never rehearsed that. It came to me. I had thought and thought about what I should say, and nothing I could think of in advance seemed the least bit appropriate. But once in front of Bill, it just came to me. I am sure I struck a chord with him.

Bill smiled and he leaned towards me in his chair, in a way you can imagine if you were one of his players and he was about to give out an important instruction, where you had better make sure you listened to every word.

"Your predecessor, Dave, saw me once a season. That was it". There were a few more seconds silence. It seemed like half an hour. Then he smiled again.

"Come and see me Monday morning before training, here in my office, and we shall see how we go, but remember, once a season your predecessor saw me."

Every Monday morning before training for the next seven years Bill Nicholson saw me and we spoke for around 15 minutes as he gave me a fully comprehensive run down on everything that went on inside the club, except of course, those issues he wanted to keep to himself, but as the years went by he confided in me much more.

It wasn't long before a string of daily national newspapers had my number and would ring me constantly for inside information. Naturally they paid me for it, but I never parted with any information I knew Bill would not want me to. No amount of money would have persuaded me or tempted me to break faith with Bill Nicholson. No way. I looked upon Bill almost as a father figure and there were times when I think he almost treated me like a son.

The papers weren't the only ones itching for the inside track, but there was one guy I did confide in, and he was an avid Arsenal fan, Lawrence Marks. He was a reporter on the *Weekly Herald*, on the news desk. Lawrence was writing a book at the time about Ruth Ellis and asked for my help, which I gave to him, and he caught me by surprise by mentioning me in the credits to that book. Lawrence and I would go out to lunch most days, to the nearby greasy spoon café, whose owners were big Spurs fans. They were also part of the big local Greek community. We loved their home made moussaka, and even when it wasn't on the menu, the dear old mama would come out of the kitchen to say hello and ask us if she should whip up a moussaka for us – and invariably we accepted. Over lunch Lawrence was hungry for his football gossip, particularly if it had any connection to his beloved Arsenal.

Lawrence went on to become one of the world's most successful comedy writers with his partner Maurice Gran with hit shows such as *Birds of a Feather* and *Goodnight Sweetheart*. In later years I was to meet up again with Lawrence and got to know Mo & Lo well. We came close to collaborating on a football book, but it never quite worked out.

One of my greatest achievements was to persuade Bill Nicholson to write his memoirs. Oddly enough, it was another Arsenal fan who helped.

Alan Samson was the commissioning editor at the time with Macmillan, and together with my good friend and *Daily Mail* colleague Brian Scovell we collaborated in writing the Nicholson autobiography *Glory, Glory – My Life With Spurs*. Nicholson was most reluctant but I nagged him for so long he finally relented. I went round to his modest semi-detached within walking distance of the Spurs stadium for a cup of tea and hours of chat about his beloved Spurs.

I now have only two copies left of his book, one of them signed by Bill and all the Double team who turned up for the launch of the book in 1984.

Among my souvenirs are three pictures of Bill Nicholson, in faded black and white.

My treasured picture is of myself with Nicholson in his office (colour page 6, B). You can spot the sparseness of it all, just a newspaper fixture list pinned to his otherwise empty noticeboard. He posed reading a copy of the official club handbook that recorded the historic first Double of the century in 1961. And, yes, it was hard to force Bill to smile for the camera, but it's a measure of our relationship that he did!

The next snap (colour page 7, C), is taken two days after Nicholson had resigned following a "humiliating" midweek 4-0 home defeat by Middlesbrough. The directors persuaded Bill to stay on for a two week transitional period, and when Nicholson appeared before the fans prior to the home game with Derby he received a rapturous standing ovation. There in the far left hand corner is yours truly taking notes in the press box.

The third image (colour page 7, D), is of John Pratt, one of Nicholson's most loyal and hard working midfield players, signing a ball autographed by the entire Spurs team as one of the summer prizes in the *North London Weekly Herald*.

It is with great fondness that I look back on the help that Bill Nicholson gave me in my career.

After one European tie, the press gathered around the manager outside of the stadium in the car park, very much as the press interviews were conducted in those days. Spurs had beaten Grasshoppers of Zurich 5-1, but in reality, Nicholson's team had actually been outplayed! Spurs had about seven break aways from which they scored five times, and the man of the match was Pat Jennings for a string of world class saves.

Of course, I was always buzzing with questions and came up with the line "Are you convinced Spurs will get through after the way Grasshoppers played?" Nicholson looked at me as if I had just arrived from Mars and didn't have a clue what I was talking about and, of course he was dead right. A man of such vast experience and knowledge knew that such a result away from home guaranteed your path to the next round, and that it would be a vastly different proposition when Grasshoppers came to fortress White Hart Lane one of the most feared venues in European football at that time. He just laughed and said "Are you mad?" and moved on to the next question.

It was a good lesson for the local newspaper boy. Think before you ask a question and don't make yourself out to look like an idiot.

One day I turned up around five minutes late for one of Bill's always illuminating Monday morning briefings, which usually digressed to other issues and plenty of off the record stuff. It was a time that you wouldn't want to miss for the world. Usually I was always sitting outside his office waiting to be called in, I am sure Bill could smell my eagerness for his company and his information. Bill was also a stickler for punctuality and I am sure he liked the fact that I was always on time. However, not this time. I was only five minutes late, and I ran the last few hundred yards from the bus stop, and must have smelt of something rather different than the normal eagerness. I started to make some excuse about transport, and also pointed out that I had an unforeseen problem with the one watch I owned; that it had stopped only yesterday and although it kind of started up again, it was not as reliable as it was which had made me miss a bus from Gants Hill.

The next Monday I came for my weekly chat in his office. Needless to say, I was about an hour early. No way was I going to be late again; far too embarrassing. Before I could say a thing, Bill told me that he was really upset that I was late the previous week, and even more perturbed that my only watch had stopped. He reached into the top draw of his desk, and pulled out a handsome looking case. He handed it over to me.

"Now," he said with a huge smile, "never tell me your watch has stopped again."

Inside the case was a gold watch inscribed with AC Milan, which had been presented to him by the Italian giants after a game with Spurs. He told me how he had been called up by the president and handed the watch in their board room with great applause from everyone present, in recognition of his stature in the English game. He had kept it with pride, but never had any cause to wear it, and rather than letting it go to waste, thought I could make good use of it. I didn't know what to say, apart from a bumbling and very humble "thank you".

Often as I made my way home from the *North London Weekly Herald* offices late at night, particularly on edition times, I would walk past Nicholson's office and I could see the light still on. He lived and breathed the club, spending more time in his office than he did at home in his own bed. He travelled the country watching games, scouring the clubs for talent, even north of the border. Now that should be done by his scouts, but he always wanted to see the players for himself, especially the ones he was thinking of signing and he would insist on seeing them a few times.

When he gave me a detailed list of the reasons why he decided to quit when he did, one of them was the stress. Personally, I didn't set much store by this reason, although I think he preferred people to think that, rather than criticise others, which was never the way he went about his job.

He told me, though, the reasons behind his long hours and devotion to Spurs, "In all those 16 years I never had a long holiday, not even during the close season. I popped into the ground every Sunday to work, and kept my house in nearby Creighton Road so I could be minutes from the ground. We could have moved out to a bigger, detached house in Hertfordshire, where many Tottenham players lived, but it would have meant spending more time travelling. Being nearby, I was sometimes able to return home for lunch with Darkie (his wife), otherwise she would rarely have seen me. Most evenings, I attended matches all over the country and sometimes in Scotland. Being in such a state through overwork was entirely my own fault. No one asked me to work all day and every day. But I ran the club and wouldn't trust the smallest job to anyone else. I wouldn't delegate, which perhaps was wrong, but it was my way of working and it had been successful.

"I had felt it was essential to have organisation and method, but now that wasn't enough. New thoughts and ideas were needed. I believed a new manager would provide them and also motivation which I felt was no longer coming from me. After our humiliating loss to Middlesbrough, I decided I could not remain any longer in my post. Not even Darkie knew of my decision. She heard about it on the radio the next morning."

I spoke with Bill about the appointment of his successor and he thought, after a lifetime at the club, that the board would have consulted him. They didn't. Yet, as we have seen with David Gill at Old Trafford, the Glazers and the chief executive, plan to consult with Sir Alex Ferguson about his successor. However there is still a distinct possibility that even Sir Alex, with all his phenomenal influence inside Old Trafford, could be treated similarly to Bill Nicholson. The problem is that Sir Alex will not have to live or die by the consequences of such a momentous decision that ultimately will have to be taken by the Glazers with input from Gill and perhaps from Sir Alex.

The Glazers cannot afford to simply go on Sir Alex's choice for his successor. For example, if Sir Alex chose Carlos Queiroz, the Glazers might want Roy Keane or Jose Mourinho, neither of whom would be top of Sir Alex's list.

Bill though, like Sir Alex, was sure he would do what was right for the club he loved. But the final decision was quickly taken out of his hands despite earlier suggestions that he would play a prominent role in choosing his successor. That hurt him, really hurt him, and no matter how much praise was heaped upon him for all of his successes, he left the club feeling that all his long service had really counted for little. He confided in me, "I naturally assumed I would be allowed to nominate my successor as manager of the club. After all, I had virtually run Tottenham for 16 years. The directors had had a comparatively easy time in those years, enjoying the matches and the glory and leaving me to take the strain. At Liverpool, the best run club in Britain (at least at the time Bill was telling me this story), Bill Shankly had attended the meeting of the directors which decided to appoint Bob Paisley to succeed him. And I have no doubt that Bob Paisley's recommendation about his own successor was heeded by the Liverpool directors and that led to the promotion of Joe Fagan to the number one job at Anfield. I did not know whether the Tottenham board had anyone in mind as the new manager. They did not confide in me. My guess is that they had no idea. The man I wanted was Danny Blanchflower. Even though he had been out of the game for some time, apart from writing a weekly column in the *Sunday Express*, it was my opinion that he would still have made an exceptional manager of the club. He had kept in close contact with people in the game, including me, and I thought he was the outstanding candidate. He had similar ideas to mine about how the game should be played. He knew the Tottenham set up and its traditions. He was a popular man with a sense of humour."

There can be no doubt that whatever the board of directors and their chairman Sidney Wale had in mind, Bill was convinced he would be given the respect he deserved and would have an enormous input. He was crestfallen to discover he had none. But, as you would expect from the man who ruled the club for 16 years without any interference, he went about the task of lining up what he thought was the best man for the job. Bill told me, "I interviewed Danny for the job of manager of Tottenham. He knew his relationship with the players would be different and he accepted that. Typically he wanted to know all the details. He was very interested and after a long talk, decided he'd like the job. He said he wanted me to stay on in a background job and I was prepared to do that."

Nicholson made the point to me how Liverpool had kept on Bob Paisley for the wisdom of his experience and his advice. Nicholson added, "I believe that it is important to have experienced managers to call upon. I fulfil that role now at Tottenham and I think Keith Burkinshaw was glad to be able to call on me when he needed to. It is a fallacy that a new manager should have his own men and his predecessor should be cut off completely. If the retiring manager has been successful, it is wasteful to discard all the knowledge and expertise he has built up over the years. Too many good men have been thrown out of the game, men with whom I shared the early FA coaching courses and who became outstanding managers. The idea that a clean break had to be made was fostered by directors who imagined that Sir Matt Busby had interfered with his numerous successors at Old Trafford. I spoke to Matt about this on a number of occasions and he assured me that he had not tried to interfere. He said his experience was available if anyone wanted it, but he did not push himself forward. I intended to be a general advisor to Danny when he took over. I would not have permitted players to seek advice from me behind his back. It would have been the ideal working relationship.

"There was another person I thought might be a good manager of Tottenham, Johnny Giles, captain of Leeds and Ireland. I rang him and asked him to travel down to be interviewed and he agreed. I spent an entire afternoon with him and was most impressed. He had all the requirements and I thought he would make a good manager. Even Danny approved. Had Danny been appointed manager, he would have wanted Johnny as his player/coach. Giles had had experience of management with Ireland and had learned from his years working under Don Revie at Elland Road. I was sure at the time that he was capable of making the jump from player to manager. He subsequently proved that with WBA.

"I felt contented that I had done my best to ensure that the running of Tottenham Hotspur would remain in good hands. During my second week as temporary manager – the two weeks extra time I had agreed to serve – a board meeting was called at the club to discuss the applications for a new manager. To my great surprise I was not called to the meeting. I really couldn't believe this because I had previously told the chairman that I had interviewed Blanchflower and Giles and would like to submit a report on both of them for consideration as my successor. I said that I felt they both had the right qualifications and had my full support. I was shocked by the response from the board, chairman Sidney Wale in particular. He was upset that I had interviewed the two men without his knowledge or approval. The other directors appeared to share his indignation. I was angry too because they had asked me to continue as manager and all the time I had been in charge they had never queried any of my decisions. They knew my motives were sound. Everything I undertook was for the good of the club. No one worked harder or longer than me in its interests. I told them in no uncertain manner that what I had done was for the benefit of Tottenham. I was using my experience of my lifetime in the game to find a man capable of taking over a great club. I felt the directors must be interested in what I had to say. Instead, my recommendations were ignored.

"I believed I was doing Danny Blanchflower and Johnny Giles a service by interviewing them, but as it turned out I was doing them a disservice. I had killed off any chance they had of being short-listed for the post. I found the attitude of the board very disappointing. The chairman said he wasn't really opposed to my taking the initiative, but was annoyed that I had done it without telling him. I countered by reflecting that I had never had to ask his permission before to do anything I thought was in the best interests of the club. Why he should have such strong objections I really do not know. I felt the directors were making excuses. Had Blanchflower taken over, there would have been a new look to the team and possibly even to the running of the club. Perhaps they felt their position had been threatened in some way.

"I also reported that I had been busy trying to line up transfer deals. I was in contact with Everton regarding their centre-half Mike Lyons. There was no commitment to let him go, but I had not received a straight refusal. I felt there was an opportunity there for negotiations. There was also the possibility of an exchange deal with QPR over Martin Chivers. For some time Gordon Jago, the Rangers manager, had wanted Chivers. I might have been willing to agree to a swap for Stan Bowles who, I thought, was one of the most outstanding players in the country at the time. But with hindsight I must admit that he was really like Chivers in that he had only two good seasons. Jago gave me the impression that he was prepared to let Bowles go as well as Gerry Francis and Don Givens. I had mentioned these proposed deals to Danny and he had been excited by them. He had also wanted Giles in his midfield but these plans were wrecked when the board decided to appoint their own man and ignore my advice."

Despite the obvious snub, Bill remained circumspect about Sidney. It was typical of him as Bill told me, "Mr Wale did not want me to leave. He asked me to stay and so did his charming wife Cynthia when I attended a private cocktail party at his house in Hadley Wood the following Sunday morning. But my mind was made up." However, Nicholson was indignant about the way his successor was handled, and at that point, his relationship with Wale deteriorated beyond repair.

But Bill was touched by the actions of his players and while Wale had no chance of changing his mind, the players nearly did. Nicholson told me, "One of the most touching moments was when the players asked me to reconsider. A delegation led by senior players Martin Peters and Pat Jennings was so persuasive that I wondered whether I was right to go. I was surprised and heartened about how the attitude of the players towards me had altered. I suppose it is true that people are vastly different when they are relaxed from when they are working under stress.

"It was said at the time that one of the chief reasons I resigned was that I had lost touch with the players. That was not the case. My relations with them were not much different from what they had been when I first took over. I had no favourites. I treated them all alike with firmness and, I hope, understanding. I think players respect discipline. If there are slack attitudes in a club, the team becomes slack and inefficient. We had a book of rules which I insisted had to be observed. But just as I never put a soldier on a charge when I was in the army, I cannot remember having taken serious disciplinary action against any player.

"Though we had a set of rules, we were not intolerant. I treated the players as men and I think they respected that. In the dressing room I liked to discuss points with individuals in such a way that other players could either agree or disagree with me. I encouraged them to take part in the debates. I was not authoritarian.

"The crowd trouble at the Feyenoord Stadium undoubtedly contributed to my decision to retire. The increase in soccer hooliganism sickened me, and the full horror of the problem confronted me in Rotterdam that night. Tottenham had a friendly relationship with the Dutch side. I had often visited the club and been entertained by the directors. We had developed a good understanding with them. While the hooligan problem was taking root, the attitude of the players was becoming more mercenary and that too, was one of the reasons why I was disillusioned about the game."

Here lies the crux of Bill Nicholson's decision to quit, listening to him intently and knowing what I did about what had been going on behind the scenes.

My gut instinct was that Nicholson was fed up with the spiralling wage demands, more so of the ordinary players. He made the point that he felt he could freshen up the side, even after the bad start to his final season, by signing new players. But gone were the days when Bill Nicholson came calling that players jumped at the opportunity of playing for a club such as Spurs and for a manager with such a wonderful reputation for the purist aspect of the game. Instead the "mercenary" instincts Nicholson hinted at became a barrier which this manager felt disgusted about. Players were looking as much, perhaps even more so, at the finances rather than their ambitions and goals in their career.

That is why it is wrong to blame someone like Martin Chivers. Even Bill picked up this point when we sat down at length to go through all the finer points of his reasons for quitting.

He told me, "At the start of my final season in charge, I was involved in a series of wearing talks with the players over contracts and one of them was Chivers. But it was untrue, as some critics claimed that I resigned over him. The fact that I told reporters little probably stirred the rumours, but that was my way. I mistrusted most newspaper reporters from the moment I became manager. I sought advice from an official of the Football Writers Association when I took over about how I should handle the press. I was told I would be able to work in harmony with most reporters providing I trusted them and made sure that anything I did not want quoted was 'off the record' and not to be used. In one of my first dealings with a reporter I told him some information 'off the record' as I thought and he swore it would never be used. Two days later it was in the headlines and I vowed never to make the same mistake again."

Fortunately Bill trusted me, and as time went on he imparted some fascinating insights into the way he operated at the club. And, one of the reasons he might have been tempted to change his mind when the players made representation to him to stay, was that he felt badly about letting down his back room staff, whom he knew would inevitably be kicked out. That was another reason, I am sure, he tried to put into place a dynasty, a Liverpool style structure involving Blanchflower and Giles, which could have meant the back room staff staying on.

Eddie Bailey was Bill's long standing assistant manager, and while quite often a figure of fun within the dressing room, he was also loyal to Bill, hard working and reliable. The players used to unkindly call Billy Nick's right hand man "Strawberry Nose", but Bill liked Eddie and so did I. I can remember as a young football writer going into the back office that Bill shared with Eddie and I was always guaranteed a warm welcome from the pair of them. In his autobiography Bill described Eddie as one of the many jokers within the club that helped to keep spirits up. But Eddie had his own unique style, and to many that was often found to be offensive. By all accounts Eddie could produce some colourful language out on the training fields.

According to Bill, Eddie just didn't get on with some players. Graeme Souness was one. Souness was at Spurs in the very early days of his career and even at an early age he was a spiky presence around the place. I can recall watching Souness when I was a mere young supporter, and you just knew he was going to be a star. There was Souness and Steve Perryman being groomed by Nicholson for the first team. Souness had all the skills, Perryman the application. As a fan you wanted both to emerge into the senior side, but while Nicholson favoured Perryman to come through first, that left Souness disgruntled, and dashing back to Scotland in a sulk. Nicholson knew this was a special talent and went after him and brought him back, but the relationship wasn't going to last with Souness remaining impatient while Perryman prospered. Souness was one of those players who made Eddie throw his coat across the dressing room and curse, much as he has done with fans at clubs such as Liverpool and Newcastle during his managerial career.

I have crossed swords with Souness on a professional level, investigating his involvement with Lord Stevens and his Quest team looking into transfers at the behest of the Premier League. I clearly rattled his cage, and when he is angry he is not a nice person to be around, I can vouch for that. Unfortunately legal reasons prevent me from going into any great detail about how I actually offended Souness!

While still at the *Weekly Herald*, I found Martin Chivers one of the more difficult characters to come to terms with. He seemed aloof and introverted. Yet, once he stopped playing I got to know a vastly different personality; charming and warm. I am not quite sure what triggered such a charismatic character change.

It was some years later after the big centre-forward stopped playing that I bumped into Martin Chivers prior to an England international at the old Wembley, where many people would gather across the road for a pre-match meal. Martin was eager for some inside information about Nicholson's reasons for quitting and how much a part he did actually play in that decision, or not as the case might be. He was intrigued by my observations based on long conversations with Bill, some that I was able to use in writing his life story, some that remain with me to this day, that I was able to reassure him that he was not, indeed the culprit.

CHAPTER THREE

Did It All Really Happen?

The East End had a mystical atmosphere, a community spirit, where you seemed to know everyone, and everyone knew you.

Brick Lanc possesscd a buzz all of its own, as there appeared to be vastly contrasting sections of the old East End.

There was Whitechapel High Road, where I would walk down towards Aldgate, passed the jellied eel stalls, of which Tubby Issacs was the most famous, on the sidewalk. If I ever headed up towards Liverpool Street station, the smell of freshly baked bread would waft through the streets from Kossoffs, mixed with the odours of salt beef and tasty potato latkas. If I fancied more adventure as I got older, there was always a long Sunday stroll passed the old Royal Mint to the Tower of London, the awe inspiring back streets of Tower Bridge and the endless imaginative games by the tower itself; naturally I couldn't afford the entrance fee to the inside of the Tower.

The East End was home to my mum. She never wanted to leave, and she returned as soon as she could. It was in these streets and familiar venues that my mum was one of many disadvantaged; widows and the like who were treated with enormous kindness and sympathy and the hand outs were given with kind hearts by the Jewish community, especially at the Jewish New Year and Passover.

Equally, it was a tough neighbourhood. Not everyone worked within the law. There were those who owned stalls in Petticoat Lane where you knew that, at best the goods were "seconds" and at worst had "fallen off the back of a lorry!" from the Essex docks.

My mum sewed together old bits of remnants which her three sisters would sell from a stall in Hackney. They pushed the stall all the way from their terraced house in Shoreditch. It was at least a mile shifting that heavy stall, and I really have no idea how they managed it. Sheer will power; the only chance of any money on which to survive apart from the hand outs. One sister was truly mad, I mean medically insane, but they refused to have Freda sectioned and instead kept her pacified with about two dozen cats that roamed the house freely creating a unique smell as you entered. It was always a "thrill" visiting my mum's three sisters. They idolised me and all wanted a kiss including Freda. Believe me that was not a great experience.

Commercial Road had a reputation of being somewhere to avoid for the faint hearted. The Krays lived there but Mrs Kray, though, was always a friendly face. There was a large area of green in front of her house, ideal for large scale football kickabouts, and a regular haunt as I got older and ventured further.

On the outside, purely as a fan, it all seemed like a starry eyed experience. Somehow that sense of occasion going to a game, and the expectancy of wanting your team to succeed didn't desert me when it became a means of earning a living. It was always something special to meet those heroes, from managers to players. Of course, working for the local Tottenham paper, there was no need to disguise the bias reporting!

On the *Weekly Herald*, I soon became friends with some of the young professionals just about breaking into the first team. One in particular was Danny Clapton, nephew of one of Arsenal's most famous ever footballer's of the same name. His father managed the local amateur side Haringey Borough, and I even ended up training there and playing in a practice match – naturally, it never went much further than that.

I went to Danny's flat, a massive tower block in Hackney, one of three all identical, and once went with him to the nearby Turkish Baths as he maintained his fitness regime during the summer, which also included tagging along on one of his runs around the local park.

Danny was a gifted midfielder, who followed shortly after Graeme Souness left, and Danny made it once to the Tottenham bench but never came on. He grew impatient and also moved on. Danny was slight of build, like John White, who could pick out a pass, and could dictate the midfield under the right circumstances. However, he could sometimes become discouraged, with pitches often heavy, laden with mud, it slowed down his ability to spread the play and gave defenders the chance to nail him in the tackle. It was such a shame, as he had all the ability, recognised by Bill Nicholson, but there was far too much competition, and a youngster had to have the right mentality and possibly even more physical presence than he might require now.

Danny and I remained close friends, he had become my best friend of that era, and we were chums with other developing players such as young centre-forward Chris Jones and Irish wingers Chris McGrath and Noel Brotherston, who made just one FA Cup appearance. Danny, though, had the sweetest of natures, and was a loyal and trustworthy friend. I never abused that friendship to find out from him anything that went on behind the scenes.

However, to meet him for a drink would often be very useful as there were invariably some Spurs stars at the same location, such as the Lacy Lady in Ilford, or a couple of pubs in the Tottenham area.

It was a vastly different era, and these days the players are VIP's in some of the trendiest and most exclusive night spots and restaurants in central London.

One summer I have this vague memory of going on holiday in a caravan with Danny and one of his close East End pals. I cannot recall, though, Ray Winstone being there. But much later when I had made my name as a football writer, and had organised a media game at Stamford Bridge, Ray Winstone approached me in the lounge and introduced himself.

I am embarrassingly ignorant of anything other than football. Ray explained that he knew me when we were all youngsters in the caravan down at the coast, just outside of Hastings. Linda was appalled I didn't know who Ray Winstone was, but we kept in touch for some time after that, and so too did his uncle who rang for chats about football.

Of course the mind does play tricks, and sometimes I have to ask myself, "Did It All Really Happen?"

So, with true journalist gusto I went in search of recollections from those who knew me at the time.

John Fennelly is still currently on the Tottenham staff as the press officer; a role he has held for so long I can hardly recall how long, but he also succeeded me on the *Herald* as the "Spurs Man".

The temptation might be to doctor some of the things people of that era might have to say about me, but to resist such folly, I asked those concerned to email their entries, which I promised would be unedited.

So here goes, the truth as they see it...

John Fennelly...

I first met Harry when I turned up to replace him on my first day at the *Tottenham Weekly Herald*. I had just finished my newspaper apprenticeship on the *Enfield Gazette* and was there to take over from Harry as the paper's Spurs correspondent.

Typical Harry, not only did he hand Spurs over to me when they had just been relegated to the old Second Division but he also took advantage of my naivety to sell me two LPs to help him pay off a tax debt. I'm sure he had some decent stuff in his collection but by the time I got there they had all gone so I ended up with a Lulu album and *Crazy Horses* by the Osmonds! Who even buys that stuff? I didn't even play either apart from the title track on the Osmonds album but, looking back, even that was rubbish. They're probably worth a few bob now! No, even collectors wouldn't touch them!

Harry then took me over to meet Spurs manager Keith Burkinshaw to introduce me as I was to produce the back page on my own the following week. But from the minute we walked into Burkinshaw's office at White Hart Lane the manager launched into a tirade of abuse at Harry for something he'd written the week before and chucked us out! That was my preparation for taking over the most important page in the *Herald* because many of the readers only bought the paper for its Spurs news and in those post-web, pre-magazine explosion days there was very little specialised coverage around.

I'd like to say that Harry stayed around to help and often called me to see if all was ok but he didn't!

In those days, sports reporters on local papers were also expected to sub and lay-out their pages themselves but I had no experience of the production process. So the *Herald* editor Peter Edwards sent me to Newcastle on a course. On the first day the tutor held up the back page of a newspaper to show us how not to do it – it was one of Harry's!

Harry was a legend at the *Herald* – but so was his dear old mum who regularly phoned in the evenings to see how her little Harry was and was he wearing his vest etc. (Harry you can expand on this, PS apologies if it's not true, this came from Dave Gold at the time, remember him?)

Years later we worked together when I did a two week reporting shift on the *Daily Mail* in Fleet Street. Harry had us walk miles to find the cheapest lunch in town, a small Austrian restaurant around the back of St

Paul's. He ate his in two minutes flat and then went back to the office and phoned everyone he knew for the entire afternoon and went on doing so well into the evening as I finally set off for home. He never gave up.

Some time further on I found out what it was like to be on the end of one of Harry's non-stop calls. Working at Spurs by now I met up with former West Ham manager John Lyall who was doing some coaching at White Hart Lane with his old pal Terry Venables. "Bloody Harry the Phone, we used to call him – he was never off it," moaned John as he recalled being consistently chased by hound dog Harry.

Well, you've guessed it. It was a wrong move to let loose people like "Fenners". As I told him in my reply.

So, I am just going to flip through Memory Lane on what has actually happened in the near 50 years I have supported the team.

My imagination was stirred by the club winning the Football League Championship and the FA Cup in the same season. That was phenomenal at the time. I can recall reading how Danny Blanchflower had been convinced before the season started that such was the talent within the team that he just knew they would land the Double. Spurs became the first club to complete the Double since Preston North End and Aston Villa did so in 1889 and 1897 respectively. So Spurs were the first team to win the Double in the 20th century. Little wonder my head was turned. More than that I was hooked. I longed to see my first match and it had to be a Spurs game.

The trophies and the glory filled games came thick and fast, even though Spurs should have won the European Cup, they did hold onto the FA Cup, no mean feat in itself in those days. And the following season Spurs were worthy winners of the European Cup Winners' Cup, the first British club to win a major European competition. Jimmy Greaves, who signed for the club after the historic Double, became Spurs' highest league scorer in one season with 37 goals.

By the time Spurs won the FA Cup in 1967 for the fifth time, I had become a regular at the Lane, and travelled to a few games within the London area but had not ventured too far afield.

By the time Spurs won the Football League Cup in 1971, I was watching every single Spurs game, both home and abroad, thanks to my job with the *Herald*. The year after the League Cup triumph Spurs won the UEFA Cup. The following season they won the League Cup again, the first club to have won the trophy twice.

In 1974 Spurs became the first English club to have played in three major European finals.

But the glory days didn't last forever, and on April 28th 1975, the Lane staged one of the most bizarre games with Spurs having to at least draw against Leeds United to stay in the First Division. Leeds, who were the reigning champions, finished in a disappointing ninth spot in the First Division that season, but were in the final of the European Cup. Although they had nothing to play for, Jimmy Armfield's team were still a massive obstacle for survival. I can recall that the manager Terry Neill tried just about everything. Even employing all sorts of pre-match mind games, including a hypnotist.

Terry Neill called Ronald Markham, whose stage name was Romark. Terry first met Romark when he was manager of Hull City. Ron told Neill that he could improve the team's attitudes and expectations through the power of positive thinking. So, when Hull played a game at Bristol City, he invited Ron to the team's hotel the night before the game. He got the players locking their fingers behind their heads, and for most, when asked to unlock, they couldn't do so. Ron had got them to believe they were interlocking steel bars. He even got a player with only a slight chance of being fit to accept the power of positive thinking.

Neill turned to Ron in his hour of need soon into his Tottenham career as manager. As I wrote in Terry Neill's life story *Revelations Of A Football Manager*, Neill told me "Tough wasn't the word to describe our task against the European Cup finalists." Neill booked the West Lodge Park Hotel from a telephone in the office of Arsenal's club secretary Ken Friar as he wanted total concentration in the final game. In reality, knowing Terry the way I did, it was the manager who was more nervous than his players. He told the players to report at lunch time on the Sunday. Neil told me, "I decided to ring Ron Markham and invited him to help ease the tension. I was half inclined to think that this smacked of gimmickry and might have a detrimental effect on the players, we had, after all, lost the match to Bristol City the year before, but we didn't have anything to lose, and if Ron handled it properly it would be a diversion from all the pressures.

"I introduced Ron to the players, saying, 'This is Ronald Markham. There's no magic but he may have a few interesting things to say to you.' Ron then spoke to them collectively, telling them that he had no knowledge of the game and couldn't affect their technical performance. A lot of the players had given everything during the course of the season and had taken personal knocks in their confidence because of the club's troubles. Ron's jocular approach and party tricks made them feel better."

Cyril Knowles had a hard man reputation, but he had, apparently, succumbed to the hypnosis, and he was told to recall one of his greatest moments, which was scoring from a free-kick. He was told that if he got a similar free-kick, he must take it, and he would score. Nearly 50,000 people crammed into White Hart Lane to roar on Spurs in their bid to preserve their top flight status. Nerves were settled after just five minutes when Cyril Knowles slammed home a free-kick from the edge of the area. When the home side were awarded a free-kick in so similar a position to that wonder goal he scored against Manchester United, no one could stop the left-back storming through the field to demand that he took the free-kick.

Neill told me how it had all been down to the hypnosis, "Ron then said he would like to try a little hypnosis on a volunteer, and Cyril Knowles stepped forward. After hypnotising Cyril, Ron told him to put his hands by his side. 'You are now a rod of solid steel,' he said to Cyril. I was sure the players would not take it seriously, but when Ron pushed Cyril over he never flinched, keeping as straight as the said steel rod. There was no laughter from the players, who were certainly impressed. We picked up Cyril, a six-footer weighing over 12 stone, and on Ron's instructions laid him across two chairs, the tips of his shoulders and head on one chair and his feet on the other. He remained rigid.

"Now it came to individual sessions. Ron was going to bring out the power of positive thinking in the form of each player's successes on the field. He couldn't improve a player's fitness or ability, but he wanted to convince them that they were going to win the match. He asked the players to recall their finest moment in football – their best game, their best goal, or anything they would be proud of recalling. Only two players were too sceptical to join in, Pat Jennings and John Pratt, who later became assistant manager at the club under Peter Shreeves. They were both determined to succeed or fail without outside influence. As Pat Jennings joked later, some of the players must have been struggling to remember anything! Ralph Coates selected a European game as his favourite moment of triumph. Cyril chose a free-kick against Manchester United when he curled the ball round the defensive wall into the top corner of the goal. *Match of the Day* had featured it in their titles for a year.

"Champagne was brought in to celebrate Martin Chivers' birthday and some cake was provided by the hotel. The players were laughing and joking. If anyone had chanced by our hotel that night they would have found it very strange. The team that was under the most severe pressure was laughing and drinking and seemed to have no worries.

"As Ron left the hotel, he said to me, 'No problems. You are assured of the right result.' Certainly he helped to prevent the players from wasting nervous energy. They were relaxed and their confidence was restored. In a very different way, the late Bill Shankly was superb at lifting the spirits of players with his powers of positive thinking.

"At the ground the next night, I noticed that some of the directors were looking extremely nervous. I noticed one taking a heart tablet, while another couldn't prevent his cup and saucer from shaking. I thought to myself that if I was similarly affected I would give up the game. I carried on to my office and poured myself a drink, laughing all the while. I couldn't prevent whatever was going to happen, so there was little point worrying about something I had no further control over."

As Terry Neill rightly told me afterwards, the game couldn't possibly have gone any better. Perhaps it was the magician Ron doing his work, or maybe, more down to earth reasons such as Leeds concentrating more on their European Cup final. Spurs dominated the opening period once Cyril had scored from the free-kick. But Spurs were unable to get the vital second goal despite their constant bombardment of the Leeds goal. The second half continued in a similar vein and Spurs finally got their reward when Martin Chivers, back in the side after a two-month lay-off, fired home from close range. The result was virtually made safe on the hour when Knowles converted a penalty after Trevor Cherry had brought down Perryman. Jordan pulled a goal back for Leeds to silence the Spurs fans but the celebrations which followed Alfie Conn's strike to make it 4-1 were as loud and long as any Championship winning season. An 81st minute Peter Lorimer goal for Leeds went largely unnoticed by the home supporters who swamped the pitch on the final whistle to mob their heroes on a memorable afternoon at the Lane.

Neill recalled, "It made me feel that bringing Ron to the hotel was worthwhile. Cyril scored two goals and after the final whistle, everyone at the club was delighted and relieved. There was a crowd of 49,886, the largest of the season, a great atmosphere, and the night was ours. They had flocked to the ground in case it was the club's last game in the First Division for a while. Fortunately it wasn't. Shortly after the final whistle, the local police chief came into the dressing room and said, 'You will have to come out and make a personal appearance. They won't go home until you do. They are all shouting for you.' My first reaction was to think how different this was from the early part of the season, when they were screaming abuse at me. It had been such a hostile atmosphere that some fans took to spitting at me while others shouted at me on the telephone. They yelled, 'You Arsenal bastard, what the hell are you doing messing up our Tottenham team?' I received abusive letters by the sack load. After one game two big fellows had come over and wanted to punch me. If it hadn't been for the prompt action of the police I might have been forced to fight both of them. I could understand everyone's concern, but I was concerned too and I was working a full day every day of the week trying to put things right.

"All this went through my mind as the police chief stood at the door, 'tell them to go and get stuffed,' I said. Perhaps in hindsight that was undiplomatic and ungracious, but at the time I meant it. I had a cup of tea and went home. It was not my intention to be abusive or abrupt to all the fans, but I was weary after the long campaign against relegation and rightly or wrongly didn't feel the need for congratulations. I was content that I had played my part in keeping Tottenham in the First Division."

I had got to know every member of that team. It would have been heartbreaking as a fan, but also from a professional view point. For both reasons I didn't want "my" club relegated. But, like every Spurs fan, one couldn't help being concerned about how much it really meant to Terry Neill. Yes, of course, it meant a great deal as a professional football manager, but it exasperated the feeling that he was the wrong man for the job, and it didn't take long for the Spurs board to appreciate that the fans didn't trust his reign as manager.

The players became very dear to my heart too. Knowing them as a fan is to idolise them. Knowing them more intimately often results in disillusionment. For me, it intensified my admiration for my heroes. Pat Jennings in goal was such a soft spoken, likable big Irishman, who you couldn't help but love, and everyone loved him. He had enormous hands, and when he first joined the club from Watford, it seemed like a huge gamble by Bill Nicholson. But when he caught the ball one handed on the stretch at the far post, it left fans like myself breathless. It was an awe inspiring sight.

The full-backs were Joe Kinnear and Knowles, with the central defenders Phil Beal and Keith Osgood. Keith was one of the players who had come through the ranks, and I had got to know him very well. Phil Beal wore these ludicrously long side burns, very fashionable at the time, and he was a hugely likable guy. He was one of those under rated players who came through the ranks when the fans wanted a big name signing to follow in the footsteps of some of the club's great central defenders, but whatever Phil Beal lacked in star quality he made up for in sheer consistency and effectiveness which made him a regular in the side.

Terry Naylor was as hard as nails, ruthless in the tackle, a typical cockney with a heart of gold.

Alfie Conn had the charisma, all showman with those flowing blond locks but he was also infuriatingly inconsistent. In his day he was the wizard of the dribble, but too often it wouldn't come off, and he could also be quite temperamental when things were not going his way.

Steve Perryman was there to provide the all energy leadership, his influence within the dressing room was total. With John Pratt, another selfless runner and tireless tackler, no team had more energy in midfield. But the entire team never seemed to get it together, and that's why they found themselves fighting off relegation even though they possessed such enormous talents as Conn and Chivers. Martin Chivers was the team's enigma. The big man often failed to punch his weight, but when he was in the mood he was virtually unstoppable. Alongside him was the hugely talented Chris Jones, a centre-forward who seemed destined never to be a great goalscorer, who seemed to miss chances through fate rather than inability.

Terry Neill was highly ambitious and after the horrific brush with relegation wanted to achieve something special at Spurs, and tried to recruit, unsuccessfully, Johann Cruyff at a time when a foreign signing was most rare in English football. Neill was an innovative thinker and his drive to recruit Cruyff was inspired, even if he was trying to convince a rather conservative board about the revolutionary capture. Neill failed with Cruyff, and also missed out on bringing Charlie George to the Lane, but did bring in Keith Burkinshaw and Peter Shreeves as coaches, fortuitously because when Neill left as manager, as inevitably he would, Burkinshaw and Shreeves were on hand to pick up the reins.

And surely Spurs would never make the same mistake again and select an Arsenal man as their manager. Surely not? Oh well, Sir Alan, that's another story.

Terry Neill finished ninth in his second season, but on the pre-season tour there were all sorts of fall outs and the suspicion he had been approached by Arsenal. With all his frustrations at the Lane, a quick switch across North London to his true love Arsenal was always going to be a big draw. So off he went.

Burkinshaw, who spent seven years at Liverpool as a player without really making the grade before ending his playing career at Workington and Scunthorpe, arrived at the Lane from Newcastle United where he worked as coach for seven years before joining the coaching staff at Spurs in 1975. Popular with the players, Burkinshaw had their full support when he applied for the manager's job and he was appointed in 1976.

Despite all of the traumas of the Leeds match, so short a time before, relegation followed in Burkinshaw's first year in 1977 but he bounced back at his first attempt and achieved one of the biggest scores in the club's history when, on 22nd October 1977, Spurs thrashed Bristol Rovers 9-0. Spurs were determined to make it straight back to the top flight and made a good start to their Second Division campaign having won six of their first eight games, but they went into this clash with Rovers on the back of a 4-1 defeat by Charlton and were desperate to return to winning ways. Only 48 hours earlier, Burkinshaw forked out £60,000 for little-known Torquay striker Colin Lee and the man who had only been playing as a forward for a season, had a dream debut putting four past a hapless Rovers side. It took Lee just 21 minutes to get on the score sheet when he swept home Glenn Hoddle's cross. Four minutes later he grabbed his second when he headed home John Pratt's corner. Hoddle was the provider once more a minute before the interval when his cross was met by Peter Taylor to make it 3-0.The second half saw Spurs simply overrun the Pirates and the bearded Ian Moores made it 4-0 on 56 minutes. The final quarter was simply an exhibition by Burkinshaw's side with Hoddle teasing Rovers with some sublime pieces of skill. Lee grabbed his hat-trick on 75 minutes and two goals in as many minutes from Moores saw him complete his first treble for the club to make it 7-0. Two minutes from time Lee capped off a memorable debut when he tapped home his fourth, but the best was saved until last when Hoddle collected Moores' pass over the Rovers defence to score a magnificent goal which sealed Spurs' record league victory.

Barry Daines kept goal that day in front of a 26,311 crowd, with Don McAllister in the defence, a young Neil McNab in midfield and Peter "Spud" Taylor on the wing.

The attack was led by the most unlikely strikers in Colin Lee and Ian Moores, two giant centre-forwards, hardly a traditional Spurs strike force. The entire team was constructed of very "nice" guys. Even the accepted "ball-winner" in midfield John Pratt, was a lovely guy off the field. The two big men in attack were mild mannered.

The only one with a touch of nastiness about his play was the slightest and lightest player of all, McNab. Yet, off the field he was also a really nice guy. I can recall the very first day he turned up at the Lane as one of Nicholson's last signings as a tiny 16-year-old, one of the youngest players Nicholson had ever purchased, and who had such enormous gifts he was destined for the first team almost immediately after arriving south of the border. It was a tough job interviewing the new signing. I took him to one of the local, and very cheap, greasy spoons in the Tottenham High Road, and could hardly make out a word through his very broad Scottish accent. But we became very good friends.

You just couldn't imagine that kind of access these days, turning up, via an introduction from the manager, and then taking a player off for a cup of tea. These days, it's the formality of a structured press conference, in front of a room full of newspaper journalists, TV cameras and crews, radio and even specialist internet providers.

Sir Alex Ferguson refused to allow David Beckham to be interviewed by any outlet for several years protecting his player from a media that has mushroomed beyond recognition from the time that young McNab turned up at Tottenham totally bewildered and looking almost lost and all alone. Now a new recruit is accompanied by agent, specialist house hunters and Mr Fix Its coming out from all directions to ensure every last detail is taken care of so the player can concentrate on his football.

Once promoted Burkinshaw knew he had to rebuild the team back in the top flight. He pulled off one of the greatest transfer coups in the club's history by signing Argentinean World Cup stars Ossie Ardiles and Ricky Villa. The team built around the talents of Ardiles and Hoddle went on to win the FA Cup in 1981 and 1982 and the UEFA Cup in 1984.

I had heard whispers from my contacts inside the game, that Burkinshaw had signed Ossie and Ricky by default. The idea belonged to Terry Neill, who wanted Ardiles, but knew Ossie wouldn't go without Ricky, and had "conned" his old mate Keith into taking Ricky. Burkinshaw was invited by Neill to tag along to Buenos Aires, who suddenly ditched his own plans of recruiting Ardiles, leaving Burkinshaw at the airport on his own. Burkinshaw decided to go through with the travel plans and ended up signing Ardiles when he only went to get Villa.

Neill told me his side of the story, "I do not regret my decision not to buy Ardiles and Villa in the summer of 1978. The deal that brought them to Tottenham proved successful for our North London rivals, but it did not enable them to take over from Arsenal as London's top club. Harry Haslam first rang me to say Ardiles and Villa were available after the World Cup in Argentina in 1978. Oscar Arce, an Argentinean coach, and former Argentine World Cup captain Antonio Rattin, who was sent off at Wembley in 1966, were friends of Harry's and had helped him set up a proposed deal. I had seen Ardiles on television and admired his skill, but knew little about Villa, who had appeared briefly as substitute in a couple of matches. Harry said Ricky Villa might be more suited to English football than Ossie because he was bigger and stronger. The deal would cost $700,000, with 15 percent going to the players and 2 percent to the Argentine FA. By transfer standards at that time, it was not an exorbitant sum.

"I rang Ron Greenwood to seek his advice. Ron said he fancied Ardiles but was less keen on Villa. At the time I was having problems with Alan Hudson and perhaps needed a midfield player but I did not need two. We had appeared in the FA Cup final and finished fifth in the First Division, we already had a strong squad. But Tottenham, who came up from the Second Division on goal difference ahead of Brighton, needed new faces. Their need was greater than ours. Harry suggested that I fly to Buenos Aires to see Ardiles and Villa, but as there were no competitive matches left that season I did not see the point of travelling that far. Denis Hill-Wood was not keen on signing foreign players, but he did not stand in my way. If I had decided to go to Buenos Aires, I am sure I could have signed them. Harry Haslam was naturally disappointed with my decision and asked me if I could recommend another club. I mentioned Tottenham. Keith Burkinshaw had just taken over at White Hart Lane and it would be a bold gamble on his part to take the Argentineans. I spoke to Keith, and though he was at first reluctant I told him if I was in his position I would consider the gamble worthwhile. He decided to investigate and the Tottenham board gave him permission to open negotiations. Keith wanted me to fly with him to Buenos Aires. 'At least we can enjoy the trip and have a few drinks,' he said. But I'd made my decision, and declined. He went alone, and within a couple of days had finalised the deal. Ossie Ardiles has adorned English football and has been a great asset to Spurs over the years, but I still maintain I made the right decision.

"Ricky Villa confirmed my fears that he was not consistent enough for our football. I remember watching him daydreaming at Highbury when the player he should have been picking up, David Price, scored a goal. He was that type of performer – brilliant in one game, infuriating in the next. He will be remembered, however, as the player who scored one of the truly great individual goals in the history of the FA Cup final at Wembley."

Well, all any Spurs fan can say to Terry is "thanks, and thanks again." Arsenal's loss was Spurs' gain. Although Terry got his revenge by taking Pat Jennings to Highbury when it was considered he might be past his sell by date at the Lane. Pat was far from finished and ended up playing for many years still at his peak with the Gunners.

The arrival of Ossie and Ricky opened the floodgates for foreign stars, a trickle at first, but more recently a deluge. Hence Terry Neill's prediction in his book published in 1985 with not his usual foresight when he predicted, "Even if there were no limit on the number of overseas players in the English Football League, I do not think there would be a significant change in the number of foreigners playing for our clubs. For a start, clubs wishing to buy them will find the same difficulties I encountered. The big name players will want salaries far in excess of what most players earn in England, and only a few clubs will be able to meet their demands. Then there are difficulties with acclimatisation, language, the style of football and everything else. Few foreigners have been successful here. Ossie Ardiles, Ivan Golac, Frans Thijssen and Arnold Muhren are exceptions. On the Continent many of the best players are mercenaries, going from country to country and being employed by clubs on short term contracts. I cannot see that happening here."

Well, Terry couldn't have foreseen the explosion of Rupert Murdoch's Sky TV cash and the advent of the Premier League. Dennis Bergkamp and Thierry Henry are examples of foreign superstars who were far from short term at Arsenal for a start, and none of them seemed put off by the weather.

Whatever Terry might boast about Spurs' Argentineans failing to elevate Spurs above Arsenal, it clearly reinstated Spurs as the great entertainers of English football.

In 1981 Spurs won the FA Cup for the sixth time. Steve Perryman set a new club record of league appearances by passing Pat Jennings' previous record total of 472.

On February 6th 1982 the New West Stand was officially opened with visitors Wolverhampton Wanderers, as Wolves had been Spurs' first league opponents 74 years earlier. Spurs won 6-1! Just like that memorable day in 1908, Wolves returned to the Black Country on the back of a defeat but on this occasion they were ripped apart by a rampant Spurs side inspired by Glenn Hoddle and Ricky Villa. Hoddle converted a penalty after eight minutes to give Spurs the lead and on the half hour mark Villa doubled that lead with a magnificent swerving volley. The big Argentinean scored his second goal 10 minutes later just before Kenny Hibbitt pulled one back for the visitors as Tottenham went in at half-time leading 3-1. Villa completed his hat-trick 10 minutes into the second half and Spurs then turned on the style with goals from Garth Crooks and Mark Falco to record Burkinshaw's side's biggest victory of the season in front of a crowd of 29,990.

By this time Ray Clemence was keeping up the great traditions of Spurs keepers, with Chris Hughton and Paul Miller among the defenders. Paul and Chris came through the ranks, so I had got to know them both very well. Entirely different characters; Paul extroverted, Chris, very much the opposite. Tony Galvin was the Graeme Le Saux of his day, a University graduate, and well spoken. A sound quality winger who could, on occasions, turn on the style. Up front Mark Falco was another home produced lad whom I got to know extremely well. He had the goalscoring gift but just fell a touch short in quality to make it to international level.

That season Spurs became FA Cup winners for the seventh time in the club's Centenary year. By finishing fourth in the league, Spurs qualified for the UEFA Cup for the first time since season 1973-74. But times were changing dramatically within the game as a whole and with the Lane in particular as Irving Scholar made more history by making Spurs the first football club to float shares on the London Stock Exchange.

Shame then when Burkinshaw became so disillusioned after a board room takeover in 1983-84, led by Irving Scholar, he announced he would resign at the end of that season. Burkinshaw went out in a blaze of glory as Spurs won the UEFA Cup for the second time in their history. It made Burkinshaw the second most successful manager in the club's history behind Bill Nicholson, and he goes down as one of the fans most popular managers for bringing the glory, glory days back to the Lane after a dismal period in the club's history.

In 1985, the club's playing strip changed to white shirts and white shorts, and the following year Steve Perryman was transferred to Oxford United after making a record 655 league appearances for Spurs. Spurs reached their eighth FA Cup final in 1987. It was a magnificent season, breathtaking goals, great thrills and excitement with a high level of skill at times. Glenn Hoddle, Ossie Ardiles, Chris Waddle and Gary Mabbutt were all on top of their game, while Clive Allen set a new club record with 49 goals in a single season and the kit returned to white shirts and navy shorts. On February 2nd 1987, West Ham were the visitors to White Hart Lane on a cold Wednesday night but it was the Spurs supporters in the ground, in a crowd of 41,995, who were warmed up by a breathtaking display from David Pleat's side who were in the running for all three domestic competitions. Belgian international Nico Claesen gave Spurs the lead on six minutes when he latched onto Ardiles' pass and chipped Phil Parkes from the edge of the area. Despite dominating proceedings with Hoddle once more in majestic form, Spurs didn't make it 2-0 until the 71st minute when the England star curled a 25-yarder into the West Ham net. That goal really opened the floodgates and Clive Allen bagged a hat-trick in the final 10 minutes to cap off a memorable night when Spurs had two Thomas' in their side, both full-backs Danny and Mitchell, and two Allen's, cousins, Clive in attack and Paul in midfield.

Claesen was one of the new imported Continental players, a tiny forward who might have made a much bigger contribution, but Pleat devised a system to get the best out of Hoddle, after initially dropping him, then bringing him back in a five man midfield with Clive Allen as the spearhead.

Richard Gough played in the heart of the defence, and the Scottish defender became one of the most influential captains at the club. A highly likable guy, I got to know Richard very well, but at times he could be extremely head strong.

Spurs made their first million plus signing, Paul Stewart from Manchester City, for £1.5m in 1988 and a year later splashed out on refurbishing the East Stand.

Spurs won the FA Cup again in 1991. In the semi-final at Wembley on April 14th, Spurs beat Arsenal 3-1 in arguably one of the club's most memorable games for Spurs supporters, denying as the team did that day, Champions-elect Arsenal from repeating a second Double.

With the demand for tickets so high, even the 80,000 seater stadium was not big enough to satisfy demand from supporters of both sides. Arsenal went into this game having lost just one league game all season and were confident of brushing aside their fierce rivals who had been beset with financial irregularities and indifferent league form throughout the season. Paul Gascoigne had been in irresistible form throughout the FA Cup run but going into this game he had played just 60 minutes of football in five weeks after undergoing a double hernia operation. Gazza's midfield partner David Howells was also coming back from injury and the decision to select him alongside the brilliant Geordie after an 11-week absence was a huge gamble by manager Terry Venables, but ultimately one which paid off in glorious fashion as Spurs' short passing game pulled apart Arsenal's game plan of trying to contain the ubiquitous Gascoigne, a player whose ability to rise to the big-match occasion made him one of the modern-day great players in the English game, and once more he proved that to be the case in an encounter which will live in the memory of Spurs fans.

With five minutes played, it was Gascoigne who put his side in the lead with an amazing free-kick from fully 30 yards which beat David Seaman and flew into the top left-hand corner. That goal settled any early nerves for Spurs and just five minutes after Gazza's wonder strike, Gary Lineker poked home from close range a second after Paul Allen's cross eluded the Arsenal defence. Spurs were now firing on all cylinders with Gascoigne and Samways dominating in midfield and Allen and Howells negating the threat of Arsenal full-backs Lee Dixon and Nigel Winterburn. On the stroke of half-time Arsenal pulled a goal back when Alan Smith profited from Dixon finally breaking forward and headed home a deep cross in front of Gary Mabbutt.

The sapping pitch at Wembley was beginning to take its toll on Gascoigne, and he left the field on 60 minutes to a standing ovation to be replaced by Nayim as Spurs desperately went in search of a third goal. Arsenal, as expected, had the lion's share of the opening exchanges in the second half but Gary Mabbutt and Steve Sedgley at the heart of the defence were magnificent in containing the dangerous

Smith and Kevin Campbell. The elusive third goal finally arrived on 78 minutes when Vinny Samways combined with Mabbutt to release Lineker whose shot squirmed through Seaman's hands and into the net. Arsenal hit the bar through Campbell and Merson late in the game but Tottenham were not to be denied a memorable victory on their route to their eighth FA Cup triumph.

Spurs became winners for the eighth time when, on May 18th 1991, the club beat Nottingham Forest 2-1 back at Wembley, but needed extra-time to do it. What should have been the Gascoigne final after his heroics in previous rounds will always be remembered for the wrong reasons as far as he is concerned – his rash challenge on Forest's Gary Charles almost ended his career. Gazza was stretchered off after that foul and to add insult to injury, Stuart Pearce unleashed a trademark rasper of a free-kick for Brian Clough's men to take the lead. Everything looked like it was going wrong. Gary Lineker's "goal" was ruled out for offside and minutes later his penalty was saved by Mark Crossley. But there was no stopping Spurs and the team finally levelled through Paul Stewart to take the game into extra-time. Then another twist as, under pressure from Gary Mabbutt, Forest defender Des Walker headed into his own net for what turned out to be the winner. The team that day was, Thorstvedt, Edinburgh, van den Hauwe, Sedgley, Howells, Mabbutt, Stewart, Gascoigne (Nayim), Samways (Walsh), Lineker and Allen.

Spurs were back in European competition. Sir Alan Sugar became chairman and steered the club away from impending bankruptcy. In 1992, Spurs became one of the founder members of the new FA Premier League, and Gascoigne joined Lazio for £5.5m – a record.

In 1994, "The Shelf" became an all-seater enclosure. In 1995 the new South Stand was completed. Record signing Chris Armstrong arrived from Crystal Palace for £4.5m when the club turned down Dennis

Bergkamp. In 1996 a new Rights Issue raised £10.9m to redevelop North Stand, complete hospitality areas in South Stand and reconstruct the pitch. The following year Spurs paid out a new record £6m for Les Ferdinand from Newcastle United. In 1998 the new North Stand was completed increasing capacity to 36,257. And in 1999 the long wait for silverware ended with a triumph at Wembley, in front of a crowd of 77,892, in the League Cup for the third time.

But on March 21st 1999, all looked lost when, with just an hour on the clock, Justin Edinburgh reacted to Robbie Savage's tackle, the City midfielder clutched his face and the long-serving defender was shown the red card. In a war of attrition, with Leicester determined to snub out the threat of wing wizard David Ginola, chances were few and far between. As the clock ticked away surely Martin O'Neill's men would take advantage of the extra man and tired legs on the famous hallowed turf? But then one last attack. Steffen Iversen burst down the right channel and into the area, his cross was parried by keeper Kasey Keller and there was hero of the hour Allan Nielsen to head home the winner. A match to forget, an afternoon to remember. The team that day was, Walker, Carr, Edinburgh, Freund, Vega, Campbell, Nielsen, Ginola (Sinton), Anderton, Iversen and Ferdinand.

With David Ginola, with all his Gaelic flair, Spurs were still an attractive team at times, but money was wasted on a profusion of bad judgement signings. For example in 2000 Spurs wasted a new record £11m for Sergei Rebrov from Dynamo Kiev. Glenn Hoddle took over as manager from George Graham in 2001. ENIC completed yet another takeover, with Daniel Levy becoming chairman. Teddy Sheringham rejoined the club from Manchester United and joined new arrivals Christian Ziege and Gus Poyet. Spurs reached the final of the Worthington Cup in Glenn Hoddle's first season as manager in 2002 but lost out 2-1 to Blackburn Rovers at Cardiff's Millennium Stadium. Jamie Redknapp signed in April before the £7m capture of Irish star striker Robbie Keane from Leeds United in August. Spurs finished 10th in the Premiership in 2002-03, successfully toured South Africa, signed Helder Postiga and Bobby Zamora and Jamie Redknapp was named captain. Spurs sacked Hoddle in September and once more David Pleat took over in a caretaker capacity. Spurs finished 14th in the Premiership in 2003-04.

Pleat departed in July 2004 as Spurs formed a new, continental-style management structure. Frank Arnesen arrived from PSV as sporting director, Jacques Santini as head coach, Martin Jol as first assistant and Dominique Cuperly as fitness coach. Santini left in November and Jol took over as head coach. In October, England started with three Spurs players (Defoe, Ledley King and Paul Robinson) for the first time since 1987.

Spurs were in the running for European qualification in 2004-05 via the Premier League until defeat at Middlesbrough in the penultimate game of the season. The team ended up ninth.

In 2006, with the likes of Aaron Lennon and Michael Dawson coming to the fore, Spurs held on to fourth place for most of the season until defeat at West Ham on the final day. Spurs went down 2-1 while Arsenal's 4-2 win over Wigan meant that the two North London sides swapped places, with the Gunners nicking the last Champions League spot by two points. The players had spent the previous night at the Marriot Hotel in the Docklands at Canary Wharf and there was a terrific uproar that the team had been "poisoned" with the club demanding the game be replayed. So May 7th 2006 goes down in Spurs long history as one of the most sickening days of all time, literally. But my inside source tells me now to forget all the conspiracy theories and that there was a logical explanation, "My information is that one of the youth team was suffering with gastroenteritis and passed on the very contagious bug to one of the senior players that day. It occurred before the squad actually arrived at the hotel and it all got out of hand from there."

For all the controversy and drama, Spurs ended that season in their highest league position since coming third in 1990, and accrued the most points in a season since 1987, when they also finished third. Jol was ecstatic with the 65 points total, and the Dutchman seemed to be the right fit for Spurs manager for some considerable time. However, the truth was that Spurs' inability to beat any of the top four teams was critical to their failure in making the Champions League, a cornerstone to the club's desire to maximise income and to increase the value of Spurs should a prospective owner launch a takeover bid.

For the 2006-07 season, Spurs signed Bulgarian hitman Dimitar Berbatov, Ivory Coast midfielder Didier Zokora, left-back Benoit Assou-Ekotto from Lens, Pascal Chimbonda from Wigan and Steed Malbranque from Fulham. Michael Carrick moved to Manchester United. Spurs matched their exploits of 2005-06 with a fifth placed league finish in 2006-07 and reached the quarter-finals of the UEFA Cup. Going into the 2007-08 season, new arrivals included Gareth Bale and Darren Bent but following a poor start, Martin Jol was asked to stand down alongside coach Chris Hughton. Highly-rated Juande Ramos was appointed head coach with coaching assistants Marcos Alvarez and former Spur Gus Poyet. The year marked Spurs' 125th anniversary. A magnificent start to the year under Ramos saw Spurs first beat Arsenal 5-1 and then topple Chelsea 2-1 to lift the League Cup at Wembley Stadium. Spurs finished the league campaign in 11th place. But it's been down hill all the way in the league since the first trophy in seven years, the sale of Berbatov and Keane, and £77m worth of new arrivals trying desperately to integrate into a new look side.

But the worst start of a season since the *Titanic* sunk tells its own story, so now it's time for nostalgia...

CHAPTER FOUR

Terry Neill... Did He Play For Arsenal? Asked Chairman Sidney Wale.

Sidney Wale was an "old school' style of football chairman. He never gave interviews and was rarely even pictured, let alone make public appearances or statements. However, as the local reporter on the *Herald*, I had known Sidney for long enough for him to trust me, well, as much as he trusted any journalist, and when I approached him in an empty Tottenham car park when he just happened to be on site during the week, I didn't miss my opportunity to ask him why he had chosen an ex-Arsenal man in Terry Neill to be the next Spurs manager in succession to Bill Nicholson.

"Did he play for Arsenal?" came Sidney's shock response accompanied by an incredulous look of horror.

Did he play for Arsenal, indeed. Good grief, you would think the man appointing such an important employee would know his CV. Perhaps not. This was an age of the last of the amateur chairmen; men who were supporters through and through, and who took little to no active role inside the club other than chairing the annual meeting and signing off the audit for the annual accounts.

If I was shocked by Terry Neill's appointment, imagine how the fans felt. I understood the fans' reaction because I was still very much a fan at heart.

But all that was nothing compared to the shock of the outgoing manager Bill Nicholson, who received a mysterious call from Neill.

Nicholson told me that the telephone call from Neill came just two days after the Spurs board had vetoed Nicholson's attempts to recruit Blanchflower and Giles. Nicholson confided, "I was surprised to have a telephone call at home from Terry Neill. At the time he was manager of Hull City and Northern Ireland. He wanted to know what was happening at Tottenham about a new manager. I told him what the directors had told me; that they would accept written applications only. He said he didn't have time to write. He was calling from a hotel near London airport. I said, 'Are you in your room?' 'Yes' he replied. 'Well,' I said, 'there should be some writing paper and envelopes there. Get your application off as quickly as you can. It won't take you long to scribble out a note. Give it to the hall porter downstairs and he will drop it in the post box for you.'"

Nicholson was very curious about that call. Eventually Neill was appointed, and Nicholson remained surprised by their choice.

He told me, "Terry Neill was the man the board appointed. It caused a considerable stir among our supporters. I wonder whether Sidney Wale really knew Terry's background. It was unique, to say the least, to appoint an Arsenal man. Even before he started, he had the problem of winning over the Tottenham supporters. Given the choice, I could not imagine any of our fans welcoming as their manager a man who had played nearly all his career at Highbury.

"The appointment of Terry Neill meant that I would no longer be connected with the club in any way. I did not blame him for that; I did not expect to be asked to stay on in any capacity. My guess was that the board took the view that as I had resigned it was better to start afresh rather than risk a 'Matt Busby situation.' I was sure it was in their minds that, had I remained, I would have tried to interfere in the running of the club, thereby undermining the authority of the new manager. I suspected if any of the directors thought that way it would have been Charles Cox, the vice-chairman, whose father George first became a director in 1907. A widower, he had worked for Car Mart, part of the Kenning car sales group and supplied the royal family with cars.

"When Terry Neill arrived he had his own advisor and assistant in Wilf Dixon. Had the club kept me on, there would have been the burden of an additional wage. Tottenham was never a club to skimp when it came to signing players, but on the administration side they had the reputation of being mean and it was well deserved."

The arrival of the Neill-Dixon regime meant that Bill's loyal assistant Eddie Bailey was also out of a job, which distressed Bill no end. In fact the whole handling of Nicholson's departure had left a sour taste for the great man.

He told me, "It was not a pleasant way to leave White Hart Lane after such a long time. I can remember receiving a telephone call from Terry Neill. He was inquiring about certain items he had discovered. It was obvious that he was in my office. I hurried round to clear my desk. I was given a certain sum by the club as a token for my years of service. All I am prepared to say was that I was far from satisfied with it."

Terry Neill's reign at Spurs was brief, just two years. Keith Burkinshaw, recruited as a coach, took over with Pat Welton his assistant. Nicholson recalls, "I was glad of the break from football but a desire to get back into it soon made itself felt. When I attended pre-season training sessions at some of the London clubs I began to miss the involvement. I went to West Ham's training ground at Chadwell Heath and also to London Colney, Arsenal's training ground. For so many years coaches from all over the globe had come to Cheshunt to study my methods. Now I had time to take a look at others'. One day at Chadwell Heath, Ron Greenwood, then manager of West Ham, asked me what plans I had. I said I was doing nothing and had no plans. He asked me if I would like to help him at West Ham. That season West Ham were in Europe, having won the FA Cup. He asked me to join the club for the season. He felt my experience of Europe would be useful. I was with West Ham for one year and I enjoyed it. I was grateful to Ron for giving me the opportunity to return to football. When Terry left and Keith took over he felt his staff needed strengthening and thought it was a good idea for me to return to the club.

"I realise there must have been a worry that I would interfere but that never materialised. Keith wanted to use my experience and when he sought advice I gave it. I did not volunteer it. Football is a matter of judgement about players. You can be sure in your own mind about a player, but it is valuable to have the backing of an older, more experienced person. Ever since I was back at the club I kept my thoughts to myself unless asked for advice. Keith may have invited me to a meeting of the coaching staff for a chat or he may have talked things over with me in private. I did a lot of scouting, looking at players of all types to see if they could suit Tottenham."

I know from my numerous conversations with Irving that the new owner was behind the recruitment of Bill Nicholson. It really didn't matter what Bill did, even if he did very little, but for Irving it was imperative for a man such as Nicholson, and what he meant to the club, that he was immediately brought back to the fold and never allowed to leave again.

But Nicholson could see that the arrival of Irving Scholar, which led to Burkinshaw's departure, was the start of a new era in football.

Nicholson told me, "The club's going public created extra pressure for the manager. Each season a profit had to be made to satisfy the City and, football being what it is, that is not easy to achieve. Keith was disillusioned with the way the team played in his last season and attendance at league matches had fallen. The wealthy directors who had taken over the club were assuming more of the managerial responsibilities, following the Continental system in which a managing director runs the administrative side and the team manager looks after the laying side only.

"I can see other clubs in England following this lead, so that they come more and more to resemble Italian clubs. This might well have advantages over our present system. Football's finances have changed so much for the worse that one man can no longer be in almost sole charge of a club as I was for 16 years. In Italy a new team manager or coach, with new ideas and methods, comes in every season, or every two years at most. He avoids disputes with players over pay and contracts, such as in which Keith was involved with Steve Perryman during his last close season and which affected their relationship for a while. In Italy the managing director deals with these problems, leaving the team manager to devote all his time to working with his players. When the players no longer respond to his ideas, it is time for him to move on to another club; there is little time for complacency among the players."

Remember Bill was telling me this for his life story which was penned in 1983!

While Terry Neill could hardly be described as a Spurs man, Nicholson was Spurs, and Spurs are Nicholson. Still are, always will be.

But there were some fun moments with Terry Neill in charge. If he had nothing else, he had a sense of humour, and a willingness to have some fun. As well as a picture of myself with Martin Chivers (colour page 7, E), at the restaurant, I have also kept a picture of a race with Terry Neill (colour page 8, A). There was never a dull moment when Terry was a manager of Spurs, believe me! Even though he wasn't around for too long. One sunny afternoon, for some reason, a challenge was thrown down and Terry and I found ourselves on the dirt track surrounding the White Hart Lane pitch, racing around it! I took the first bend ahead and that spurred Terry to kick in and he ended up the winner by some distance as the picture will testify.

Terry was never going to be a managerial norm, but my relationship with him continued when he became Arsenal boss, and long after his managerial career came to an end, when he opened a wine bar restaurant close to the *Daily Mirror* building in Holborn. That meant I actually saw much more of Terry than I had when he was in the game.

The publishers held a book launch at Terry's bar, when I co-wrote an account of Terry Venables' life in football and also his business affairs with Steve Curry, and Steve and I are pictured with the launch editions of the books outside of the bar (colour page 8, C).

After a good few years Terry sold the wine bar and headed off back to Ireland.

The fact that the *Mirror* Group sold off their traditional Holborn HQ and headed off to Canary Wharf sounded the death knell for Terry's bar, a watering hole for many of the football mad *Mirror* boys of the time.

CHAPTER FIVE

G-Men Greaves And Gilzean, Nice One Cyril Knowles And Danny Blanchflower.

Sometimes even the most experienced and knowledgeable can miss a story that's right under their nose. I literally missed one right under my nose when I was still very much a novice, so perhaps I can be excused, a little bit at least. I was so nervous about presenting a bag full of footballs for the lucky *North London Weekly Herald* prize winners on the White Hart Lane pitch before Alan Gilzean's testimonial match, that I didn't notice how one fan had run onto the pitch and kissed the feet of legendary striker "Gilly". The first I knew of it was when I picked up the *Evening News* the next day and there was the picture on the back page. The young girl was one of the recipients of the prizes, and the long haired bearded guy in the background on the far right was the *Herald*'s resident photographer Nick Townsend, who went on to become a writer and whose last position was as columnist on *The Independent on Sunday* (colour page 9, D). There is another picture of me actually looking up to see what was going on and pulling out one of the footballs to hand out to the queue of prize winners (colour page 9, D).

Gilly was one of my all time heroes. His grace and artistry was awesome. His bald head belied his athleticism. Often Berbatov has been likened to Gilly but Gilly was pure magic, and very consistent, unlike the sulky Bulgarian. Gilly was also more devastating the bigger the occasion. The Scot processed a telepathic understanding with Jimmy Greaves, who was lightning fast over a short distance, and never seemed to miss when in front of goal. The G-men were mind-blowingly good and they were a joy to watch. I would leave White Hart Lane bitterly disappointed if I hadn't seen them perform to their brilliant best in every game. At least, that's how it seemed in those days. The real glory days, the days of the European Cup, magical clashes in the semi-final against Benfica and the Black Pearl, Eusebio. Even glory in defeat. It would be glorious attacking football, out playing the opposition, even when they failed to make it to the final they deserved to grace.

I met Jimmy Greaves briefly in my privileged days as a journalist but never really had the chance to chat with Gilly, or many of the Spurs heroes of the early 1960s.

It was not until I made it to the local *Tottenham Herald* newspaper that I acquired an intimate knowledge of the players.

I had the chance to interview one of my boyhood heroes, Spurs full-back Cyril Knowles, in the back of a cab during my days as a novice reporter. The fans would sing Nice One Cyril, and the mild mannered guy off the field would be a demon on it launching into rock hard tackles that would intimidate any winger in the world.

But tragedy struck when Cyril's son was killed by a stray stone that flew through the front windscreen of his car, and struck him on the forehead. Cyril was unable to play for some time, and it was impossible to convey to him how sorry you felt. I would watch him wandering around the ground in a daze, before he was in a fit state of mind to resume his football career.

My career was taking an unusual turn. The *Weekly Herald* was part of a chain of local newspapers owned by Thompson, with their training school in the North East. I loved being the Spurs local reporter so much I never envisaged ever leaving, but for personal reasons I moved from the *North London Weekly* Herald to the *Newcastle Journal* and stayed in the North East for just over a year before returning south, moving to Croydon to begin work for the *London Evening News*. In those early days there were seven editions a day, the first was on the streets to greet everyone going to work in the capital. I would need to leave Croydon at 6am to be assured of being at my desk by 7am to prepare for the first edition, which was really much of an overnight, but to work hard on the second edition. My usual route was to take the fast trains from East Croydon which was a short bus ride or long walk from home, then from Victoria to take the tube to Blackfriars, and from there it was walking distance to the old Associated News building. My first sports editor was Peter Watson, next up was Vic Wakeling who went on to a TV career and to become head of sport for Sky.

I got to know Danny Blanchflower very well when he became manager of Chelsea. I always thought he was the right man for the wrong club. He was a perfect fit for Tottenham, but not so for Chelsea. And it showed.

Although not many people, including his own players and especially the media understood him, I found his bizarre conversations and thoughts absolutely enthralling. Perhaps, it was because he was one of my all time heroes, captain of Spurs' fast flowing, entertaining and winning 1961 Double side that I warmed to him more than most. Maybe, it was because I liked to listen to him, because somewhere there was enormous insight, if you were able to decipher it. He didn't last too long in management; he was far too intelligent, years ahead of his time. But he did put up with me, which was something, as I was young, over-enthusiastic, and probably over the top, ringing managers like Danny at 6am in order to check out national daily newspaper stories, mostly tittle tattle, for the first of the evening editions of the *London Evening News*. The first edition "copy" deadline was something quite bizarre in itself, at 7.15am, which meant that I prepared the stories overnight at home, on one of those old fashioned typewriters, and brought them into the office to be immediately subbed and to be raced off for the extra early edition.

Eventually Danny's wife must have complained, because he picked me up on it and told me that he couldn't take any more 6am phone calls. I was surprised that he didn't do this after the first one. I suppose he understood my predicament. That was Danny all over.

He told me that he had actually had a plaque made which he hung over his bed, and it said, "Don't take any calls from Harry Harris before 7am".

I didn't believe him. But with Danny you just didn't know for sure.

CHAPTER SIX

My First Cup Final.

True to her word, when it came to the first all-London FA Cup final between Spurs and Chelsea, I had a ticket. My mum took me and a friend to Wembley and waited outside while I sat there with my pal from school who also supported Spurs and from our semi-obscured vantage point loved every minute of a game all the pundits branded boring, one of the worst Wembley finals of all time.

But it didn't stop me rushing around to the local newsagents when I got back from Wembley to queue up for a copy of the evening papers "Pink" edition with much of the games match report and early pictures. As I was to discover later, the intensity of putting together a match report virtually as the game is still in progress, meant that there was no time for real analysis, so the evening paper report passed little comment on the quality of the game. However the Sunday papers and the Monday editions were scathing about the lack of quality and excitement as both teams cancelled each other out in their determination not to lose the all-London final which meant so much to both sets of fans.

I kept every one of those less than flattering match reports. In fact, I had dozens of scrap books filled with the programmes of each game, and the newspaper cuttings. I loved the *Daily Express* reports which carried a little star with a number in from one to five as a rating for the match and its entertainment value.

Incredibly some of the names that would appear on those reports, Steve Curry from the *Express*, Nigel Clarke in the *Mirror*, were still around when I finally broke into Fleet Street.

And, some of the players in that final became more than heroes on the pitch but people I grew to know extremely well.

One of them was Joe Kinnear who went on to become manager at Wimbledon and Nottingham Forest and more recently, caretaker manager at Newcastle. Joe was the pin-up boy of the Spurs team that year. He then became an outstanding manager with the Crazy Gang and he was a nice bloke. I liked him a lot.

Unfortunately, Joe is responsible for one of my biggest howlers during my time at the *Mirror*. Joe was coaching abroad and wanted me to write an item in my column informing everyone back home how well he was doing and wouldn't it be a great idea to hire him in England. I was more than willing to oblige, but in the article I suggested he had a wonderful lifestyle, to go with his managerial success, from his luxury apartment "overlooking the Himalayas." Yes, I hold my hands up... not easy overlooking the Himalayas, is it? Well, you might have thought one of the sports sub-editors would have spotted it. Maybe they did, and thought it too good to change!

Joe was coaching in one of the world's most unlikely spots at the time, Mongolia, and was just about forgotten back here. I like to think I helped him more than a touch, and when he eventually returned to English football, it wasn't long before he was managing Wimbledon and making quite an impact there.

Spurs became synonymous with the FA Cup, and thanks to my job, it became a double whammy for me as my club enjoyed such triumphs at Wembley.

None more so than when Spurs beat Manchester City 3-2 in a magical night at Wembley in a reply that all genuine football fans will recall with great warmth... the solo goal from Ricky. Tears of despair turned to tears of joy for the bearded Argentinean as Spurs went marching on to lift the trophy in the 100th FA Cup final.

Ricky was so often overshadowed by his fellow countryman, Ossie Ardiles, but not this time. Ricky became the most unlikely hero in the Year of the Cockerel. Off form and finally substituted in Spurs' first Wembley clash with gallant Manchester City, Villa came back with enormous courage in the replay to score two goals, the second and eventual match winner, is now accepted as the best ever to grace the old famous Wembley turf, and it will take some beating in the new one.

Ricky said modestly immediately after his personal Cup final triumph, "I wanted to score a goal but I think I was a little lucky, having two defenders so close to me." As I got to know Ricky better, this was genuine modesty, believe me.

Ossie commented after the final, "I have always wanted to play at Wembley and I have now played in two finals. To win the Cup is marvellous."

Captain Steve Perryman observed, "I was conscious of the fact that Spurs had won all their five previous FA Cup finals, but I think we were worthy winners in the end."

Spurs won back to back FA Cup finals, beating QPR in another replay, which was the team's 66th match of the season. Underdogs from the Second Division made Spurs battle all the way. Graham Roberts was fouled by a tackle from Tony Currie and Glenn Hoddle sent keeper Peter Hucker the wrong way from the penalty spot to score the Cup winning goal.

Of course it was also a time of enormous controversy as Ossie was forced to move out of the country during the Falklands conflict, returning in January the following year from his war-imposed loan spell with Paris St Germain.

Graham Roberts lifting the UEFA Cup with Tony Parks' match winning penalty save, Keith Burkinshaw quitting the Lane, Spurs being listed on the Stock Exchange in September where all 3.8m shares at £1 each were sold out within minutes of trading, the game had changed completely.

I bought my 100 shares, persuaded by Irving that it would be a good thing, and only recently cashed in those shares. I was persuaded to do so only because of the way foreign ownership now moved into the Premier League, and because the paper work that landed through the post promised that the original share certificate would be returned. It wasn't. It has got lost in the post. They hadn't even bothered to protect it with a recorded delivery. Cheap skates! A piece of precious nostalgia lost. Should never have sold those shares; I'm kicking myself.

Anyway, after Irving took the club to a full Stock Exchange listing, the game was destined never to be the same again.

Change continued after the Bradford fire, Heysel and Hillsborough, with Spurs one of the club's along with Liverpool, Norwich and Southampton affected by the UEFA ban, as they were the four barred from the UEFA Cup, with Manchester United unable to compete in the Cup Winners' Cup and Everton deprived of a place in the European Cup.

Spurs, though, were still a major force to be reckoned with. In the 1986-87 season Clive Allen, who hitherto had failed to fulfil his promise, was given a new formation under David Pleat, with Glenn Hoddle playing as a second striker, supported by Ardiles. Allen bagged 49 goals in the season, although he was sold a year later.

Spurs' proud record of never losing a major Cup final at Wembley was surrendered to Coventry City, who won their first final in their then 104-year history. Clive Allen had opened the scoring, but Dave Bennett equalised, Gary Mabbutt claimed the Spurs second, and a flying header by Keith Houchen equalised again, while Mabbutt's own goal sealed Spurs' fate, and put poor Mabs in the record books, scoring at both ends.

CHAPTER SEVEN

Ossie Ardiles And Ricky Villa... Ossie's Going To Wem-Bley, His Knees Have Gone All Trem-Bley, Come On You Spurs, Come On You Spurs...

Ossie was one of my footballing heroes as a winner of the World Cup with Argentina in 1978. His arrival at White Hart Lane with compatriot Ricky Villa was a landmark in English football history. It is credited with opening the floodgates for foreign footballing imports. Ossie and Ricky were one of the main reasons for a change of direction for me, as their arrival convinced me I needed to return to London to cover this momentous event, rather than remain in the North East.

The call to return to the capital and back to the Lane was over powering. Spurs had been promoted and somehow recruited two of the world's best players. It was too much. I was mentally packing my bags as soon as the news of their signings broke in the press and with wall to wall TV coverage of the amazing events.

A switch to the *London Evening News* was the start of my journey through some of the major tabloid newspapers in Fleet Street, the street synonymous with national newspapers as it was there that the majority of the offices were situated until the late 1980s exodus to wherever they might have relocated, Wapping, Canary Wharf and the City.

And yes, it was all worthwhile. Back to my spiritual home, and the football was breathtaking, not at first, but eventually there was a new dawn of exhilarating football with the likes of the Argentineans combining so beautifully with the flamboyance of Glenn Hoddle. A wonderful Cup final triumph. And who can forget the build up with "Ossie's Going To Wembley, His Knees Have Gone All Trem-bley, Come On You Spurs, Come On You Spurs"; Chas and Dave ruled the airways, it was magical.

It was a good career move too. Four fabulous years on the *Daily Mail*, 18 on the *Daily Mirror* and nearly seven on the *Daily Express*.

The Spurs team of the 1980s brought back all the old memories of stylish football, exhilarating goals, and mouth-wateringly good individuals.

Up front Spurs boasted a lethal combination in Steve Archibald and Garth Crooks. They called Archibald the "White Rat" because there was always a suspicion he was up to no good, but Garth Crooks was a lovely guy, whom I got to know on a personal level after he had finished his playing career. Garth is now with the BBC, and takes an awful amount of stick for his long winded questions to managers and players after games, but at least he is a highly respected figure, who has been chairman of the Sports Institute.

Garth regularly calls for some inside gossip on certain subjects he is featuring on *Football Focus*, and he has been around to my home a few times to conduct interviews for the Saturday lunch time programme.

At the end of their playing careers, Ricky returned to his homeland to buy a ranch, while Ossie moved into management. I've seen Ricky many times since, he often returns to see Ossie and to make some personal appearances.

After a successful stint with Swindon, followed by spells at Newcastle and West Brom, Ossie was welcomed "home" as manager of his beloved Tott-en-ham. Ossie took on the challenge that Glenn Hoddle had, at first shied away from, quite wisely. Hoddle had opted to sign up for Ken Bates at Stamford Bridge at the time, but a phone call from Sir Alan Sugar nearly scuppered Ken's plans and Hoddle's move to the Bridge where he was destined to start the Chelsea revolution with the signings of Ruud Gullit and Mark Hughes.

I had managed to arrange an audience with Sir Alan at his Chigwell mansion. I went there with my then sports editor Keith Fisher. It was a great interview with headlines such as "They Think I Am The Man Who Killed Bambi"; it was his first big interview after he axed Terry Venables as his business partner and chief executive at the Lane.

During our chat, I suggested that Glenn Hoddle was the man to take over from Venables. Sir Alan loved the idea. Keith and I popped round to a pub in Chigwell close to Sugar's home, where I filed my interview and, at the call box in that pub, contacted Glenn to offer him the Spurs job. Glenn said he would come back to me after he gave it some thought overnight. I relayed the message back to Sir Alan.

The next morning Glenn said how tempting it was, but there were two major problems which he found insurmountable. Firstly, he had given a commitment to Ken Bates and didn't feel he was able to break it even if he wanted to, which I took to mean he probably had already signed the contract. And, secondly, he didn't feel the time was right to become Spurs manager, no matter how tempting, even though he thought he was destined to return to the Lane as their manager, and it must have crossed his mind that the chance might never come again, Glenn felt, intuitively, that it would be far too "political" to be the one taking over from Venables after all the problems with the fans and the war with Sir Alan. The supporters had sided with Venables in the High Court battle with Sugar. He had made the right judgement call alright.

Ardiles, though, was eager to take up the baton. He was by far a more political animal than most footballers, and he felt he could handle it; that his own popularity with the fans would see him through, and see off Venables. Ossie won the hearts of the Spurs fans from the word go with his cavalier style. With Jurgen Klinsmann flourishing in front of goal, and an array of attacking talent, Spurs were often a joy to watch going forward, but defensively they became a nightmare, and, for all of their attacking flair, there were large gaps at the back for opponents to exploit. It was a throw back to the first few games of the Ossie and Ricky show, the ticker tape reception making it just like the summer's World Cup in Buenos Aires, the tingle of anticipation as Ricky beat Peter Shilton in the opening game at Forest which ended 1-1, but the second game at home, Spurs lost 4-1 and in September they were thrashed 7-0 at Anfield.

When Sugar was still plain old Alan, he had the good sense to consult the professionals when it came to some of his major decisions concerning the appointment of managers. Shame then that he didn't take more notice when he asked my opinion! Sir Alan's forte was that he was one of the nation's best businessmen. He might have been able to appoint the best men for the job at Amstrad but he was clueless when it came to appointing a manager, and if he was honest with himself, he would admit it.

With Ossie, however, it was a question of the manager not taking my advice.

Determined to help Ossie as the sack rapidly approached in 1994, I convinced Sir Alan that all that was required was a strong-minded, top of the range, wise old hand, an experienced defensive coach to organise a way of halting the leakage of goals. I suggested former England assistant coach Don Howe, and yes, a former Arsenal manager. Times had moved on to the point where even the Spurs fans would accept someone like Don, highly respected, very well liked within the football industry and someone who would also carry the supporters who had become knowledgeable enough to have accepted The Don. Yes, Sir Alan said, he could see the logic of having someone like Don Howe onboard. But the Spurs chairman stressed that he couldn't just simply pull someone in like that without consulting Ossie and that it would have to be Ossie's decision to proceed with the idea. I suggested that the first step would be to sound out Don, to ensure he would be interested in considering the task. I was given the go ahead by Sir Alan to sound him out (I think you can see how I would come across some of my big exclusive stories – it's not all about just sitting there waiting for the phone to ring, the best approach is to do the ground work yourself, and when the time is right your reward is the story).

I contacted Don, whom I had known and liked for many years, and had come to respect, not just for his extraordinary prowess as a coach, but for his honesty and integrity and I knew he was someone who could keep a confidence. Too many people in football loved to gossip and leaks were all too commonplace.

Typically, Don Howe demonstrated all the characteristics I had defined above, when he insisted that he would like to become the Spurs defensive mastermind, on the proviso that Ossie himself made the request personally. I couldn't help but agree with Don. In fact, most of the time I couldn't help but agree with Don. He was that type of guy. He, like, the chairman, was uncomfortable to press ahead unless this stipulation had been met by Ossie.

Once again I tried to set up a call between Ossie and Don.

I contacted Ossie and as diplomatically as I could put it, told him that his job was on the line unless he could sort out the defence and that I had the perfect guy who could come in and assist, that it would only be on a part-time basis, and that it need only be short term. Why not see how it goes? Ossie said he would think about it and come back to me. The next day, I heard nothing, so the day after I phoned Ossie again. Ossie gave me a firm "thanks for trying to help, but no thanks".

Ossie had teamed up with playing pal and coach Steve Perryman, and the manager felt he would be undermining Perryman's position. He went even further and suggested it would be an insult to Steve Perryman, who had played a record number of times for Spurs as a midfield star, or at times at full-back, and had sufficient experience to organise the defence. I didn't ask Ossie whether he had run the idea past Steve Perryman. It was hard to assess by his tone whether he had or not. But my gut feeling was that he had not. Ossie had, though, passed by the opportunity to recruit Don and in my view, save his job. Results took another turn for the worse. Spurs were dumped out of the FA Cup at Notts County and I was there to see it. It was not a pretty sight, I can tell you, for myself, and for all the Spurs fans. It is tough to be dispassionate under these circumstances. I have to think like a journalist, rather than a fan. I needed to take a cold hard look at it, and assess whether a change of manager was required, as Spurs fans were now generally turning towards that view, whereas they had supported Ossie despite some dire results. Ossie was heading for the sack.

Sir Alan told me at the time that it was one of the toughest decisions he has ever had to make in football because he liked Ossie so much, and there was always a nagging feeling at the back of his mind, along with the fans, that Ossie could have succeeded at his beloved club, given more time – and a Don Howe type defensive coach!

Despite the deep hurt at being sacked by Spurs, Ossie continued to strive to be successful in management, even though he was forced to leave the country to try his luck in Japan, and he has managed in a number of other countries since. Ossie and I have remained firm friends.

I have become reacquainted with Steve Perryman through a mutual friend Barry Chauveau, a life-long and passionate Spurs fan. As the legendary Spurs captain of the 1970s and early 1980s, and the club record appearance holder, Steve P was the shop steward of the Tottenham team that produced arguably the best Spurs team since the Double side of the 1960s. He enjoyed a firm grip of events inside the dressing room as skipper of the team when I was a regular at White Hart Lane. We got to know each other well. I respected Steve for his enormous influence within the dressing room, as well as being an accomplished footballer and leader of the side on the field. I am sure he respected me as a journalist, even though players and those within the industry would never admit it.

When Steve moved on from Spurs in March 1986, he and I became involved in one of the most bizarre incidents of my journalistic career when Robert Maxwell, then proprietor of the *Mirror*, and, as it happened, chairman of Oxford United FC, rang down from his lofty, opulent, marble-pillared, penthouse offices and overnight accommodation to request my presence in his private apartment above the *Mirror*'s Holborn editorial offices and headquarters.

He gave a rather mysterious reason for wanting my presence; he told me that he had something related to football that would require my expertise. The only hint he gave me was to suggest he would need my vast experience and knowledge about players' salary levels. It was all very intriguing. When I arrived, via the private lift, escorted through to his suite by the butler, Maxwell was sitting in a big, comfortable leather seat in a room adjacent to his offices, and he beckoned me to join him in an equally relaxing seat. He told me that Oxford's newest and biggest signing was about to come through another door in a few minutes and, as he was unfamiliar with the terms and bonuses expected by a top First Division star, he wanted me to help him negotiate the player's wages. Wow. Now that was a first. I'd never heard of anything like this before. My first thought was this is going to be an even bigger surprise to the player who walks through the door, than it has just been to me. My mind was racing with all the ramifications of such a task when before I could come to any real conclusions about how I was going to play this whole tricky scenario, in strode Steve Perryman.

I was not sure who was the more shocked, him or me. After a few minutes getting used to this surreal environment and circumstances, it was hard to keep a straight face. I just kept thinking that Stevie P must be absolutely mortified to see me there with his prospective new chairman, with the touchy and delicate subject of the meeting being the terms of his contract.

Fortunately I didn't think his wage demands were particularly excessive, just right in fact, par for the course of such an established, yet aging superstar. Clearly, Maxwell thought them excessive, and that's why he needed me there to gauge whether he was being taken for a ride. I told Maxwell I didn't think Perryman was making undue demands. Maxwell was actually quite generous when it came to matters such as this. If his manager had identified Perryman as a key signing, I am sure Maxwell would have probably gone even higher in the payments. However, Maxwell was also mindful of the financial limitations of a club like Oxford. So, he needed to strike a happy balance.

After I gave my verdict on Perryman's wage demands, pointing out that I thought them to be fair, Maxwell agreed the deal on the spot.

Time, then, I thought for a quick interview. How could Steve refuse?

CHAPTER EIGHT

Irving Scholar, And How I Signed Chris Waddle.

Irving Scholar and I share one deep and meaningful relationship outside of marriage – a love affair with Spurs.

It was this common ground that bonded us together to become great allies during his seven years as Spurs chairman, and well beyond that point to this very day. If there is ever a time when I need a friend, need advice, or just someone to talk to, Irving is always there. Well, there if you can track him down between his home in Monaco, his frequent holidays in the States, and his roaming between London hotels, usually staying at the Millennium in Mayfair.

During Irving's seven years in charge of Spurs, I was in the privileged position of knowing so much of what was going on, with the then chairman increasingly informing me of the inside information assured that it would go no further – and certainly not into the *Daily Mirror*... unless he specifically gave the ok.

It led to a string of blockbuster exclusives that left our rivals trailing behind. It also underlined my strength when it came to accurately reporting events at the Lane. Spurs fans came to trust my stories as gospel, and they had every reason to believe them. In some cases, I even helped create the stories!

For example I broke the story in the *Mirror* in 1986 that David Pleat would be the new Spurs manager following Peter Shreeve. Unfortunately for David Pleat, I also knew that he was going to get the sack, something that hurt him very deeply, arguably more so than the run of the mill dismissals which are hard enough to take for the manager. On this occasion David Pleat was still very much the right man as Spurs manager. In fact he was being touted as the next England manager. It also hurt Irving Scholar to get rid of him, because it was due to non footballing matters; David Pleat had been accused of kerb-crawling. It was also a very difficult period for me; I liked David, and no one wanted him to survive more than I did. I was the journalist putting Pleat forward as an outsider coming through rapidly on the rails as a contender to become England manager once Bobby Robson retired. I doubt whether he would ever have made it right to the top of the England pile, but he might have come very close. I have kept in touch with David, who is now an expert TV pundit and analyst. I know how bitter he feels at times because he never quite fulfilled his potential as a manager.

One of those more unusual episodes came when Irving called me to help him in his excruciatingly difficult quest to sign Chris Waddle from Newcastle United. There were other top clubs chasing the winger's signature, but Irving had set his heart on the Geordie star.

As I had lived and worked in the North East I had a rare insight into the Geordie psyche. Irving wanted to tap into this local knowledge. Irving had discovered that Waddle had a great reluctance to move to London. I could understand why. Certainly at that time there was still a great deal of subconscious mistrust of the southerners, and their lifestyle.

Waddle had been selected to play for England at Wembley and his wife wanted to surprise him by leaving work early that Wednesday, travelling down to watch him play – without telling him.

Irving was arranging the tickets at Wembley, and asked if I would forsake my usual place in the press box, covering the game, to sit in the stands with Mrs Waddle to keep her company, but more importantly, to subtly talk to her about my experiences living in Newcastle – and then to convince her it would be the right move for Chris if he signed for Spurs.

The deal was that I would convince my sports editor of the merits of forgoing the normal match report on the England game, in pursuit of the big transfer story.

The whole escapade worked. I chatted to Mrs Waddle about life in Newcastle and how easy it would be for them to settle in the south, and how wonderful Spurs would be and how supportive the chairman is.

Chris Waddle signed for Spurs – and I got the exclusive story. Job done. What a coup for the club and for the newspaper. More importantly, it gave me enormous pleasure in playing my role, however small, in securing one of the most talented individual players for my club.

As for Chris, he didn't forget the part I played in persuading him to move. Chris inscribed in his autobiography "To Harry, thanks for being around."

Irving was regularly accused of selling Spurs stars, but actually his only interest was buying them. He never interfered with the decisions of any of his managers to the extent that people thought he did. After all the trouble Irving went to in acquiring Chris Waddle, he hardly wanted to flog him, irrespective of how much profit he would make.

The truth is he did not want to sell Waddle to Marseilles in 1989. Spurs had been approached with an unbelievable offer from Marseilles, who had established themselves as a major European force at the time, and he felt it was an obligation to the player he particularly admired and with whom he got on with, to at least inform him of this unique opportunity. Irving hoped Waddle would turn it down and he made it absolutely clear to him that he didn't want the England left-winger to go. To help put the French club off, his manager Terry Venables was mandated to put a ludicrously high valuation of £4.5m on 29-year-old Waddle's head, and no one expected Marseilles to come up with that kind of money, which then would have been the third highest fee of all time. It's like Real Madrid offering Manchester United £100m for Ronaldo; they might want him and do everything they could to get him, but Real were never going to offer anywhere near that kind of silly money. But when Marseilles came back to match Spurs' valuation, it was a staggering amount of money at the time. It would have been financial madness not to take it. Don't forget Spurs actually paid a mere £600,000 for Waddle from Newcastle.

The funny thing is that, following the sale, Spurs then came third in the league the following season and won the FA Cup the year after.

The banning of English clubs from European competitions for five years from 1985 proved a real setback for a club with such a fine European pedigree as Spurs had, having qualified more often than not. It is ironic that in the first 15 years since Irving left the club Spurs had only qualified twice, the second time in 2006. With Juande Ramos winning the League Cup, the club were back in Europe on a more regular basis, but the goal to qualify for the Champions League still looked some way off.

As Spurs were the first British club to win a major European title, it is imperative for the club to resume their status as one of the big clubs in Europe. The real power lies within Europe. When once it was the possibility of a European Super League breakaway, the Champions League has managed to cement UEFA's authority with the GI4 club movement fading all the way out of existence.

Irving and I share a fascination with the politics of football, the intrigues, the plotting, the television deals, the unscrupulousness within the industry.

For both of us it has been an eye opener, just how many people were desperate for power and influence, and how far they would go to attain it.

One aspect in particular intrigued me as a journalist; the bungs. And the pursuit of those who perpetrated such "crimes".

Sir Alan Sugar coined the term "bung" in his High Court battle with Terry Venables, but Irving came across the boot money philosophy that had existed in the game before he took control of Tottenham, during his tenure of office, and long afterwards.

After my former *Daily Mirror* colleague Brian Reade penned his account of his life with one bird – the Liver Bird, it inspired me to write this account of my affair with one bird – the Cockerel. I know from first hand Brian's passion for Liverpool, and I am sure he feels the same about my affinity with Spurs. Brian wrote a column for the sports pages of the *Mirror* and I was more at the sharp end of the news gathering and know from my investigations that the bung culture existed far more profoundly than anyone within the game has cared to admit.

Irving Scholar knows from his first hand experiences of the bungs, and he has told me the names and the details – none of which I can repeat here for legal reasons. However, Irving can only go so far with his expose into the murky world of football and bungs.

His first Tottenham manager Keith Burkinshaw is credited with labelling agents as "leaches" but Irving soon discovered how managers were on the take as the game began to be taken over by greed and crooks. The game was awash with agents spreading around the money in illegal payments to smooth deals, but only Arsenal's George Graham got caught red-handed with his fingers in the till.

But then it was the Inland Revenue and not the football authorities who closed the net. The football authorities have proved to be notoriously bad at nailing the villains, and even when they have the best intentions it always seems to go pear shaped.

With the Lord Stevens/Quest team pawing over 362 transfers from

January 2004 until 2006, and *Panorama* desperately trying to snare Big Sam Allardyce and Harry Redknapp, the issue of bungs led the national news bulletins in the early part of the 2006-07 season, just as they had done in different periods, without really amounting to very much.

For Irving, it has been amusing to see so many within the football industry shrugging their shoulders and suggesting that it doesn't happen now and perhaps it might have existed in the not too distant past but only very limited. Talk about sweeping the bungs issue under the carpet.

Irving knows the truth after his period as Spurs chairman, he knows of two unbelievably big name superstars and equally major managerial legends who have asked him directly for bungs – of course, Irving refused them without a moment's hesitation.

Here are the details of the offers of bungs, but clearly, for legal reasons, the names of everyone concerned are not mentioned. Nonetheless, the football authorities should take note, not that they would do anything about something that happened so long ago. The great get out is that the FA would find it hard to act retrospectively against clubs whose ownership has changed hands, managers who might no longer be in the game, and players who also might have long since retired and not be involved in football. All these scenarios, though, are merely hypothetical, and in no way attempt to identify those who were involved.

Bung One... Irving's manager went to see him with a transfer target in mind, but with a problem.

"I can't deal with this manager. He is so difficult. Can you speak to his chairman? I really want the player."

Irving approached the chairman of the club concerned and, after a few conversations thrashed out a price of £500,000 for the player, a lot of money at that time.

A couple of weeks later, Irving's Tottenham manager at the time came back into his office. "I've just had a call from the manager's assistant with a demand for £30,000 in cash."

A furious Scholar told his manager, "There is no way I will put the club or myself in that position. I will not contemplate getting involved in anything illegal", Scholar told his Spurs manager.

Scholar insisted that there would be no back hander to the other club's manager. Scholar told his manager that everything would have to be done in the normal way. The manager left with a flea in his ear for even having the nerve to suggest to Scholar that he should pay the rival manager a transfer back hander. But Scholar's manager totally accepted and understood Scholar's stand, even though the chances of acquiring the player were now miniscule.

The matter of a back hander for this manager was never raised again. The transfer did not go through.

Scholar declined to tell me who the manager requesting the back hander had been. However, I guessed it in one. And, to be fair, it doesn't take an awful lot of guess work. This manager was notorious for asking for bungs, and was well known within football circles for liking his cash in hand, usually handed over to his assistant.

Bung Two... This time Irving wanted to sign one of the best young strikers in Britain, one destined to become one of his country's greatest ever strikers. But the deal fell through because he refused to pay a bung.

Now here's the twist. Usually an agent, or the manager himself, through his assistant, would ask for the cash. On this occasion Irving received a call from a director/chief executive of another club NOT involved in the purchase of the player. Mr X, a very well known figure in board rooms, suggested that if a £50,000 cash payment was made to the manager of the player's club, the star striker would be on his way to Spurs.

It's interesting to note the rationale behind this particular demand for an illegal payment. The striker was on his way out because he was just too good for this club and was on the move to bigger and better things. His manager feared that without this striker his club would be relegated, and he would get the sack. He was seeking some "insurance" for the inevitable consequence of selling the striker. The proposed deal was a £750,000 fee plus £50,000 for the manager – and this proposition came from the senior figure of a rival club! Quite what it had to do with him is a mystery to this day. However, when Irving started negotiations with the club actually selling the player, the price suddenly rose to £1m and the deal was dead.

This snapshot of how major transfer deals regularly occurred a few years ago is the backdrop against which the Lord Stevens/Quest "bung" enquiry was set. The problem has been endemic for a long time. The question is how do you prove things when there are no records and while managers, players, agents, and even chairmen and chief executives keep their lips tightly shut about what they know? Perhaps, they were all in it together? Now, the conspiracy theory is the one that the City of London police have been investigating for quite some time.

Of course, Irving himself once fell foul of the football authorities when it emerged that Spurs had paid interest free loans to induce players to sign for the club. But Irving has always told me that if he had known he was breaking the rules he would never have done it. He had been told by the professionals inside White Hart Lane that this practice was perfectly acceptable. The club notified the Inland Revenue and actually paid the tax due, which was how the problem came to light. Irving insists he never intended to break the rules, and once he discovered that the loans contravened the rules, ordered them to cease immediately.

Irving quickly discovered that in football, you could trust no one. After being brought up in the world of property and having dealt with City institutions and high flying businessmen, it was a shock to his system to discover that in football a handshake means little; sometimes absolutely nothing. A handshake in Irving's business world, was a man's word, which was as good as a done deal. Then, Irving came across agents, managers, players and even fellow chairmen, where he began to learn the true meaning of the phrase "bung".

Irving once shook hands with Sir Alex Ferguson, when he was still plain Alex, to become his Spurs manager, only to discover it didn't actually mean anything when the Scot changed his mind and left Aberdeen for Manchester United instead. Irving was deeply upset. He wanted to take his club back to the top and, when he left, Spurs were still rated as one of the Big Five. But they were far from the summit of the English game, where he really wanted to take them. Had Scholar been successful in landing Ferguson, it might well have been different, who knows?

On a personal level, Irving Scholar is one of those true football enthusiasts, who is in love with Spurs, and I hate to say this, but I have discovered someone more obsessed with the club than myself.

Irving also fancied himself as a footballer, and to be fair he wasn't bad. Eighteen months before he bought the club, Irving played in a Tottenham shirt on the White Hart Lane pitch and scored two goals in a charity match. That, no doubt, persuaded him to go off and buy the club! Just two weeks before the 1984 UEFA Cup final, he played in the same team as Ossie Ardiles at Leyton Orient in another charity game but it didn't end in glory this time, as unhappily for Irving, he snapped his Achilles and ended up on crutches. He was, in turn, snapped hobbling out of the ground on those crutches with his lower leg encased in plaster with physio Mike Varney finding it extremely hard to suppress a grin. However, Irving also saw the funny side of it, and he was also smiling as he hobbled out of the stadium. In fact when Spurs lifted the UEFA Cup trophy after a thrilling penalty shoot out at White Hart Lane, Irving had to be wheeled around the stadium in a wheelchair and was determined to be in the dressing room to celebrate along with his players, despite his painful handicap.

Despite all the problems I inflicted on Irving with my probing questions and incessant "begging" of him to allow me to publish some of the stories he told me about, the former chairman remained a true friend and confidante many years after his break from any business involvement with football. His biographer, Mihir Bose, called him "the Martin Peters of the board room", reflecting Sir Alf Ramsey's comment about his midfielder being 10 years ahead of his time.

In his biography *Behind Closed Doors*, this is what Irving had to say about me...

"The only journalist I was close to was Harry Harris. He had been on the local paper in Tottenham and shared my deep love for the club. Almost from the beginning we got on very well. Harry, by this time, was the chief football writer of the *Daily Mirror*, which meant that like all Maxwell employees, he was at the beck and call of Captain Bob. How Harry balanced Maxwell's dictates with his own journalistic need is a story that he must tell one day himself, but all I can say is that, despite everything I went through with Maxwell and others, my friendship with Harry remained unimpaired. If anything, I came away appreciating how well he understood my own, and Tottenham's predicament."

CHAPTER NINE

Keith Burkinshaw, Peter Shreeve, The Ray Clemence Secret And The Gerry Armstrong Wind Up.

Terry Neill's reign at Spurs was brief; just two years. Keith Burkinshaw, recruited as a coach, took over with Pat Welton his assistant. Burkinshaw, with the new power within the board room and Irving Scholar pulling the strings, brought Bill Nicholson back into the fold as an advisor. In his time at the club Burkinshaw won the FA Cup twice and Spurs went out, in his final game, as winners of a European trophy. After eight years Burkinshaw was disillusioned about how the team performed in the league in that final season, he was engaged in a long running contract dispute with the influential captain Steve Perryman, and also saw the whole dynamics of the game change.

Burkinshaw was though, a one-off in managerial terms, and his time at the club was filled with oddities...

Burkinshaw and Peter Shreeve were pacing up and down at the airport. I was part of a small contingent of football writers who had accompanied the Spurs official party on one of their major European adventures on the way to winning the UEFA Cup. Keith and Peter were serious types. No mickey taking, no practical jokes, no mucking around with these two in charge... especially the manager. Shreeve, a former taxi driver, had a much more sociable streak to his nature, but Burkinshaw is a deadly serious Yorkshireman. So, on the morning of our return to England, it was hardly surprising to find the pair together in an agitated mood. This scene went on for some considerable time, and it dawned on us that the club's charter flight, which carried the players, the directors, the media and a handful of elite supporters (all of whom footed the entire bill for the journey) was being held up for some reason or other.

Enter Ray Clemence to the airport departure lounge being supported by two Spurs staff members. It was now perfectly apparent what had been going on. The England goalkeeper had a stupid grin on his face, as he was bellowing out a song or two.

Ray did not stop singing at the top of his voice, all the way up the stairs to the plane, and he had to be helped to his seat by his two aides. Once seated he fell into a deep sleep and all was peaceful again; except for Burkinshaw's mood. Not surprisingly, he was fuming.

It transpired that Clemence had been out all the night before and had got back to his hotel bedroom just as the Spurs party had left in a convoy of two coaches, the players and officials heading the way, followed by the media bus and the few fans. Oblivious to the time, Ray went straight to his room and fell fast asleep and was still in his bed when a couple of the Spurs staff were assigned to return to the team hotel to find him.

Peter asked the handful of press present if we would oblige him and the club and not report the incident. We agreed. It was a vastly different era back then in the early 1980s. The barriers have been growing higher over the years. Now there can be five or six representatives from one newspaper, depending on how high profile the event, whereas back then there was just one. It was far more controllable. We would then often go out drinking with the players ourselves, and we could tell a few tales about that, but, of course, we didn't. We would keep all the minor indiscretions to ourselves.

Ray Clemence, though, has progressed in the game to become England's goalkeeping coach, and all credit to him to bounce back from a rocky period when he was banned for a time from receiving FA Cup final tickets. Unfortunately, I was the journalist who broke the story in the *Daily Mirror*. I say unfortunately because such articles are never going to endear you to the person who is the central character, and in this case it was Clemence. Of course, from a pure journalistic view point it was a story that made headlines and was followed up by every conceivable media rival. But Ray was furious. He maintained that he had parted with his precious Cup final tickets as a gesture of good will to a relative, who had let him down and sold them on the black market, as it transpired. Ray put up a powerful case for his defence, but the FA insisted that the Cup final tickets were the responsibility of those to whom they were allocated.

I bumped into Ray many times within the England camp over the years, and although I would never say our relationship regained its friendly nature, he was always polite and would greet me with a smile.

For all those within the football industry who had reason to dislike me for whatever reason, there are just as many with whom I can say I have forged a special relationship. One of these is Gerry Armstrong. I first met Gerry when he signed for Spurs as a raw centre-forward from Irish football. We seemed to hit if off immediately. Gerry is an amiable fellow, and good natured. I liked him a lot. Once you've struck a friendship with Gerry, there is no one more loyal.

From time to time "offending" journalists are placed in a manager's sin bin, banned from a press conference or two, kept out of the loop of any inside information the manager might have wanted made public, usually for his own ends, and, of course, generally treated like shit for having the audacity to step out of line in some way. Often the "offence" might be trivial; being ultra critical of the team and more importantly to the manager or the tactics, maybe a mis-quote here or there that he has taken the wrong way, perhaps an over the top headline that caused him some kind of embarrassment with his players or worse still with his chairman. Quite often it doesn't take an awful lot to trigger a fit of pique from a manager, particularly one under pressure, and the majority are always under some sort of pressure. Some deal with it with a deliberate hard line approach designed to keep the media pack under his control, and one of the best control freaks with the media is Sir Alex Ferguson. He will use the most effective punishment for anyone who steps out of line, by causing them as much grief as he can in preventing them from performing their job. In the case of the BBC, he has refused to speak to them for years after an offending broadcast.

I was relatively new to the job of football reporting, still working for the *North London Weekly Herald* group of newspapers. For some reason around this time the then Spurs boss Keith Burkinshaw had got the hump with me about something I had written, and I was being shunned by him. Now, that was pretty damn tricky for me, as I was covering just about everything that moved in relation to the club, and it was tough if you were being ostracised by the most important man there – the manager. In fact, he even told me that he would not cooperate with me for a full month; that was my punishment for upsetting him.

Players at any club like nothing better than to "wind up" their manager if they can, and at this time the Tottenham stars were expert at this irritating little game, and they liked nothing better than winding up Keith, who didn't see the funny side of their many practical jokes.

On this occasion several players were in the treatment room, and Gerry decided he would use me as a means of winding up the manager. He kept look out at the door awaiting the manager's arrival, as Keith was always quite predictable about the time he would check out the injured players prior to the weekend's game. When Gerry spotted Keith, he rushed over to the phone, pretending to be deep in a meaningful conversation with me, and also pretending not to have noticed Keith entering the medical room.

"Sure Harry, no problem, we'll let you have the team for Saturday." It was hard for Gerry and the treatment room full of players to hide their sniggering, but Keith hadn't noticed the players mocking him, his blood pressure was quickly rising, as Gerry continued, "We've got some injury problems Harry so I will have to make a shrewd guess based on our training this morning what the team will be; Jennings..."

Keith was bright red by this time, according to Gerry, who loved telling me the entire story afterwards. Keith was shouting at Gerry, who told him that the players always gave this particular journalist the team every week. As it was intended to do, that only made Keith redder in the face, angrier, and on the verge of exploding with rage. It went on for quite some time with Gerry never letting on he never actually talked to me, until the players couldn't restrain themselves any longer, and when, finally, Keith realised it was just one elaborate wind up, he stormed out of the medical room.

The real funny side of it, of course, was that the players did feed me some inside information, and Gerry would often help me out with team news without giving too many secrets away. Gerry liked a laugh, but he was a true professional, and would never damage the team's chances of success by giving away the kind of information that the opposition needed to know.

CHAPTER TEN

Terry Venables And The Truth About My Revelations.

Spurs fans booed Terry Venables soon after he arrived at the Lane from London rivals Chelsea, but I was too young to fully appreciate why supporters took such a dislike to one of their own, and let them know about it.

I thought Venables was a skilful new star but even someone as young as I was could differentiate between Venables and his predecessors in the Tottenham midfield who were such colossus' of their era that it was tough for someone new to fit in. He just didn't seem to raise his own standards from his outstanding career at Chelsea. It was a demanding role to fill the shoes of players such as John White who had gone before him. Yet, he was part of the Spurs team that beat Chelsea at Wembley in the first all-London FA Cup final which was also my first final, so I have nothing but fond memories of an exciting day out. The match itself was hammered by the critics and, looking back, quite rightly for a stalemate of a contest, but for me it was the thrill of a lifetime just being there to soak up the atmosphere with that unique adrenalin rush of the build up to such a big day, at least the biggest day of the football calendar in those days before the Champions League mushroomed in format to ensure the biggest English clubs were always in contention towards the end of the season.

In those days, the London evening papers produced a football special edition, so arriving back home, I was allowed to stay out waiting patiently at the newsagent for the "Pink" with the early pictures and the report of the Wembley final. To me all those Spurs players; Pat Jennings, Joe Kinnear, goalscorer Frank Saul, even Terry Venables, were my heroes. Somehow the standard of the match didn't seem to matter. Never mind the quality, I was there, and it was special.

Venables left the Lane after a short spell of personal torment, and I never really, as a Spurs fan, followed his career much after that. It never crossed my mind that he would play such a significant part in my career as a journalist.

From a professional point of view, of course, Venables and I seemed to be joined at the hip! A lot of people felt that I had a vendetta against Venables. He certainly thought so after my investigation into his private business affairs and his sporting business practices during his time as chief executive at Spurs.

My investigations into Venables though, brought me into contact with some fascinating characters. One of them was TV journalist Martin Bashir. My first contact with Martin was as a rival! Unknown to me, Bashir was heading up his own TV documentary with the BBC investigating Venables. At the same time I had already been employed as a consultant by Roy Ackerman at an independent TV documentary makers, Diverse, to make a special on Venables for Channel 4's *Dispatches* programme.

After a couple of months it became apparent that *Dispatches* were in a race to screen the Venables story on TV ahead of *Panorama*, where Martin Bashir was working on the same expose. *Dispatches* was screened first only a week ahead of *Panorama*, and while the *Panorama* documentary was highly acclaimed, no doubt because it appeared on BBC, I always felt that the *Dispatches* programme had come closest to unravelling the complexities of business interests and practices inside Spurs.

Afterwards I became very close to Martin and got to know him well enough to call him a personal friend. We often talked about collaborating on a number of other football-related exposes, but never quite found the right subject. Martin was working as a freelancer for the BBC at the time, and was very ambitious and, of course, his documentaries on Princess Di and then Michael Jackson brought him global recognition and prominence which eventually manifested itself into a lucrative contract to work in the States.

Not just Venables, but all of his close associates, came under my *Mirror* investigation, and some who were friends and close contacts prior to it became instant enemies at first, although they mellowed as the years went by.

Frank McLintock might have been captain of Spurs' great rivals Arsenal, but I knew Frank well; a highly articulate and very approachable player and then manager but when he became an agent linked to the Venables saga my relationship with him deteriorated. Frank naturally took great exception to being drawn into this controversy and felt he had been victimised by me in the *Mirror* articles. We didn't speak for some considerable time. But credit to Frank, he has appreciated that I was doing my job, that I had got all my facts right, and we have spoken, although hardly what I would call any deep or meaningful conversation.

The *Daily Mirror* labelled Venables "El Til" in one of the hardest ever hitting back page headlines in my series of exposes.

The five year Premier League enquiry team handed over their extensive files to the FA. Graham Kelly was the chief executive of the FA at the time and he allowed me to deliver files in a big black case, marked with a huge *Mirror* logo, on our investigations into irregular payments and dodgy invoices in football. Graham seemed keen enough and most definitely sincere in his desire to clean up the game of any sleaze. We were pictured together outside the FA at Lancaster Gate and inside his office and he promised to act upon our findings. We reported his interview in great length in the paper. The FA, under Graham, did not, eventually, push the boat out in this area and it took the accusations by Luton manager Mike Newell in early 2006 to finally spark a proper investigation into transfer dealings.

The DTI declined to pursue the matter of Venables' financial affairs in the criminal courts. A number of cases against celebrities of this nature brought by the DTI had failed in front of star struck juries, so the DTI wisely opted for a civil action against Venables instead. However, when the charges were made in the civil court, they referred to them as "criminal" charges. Venables was found guilty in the civil courts and banned by the DTI for seven years from serving as a company director. That ban expired in January 2005. Wisely, from Venables' point of view, there is precious little one now hears about his business affairs.

The general perception at the time was that I was anti-Venables. Worse, that I had a personal vendetta against him. Nothing could be further from the truth. But Venables clearly believed it, and I had problems from a section of the fans whipped up by the propaganda.

It was even reported in some papers that Venables had, in fact, issued legal proceedings or was about to do so, and that the whole issue he had with me and the *Mirror* would end up in the High Court. I never actually received a writ. Well, that isn't strictly true. Despite numerous placings of times in the media that he had actually sued, he never quite got round to it... until the very last minute.

Libel actions can be brought up to three years after the event of the article being published. On the last possible day inside the three year limit his lawyers dispatched a messenger to deliver the writ, which I would need to take hold of personally for it to take effect. The messenger somehow got through the security at the *Mirror*, reached the third floor editorial offices where I would normally be found and asked for directions to my desk.

Now, came the crunch, he had to find me and hand over the legal documents personally, which I would then, in turn, pass on to the legal department to handle.

So where was I? I was at home on a rare day off. We football writers and indeed most journalists in general, do not work nine to five and certainly don't keep regular "normal" working hours.

It may be a huge surprise that my declared opinion of Venables is not clouded or prejudiced by my investigations into his business dealings; I believe he is an outstanding coach. I thought he did a marvellous job with Barcelona and England, and that he wasn't that bad as a Spurs manager, actually. It was only when he became an owner of a club that he bit off far more than he could chew in my opinion.

In fact, I recommended him to be England coach. Kelly, made an audacious decision that it was time the FA came down from its Ivory Tower, as he put it to me and a few of my journalistic colleagues, and consulted with some of the constituent parts of the footballing industry about the selection of the new England manager, and as such asked a group of three respected football writers to give him our opinions. We were invited into Graham's hotel room when we were all together covering an England game. Unanimously we agreed that Venables was the right choice, strictly on his prowess as a coach, and someone who would be able to galvanise the players together into a team.

Venables, was, indeed, appointed England coach and had a good tournament when England hosted the European Championships in 1996, although it can be argued that he had a fortuitous tournament too, and that the highlight, the thrashing of Holland, was against a nation on the downward spiral. Perhaps so, but Venables succeeded in bringing the nation to its feet singing *Football's Coming Home*.

Long after the dust had settled on my investigations into Venables, it seemed our paths were destined to cross.

We dined at the same Indian restaurant early in 2006, the Bombay Brasserie near Gloucester Road tube station. I walked past his table, his jaw dropped open and all he could manage was one of his usual cheeky smiles. "Not stalking you, Terry!" I said cheerily as I walked on.

Yes, I can forgive Terry for thinking I was stalking him because this was not the first time we seemed to bump into each other…

One of the funniest was when Terry was strolling along in the sunshine, outside of the five star La Manga hotel, oblivious to all around him as he concentrated on the business deal he was hatching on his mobile phone. El Tel was back on his Spanish beat putting into place the final part of his master plan to construct a La Manga-style resort that specialised in coaching young players. My sources had told me that Tel wanted to import poor African kids with outstanding footballing promise and develop them into future stars, and then have part-ownership in them to sell onto the elite European clubs. Naturally, my chances of discussing this grand scheme with Terry were zero considering our history. Although I knew in advance of Venables' mission in Spain, it was sheer coincidence that I just happened to be spending some time in the resort also. Suddenly our paths crossed outside the hotel as there was no way I could avoid him. Linda and I were walking towards the hotel entrance, and I hoped he might continue his conversation and not notice us. But Terry turned and caught my eye. His voice stopped, his jaw dropped, and off he dashed cutting short his mobile phone conversation for fear I might overhear. "Don't worry, Terry, I'm not stalking you". I said. Venables, to his credit, smiled, unable to speak as he was making his hasty exit.

My battle to uncover the truth at Tottenham left its scars. Deep scars. It was one of the reasons my love-affair with Spurs, and with football in general took a nasty turn for the worst.

You have to recall how temperatures had been raised to boiling point by the Venables-Sugar war. Sugar was vilified as he walked to the court, his car pelted with rotten eggs, and he suffered personal abuse. Venables was hugely popular with the masses, Sugar was viewed as the villain. Anyone siding with Sugar was instantly branded as a traitor to the Spurs cause.

It wasn't that I sided with Sugar but I must confess, it certainly looked that way. I had my concerns, but as a journalist, my objective was to view the facts. As a fan, I was torn. In my opinion Sugar was in the right, but the fans also had a point; they wanted him to spend even more cash on players, while Sugar knew that it was prudent to balance the books and he refused to gamble with the club's long term financial security. I was also in the privileged position of having the inside track, whereas the fans were largely in the dark. While I could publish most things, I could do so only providing I had the evidence. It was tough enough even with the evidence with Venables' lawyers threatening legal action; their purpose to slow me down, or stop me completely, rather than actually really wanting to fight a legal action in court.

Some of my best friends, those closest to me for many years, suddenly turned on me. At first they tried to persuade me to back off, but it soon became nasty.

One of my greatest pleasures had been to stroll along the route towards the Lane, relishing another match and all the thrills and twists and turns the afternoon's entertainment might bring. It would be followed by listening to the managers in the main press conference, and then hanging around to catch an interview with the odd player who felt inclined to stop for a chat with the media. It provided a wonderfully rounded account of the game, which provided the basis on which to write a match report.

This whole experience was soured by the level of abuse I would suffer at the hands of the fans, although I must say it was a tiny section of the Spurs support, who had turned against me, in favour of Venables and deeply opposed to Sugar. Fans who recognised me from appearances on Sky, more so than the postage stamp by-line picture in the *Mirror*, wanted to scream abuse at me, or more menacingly stride up alongside to whisper dire consequences for maintaining my stance against Venables in favour of Sugar.

I started out by trying to explain my stance with anyone who did not raise the debate beyond acceptable politeness but it was to no avail. Few of the pro-Venables mob wanted to hear my version that, as a coach, I admired his talents, but as a businessman, his practices needed to be exposed in the public interest. After that it was up to everyone to make up their own minds.

The Venables-Sugar saga soured my love-affair with Spurs to such an extent that it put the thought in my mind that there would come a time, long before retirement, when I would seek a life change, that continuing "on-the-road" was no longer something that inspired me, nor did I enjoy. Therefore, when the chance emerged with the *Express* Group in 2000, I left the *Mirror* to write a column with the Daily and the Sunday titles without having to cover the games. It was an investigative, news led Ahead of the Game column which meant I could work from home. I became the first and probably the last football writer, who did not actually go to the games, which threw my colleagues, it must be said.

However, I did go to far more games than my rivals imagined, but instead of rubbing shoulders with them in the press box, I was in the more influential sections of the grounds, either in the director's box, or with the leading sponsors in their executive boxes. Believe me, I gained far more insight there than ever I did in the press room, where most of the gossip came from fellow journalists.

I have, after a while, regained my enthusiasm for football, and for Spurs in particular. It is also long past the Sugar era. Sugar has sold his shares and apart from popping up in the director's box for home games now and again, very little is seen of him, and certainly precious little, if anything, said about him in connection with Spurs.

Spurs fans have come to change their opinions of Sugar as the years have rolled by. They no longer seem to have such partisan views with regards to Sugar and Venables. However, the Spurs supporters still mistrust Sugar's motives for being involved with "their" club and will never be won over about the reasons he held back in the transfer market as a prudent financial policy.

I deal very little now with Sugar, who has moved on, as indeed have I.

In retrospect, it is easy to criticise Sugar for riding to Spurs' rescue to raise his own profile. He has been knighted for his business acumen and for what he has done for the country taking that business abroad. But, it can be argued, that he shot to real fame because of his involvement with Spurs.

CHAPTER ELEVEN

Gazzamania!

Gazza has been a hero of mine and many Spurs fans who would have witnessed him dribbling into the opponent's box, getting down to the by-line, turning and dribbling his way back out of the box past the same defenders, before turning again to face the goal, and shooting into the corner. Such invention and impishness endeared him to the Spurs faithful right from the start. Irving Scholar wanted to buy Gascoigne from Newcastle, but knew there was strong opposition lurking in the background in the form of Manchester United. But Irving told me how he pulled out all the stops and made it his personal mission to persuade the Geordie boy to come to London and play for his beloved Tottenham. Irving made it happen and no one really knows the inside track on how hard he fought to pull off the transfer.

Gazza thrilled me immensely in the Lillywhite shirt of Spurs, that's where he belonged, and how every Spurs fan rejoiced when he fired that long range free-kick over David Seaman's head in the FA Cup semi-final.

It was such a tragedy to see Gazza wound up like a man possessed when he came out for the Wembley final and inflicted that horrendous knee injury upon himself with that ludicrous flying tackle on Gary Charles. Gazza was never quite the same force after that.

A measure of my admiration for his talents, is that when I received my first PC at the *Mirror* offices and had to use a password for the first time, I chose G-A-Z-Z-A, and used it throughout my stay there.

For my part I invented the phrase Gazzamania. Mel Stein was his agent, friend, minder and advisor for more than a decade. I know Mel exceptionally well. I would consider Mel, a well known sports specialist lawyer, among my confidantes, and you know anything confidential with Mel will stay that way. Mel knew that it was a two-way street. In many ways Mel was responsible for ensuring Gazza shot to fame and into the superstardom stratosphere, by keeping him out of as much trouble as he could, and certainly in his younger days wielded greater influence.

Stein wrote Gazza's first of many autobiographies and in it said, "*The Sun* started Gazzamania officially with their constant use of the phrase, but Harry Harris in the *Mirror*, had probably been responsible for coining the phrase almost a year before. All *The Sun* was doing, as it did so often, was reflecting opinion."

I first noticed Gazza's talents when he turned out for England's under 20s in the annual Toulon Tournament. People knew of this impish young Geordie in the black and white, but it was during this tournament when you noticed, not just his extraordinary talents, but his sheer cheekiness. The stadium had concrete layers to sit on, and precious few facilities, and one side was open to the motorway with a wire mesh and stretch of grass between the players and the cars. After scoring a spectacular goal, Gazza ran across to the side line looking out to nobody to begin his celebrations to an imaginary crowd.

Back at the team hotel, where a handful of Fleet Street's more junior journalists had gathered for a daily briefing, Gazza didn't simply look out of his window above us, but decided to urinate down in our direction. Talk about taking the piss out of the press!

At the airport, the players managed to wander off in groups to board the little buses to take you to the plane. Not Gazza. He managed to get himself a little lost, and ended up on the bus full of journalists and assorted FA officials. He was a bag of laughs, always smiling, and you

A: Dad and his little lad. My father, Jack, who died when I was five.

B: Keeping a tight rein on a four year old on Brighton Pier. But Jack, with fag in hand, was to die painfully from lung cancer because of his 60-a-day Woodbine habit.

A: The Harris Family. Jack is seated because, although always dapper in suit and tie, or in this case, evening dress and dickie bow, he was on the short side, so my mum Sara would always stand when photographed next to him. That must be Jack's mum in the picture.

B: All the kids at Canon Barnet Primary School look angelic, but this was a posed pic. School was more like a bare knuckle fight with bullies and rough house football in the playground. I'm in the second row on the left, up against the wall.

C: My school reports dating back to 1968 from Davenant Foundation Grammar School for Boys, which, for a century, was in Whitechapel High Road next door to the Salvation Army, until it moved to Debden in Essex, stressed my aptitude for helping out with the school magazine, my first rung of the journalistic ladder!

C

DAVENANT FOUNDATION
GRAMMAR SCHOOL FOR BOYS

Report for the TERM/~~HALF TERM~~ ending July 24th 1968

Name H. Harris — Form V

Age 16.2 — Average age of Form 16.7 — Number in Form 26

Position — Position for the previous Term/Half Term

SUBJECT	Examination %Marks	Examination Position	Effort	Comments	Subject Master
ENGLISH			B	Works steadily	EA
HISTORY			B	A conscientious worker.	[illegible]
GEOGRAPHY				He has worked well and deserves success.	P.J.B.
FRENCH			B	Worked well, but appeared more & more confused, probably owing to earlier failure to learn thoroughly.	[illegible]
GERMAN			B.		
MATHEMATICS				Has worked ne[...]	
ADDITIONAL MATHEMATICS					
CHEMISTRY					
PHYSICS					
BIOLOGY			A	He deserves [...] successful [...]	
TECHNICAL DRAWING					
WOODWORK					
MUSIC					
PHYSICAL EDUCATION					

Absences — Possible att[...]

A Good — B Satisfactory

We hope for a good result. Gave most useful help in preparing the School Magazine

J. Fyson — Form Master

DAVENANT FOUNDATION
GRAMMAR SCHOOL FOR BOYS

Report for the TERM/HALF TERM ending 16th July 1969

Name H. HARRIS — Form Lwr VI

Age — — Average age of Form — — Number in Form 17

SUBJECT	% Marks	Position	Standard of work	Comments	Subject Master
GEOGRAPHY	46		A	Although there is still a lot of work to be done, he is making good progress and is developing a mature attitude to his studies.	P.J.B.
ENGLISH	40		B	His language papers were satisfactory but in the Literature section his work is below required standard – he must plan his answers and set out his knowledge better	EA
HISTORY	21		B	He seems to find difficulty in expressing himself fluently. Also he is inclined to get confused when dealing with basic facts.	[illegible]
Physical Education			A	Good ability	[illegible]

Absences 6 — Possible attendances 117.

A Good — B Satisfactory — C Unsatisfactory

It seems that the next step in his work must be to improve arrangement & setting out.

Spurs' young up and coming winger Jimmy Neighbour, Chingford born, so one of the local lads made good, appeared on my Whipps Cross Hospital Radio programme which I did once a week along with Steve Tongue, free of charge, who worked on the rival local Walthamstow paper. Steve went on to become a well known national football writer.

A: Terry Neill didn't hang around very long as Spurs manager, and didn't hang about when he challenged me to a race around the perimeter of the Lane's pitch in pre-season. Although I was ahead on the first bend, the fit looking Neill tore away and won by a "smile".

B: Interviewing the team's left-back Cyril Knowles in the back of a cab. Nice One Cyril was a fabulous overlapping full-back but suffered personal tragedy while a Spurs star.

C: The launch of my book on Terry Venables. The launch took place at Terry Neill's bar/ restaurant in Holborn opposite the offices of my former newspaper the *Daily Mirror*. I was close friends at the time with the *Daily Express* football correspondent Steve Curry who co-wrote the Venables book. Steve concentrated on Venables the man, footballer and manager, while I delved into Venables' business affairs.

D: How to miss a story right under your nose! I was giving out the prizes of autographed footballs to the winners of the *Weekly Herald's* competition prior to the Alan Gilzean testimonial night at the Lane. I was so nervous standing out there in front of the big crowd on a cold night, that I completely missed a fan running onto the pitch to kiss the feet of the balding striker with the deft heading ability. Didn't see this picture or know anything about what happened until I saw it in the *London Evening News* the next day! In the far right hand corner is the *Herald's* photographer at the time Nick Townsend, who went on to become a well known football writer; the only snapper turned scribe I've ever come across.

E: The then Chelsea chairman Ken Bates enjoyed the hospitality aboard Alan Sugar's yacht so much he was conned into holding up a Spurs shirt giving a thumbs up! At least dear old Ken has a sense of humour. Sir Alan sent me the picture for a laugh too.

F: Former Spurs chairman Irving Scholar celebrated his 50th birthday with a private party in an exclusive upstairs room at The Ivy, not far from his London offices. I presented him with a special Magnum from one of the sponsors who had a label written to commemorate the occasion.

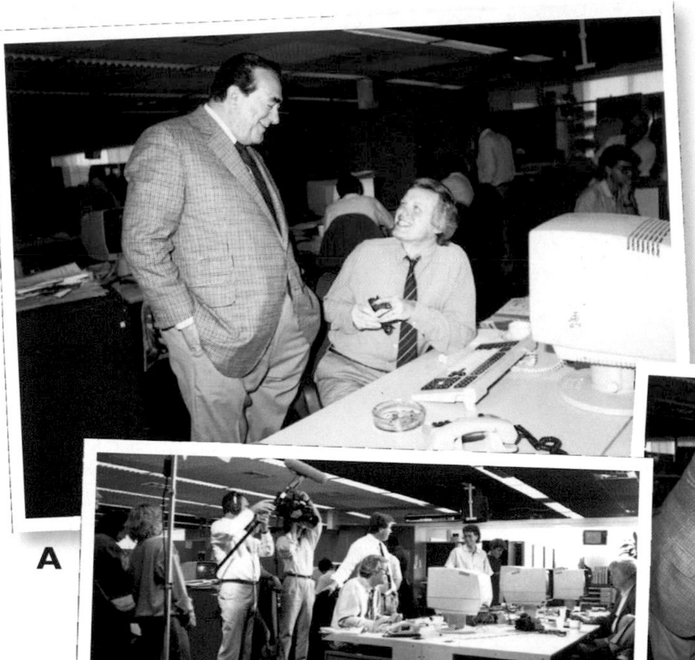

A: The mighty *Mirror* proprietor Robert Maxwell breezes onto the editorial floor to see what we are up to. Sir Michael Grade began his journalistic career on *the Mirror*, and we had brought him back to pen an article. You can see me at my desk in the right hand corner. Grade's return made some great TV as you would expect from the head of a number of TV networks.

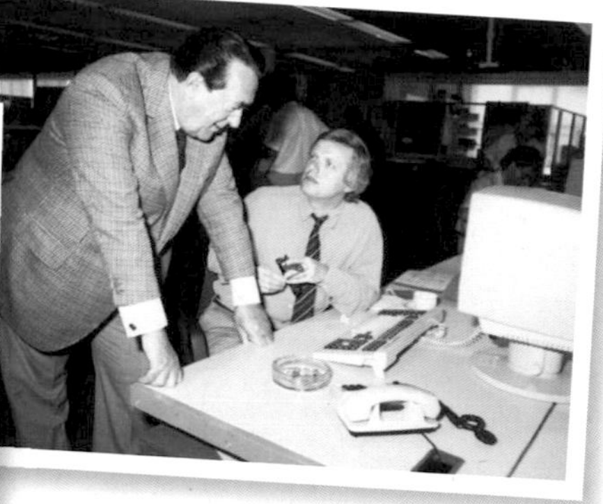

A

B: My guests for the Football Writers annual awards dinner, when the Footballer of the Year was presented with his glittering trophy, always attracted a star studded table when I was on the *Daily Mirror*. No expense was spared back then. On the far left I am seated next to plain old Sugar in those days who in turn was next to Richard Desmond when he was merely the boss of *OK* and whose editor was Martin Townsend, now editor of the *Sunday Express*. Football agent Jon Smith is also there plus the more recognisable face of Graeme Souness. Alan's son wanted to sit next to the former Spurs player, albeit youth and reserves.

B

C: Another awards dinner, and again Sugar is next to me. On the other side is the then minister of sport Kate Hoey. Next to Kate is Alan's PR advisor, Nick Hewer who shot to fame on *The Apprentice*. Ken Bates is also there flanked by his wife to be Suzannah, and my editor Colin Myler, one of the best and most controversial editors of his generation. Next to Suzannah is Bob Blair, a veteran at the *Mirror* until he retired, and next to him is Spurs legend Garth Crooks. There is an Arsenal element there too, a great personal friend in David "Rocky" Rocastle and his agent Jerome Anderson who is sitting next to fellow agent Jon Smith.

D

Sir Alan and Lady Sugar
request the pleasure of your company
at the marriage of their daughter
Louise
to
Mr Mark Baron
at "Bramstons", Roding Lane
Chigwell, Essex
on Sunday 5th August 2001
Ceremony at 4.00 pm
Reception and Dinner to follow

RSVP
"Bramstons"
Roding Lane
Chigwell, Essex
IG7 6BE

Carriages 12.30 am
Black Tie

LOUISIANNA
LONDON

Mr & Mrs Alan Sugar
requests the pleasure of the company of
Mr. H. Harris & Linda
on board the Motor Yacht Louisianna at
on Tuesday 23rd April at 8.00pm
RSVP 01277 208004
(Louise)

MRS ANN SUGAR AND FAMILY
HAVE PLEASURE IN INVITING YOU
TO A SURPRISE 50TH BIRTHDAY PARTY FOR
ALAN SUGAR
AT THE REFORM CLUB, 104 PALL MALL, SW1
ON SATURDAY 15 MARCH 1997 AT 7.30PM

R.S.V.P. BY 28 FEBRUARY 1997
ANN SUGAR
C/O LINDEN COTTAGE
125 HIGH ROAD
CHIGWELL, ESSEX
IG7 6QQ

BLACK TIE
CARRIAGES 2.00AM

E

D: Invites from the Sugars; to Alan's 50th birthday party, to his daughter's wedding and as a guest to a party aboard his yacht *Louisianna*.

E: Outside and inside the House of Commons with the minister of sport at the time Kate Hoey, who took up the *Daily Mirror* campaign to expose corruption in football.

My *Daily Mirror* sports editor Keith Fisher told me to stand in for Gazza when the unreliable Geordie failed to turn up at the newspaper's Holborn headquarters for a photo shoot organised by England shirt sponsors Umbro. Gary Lineker, David Seaman, Paul Parker and me... I have played for the England Press team, but this picture was something unusual!

A: I must confess that I had a very unusual working relationship with Robert Maxwell, who treated me with more kindness than he did his own boys!

B: The day and venue for the infamous Hand of God goal by Diego Maradona. I was there. And here's the picture to prove it, outside of the Azteca Stadium in Mexico City.

C: One of my many interviews with Pelé, courtesy of my great friends at Umbro, this time at a trade fair in Germany, where there just happened to be a picture of Gazza. This was a great picture opportunity as Pelé had been talking about Gazza and his England career.

D: In the days of the Rumbelows Cup, the trophy had been delivered to the *Mirror* building for a photo shoot, so a chance for a Monte Fresco, put the Cup on your head, snap. There is no snapper more famous than Monte.

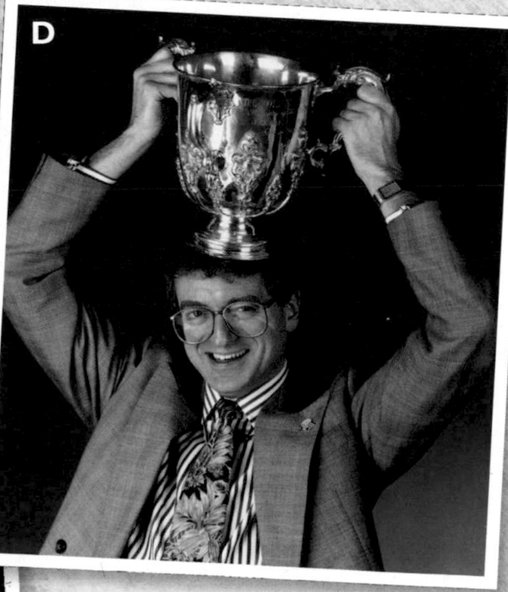

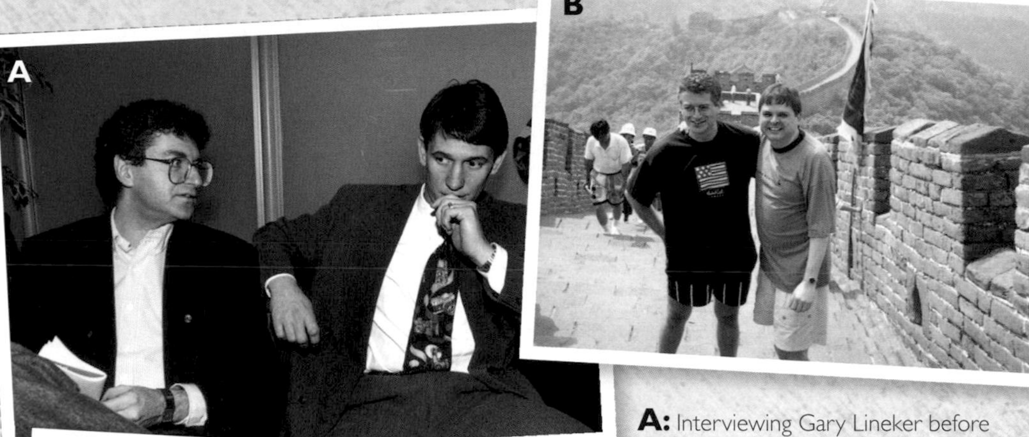

A: Interviewing Gary Lineker before he boarded his flight to Japan to see his surroundings after signing for Grampus Eight in the "J" League.

B: England were on tour in China, and here I am at the Great Wall of China with friend and journalistic colleague Alan Green from Radio 5 Live. One of the most genuine guys in the business.

C: Spurs fan and journalistic colleague Mihir Bose, now sports editor for the BBC, pictured together at Irving Scholar's 50th birthday bash.

D: Transformed into a cartoon character on the *Daily Mirror*'s daily strip cartoon. The one and only journalist in the fabled chronicles of Striker, aka Dave. If Striker needed advice, I was the one he would turn to. If Striker had a story, I was the guy he would contact.

E: Invited by the FA and one of their sponsors to try out my skills with the then England coach Glenn Hoddle. The then *Sun's* football writer Brian Woolnough, soon to move onto the *Daily Star* is pictured with me and Glenn. Here I am showing off my left foot.

F: Yet another happy snap at the Football Writers annual awards night. I am at the far end with football agent Geoff Weston. Spot my *Daily Mirror* editor at the time Piers Morgan, and in the front is the world's No I football agent Pini Zahavi, rarely, if at all ever photographed. Sir Alan Sugar's son Daniel is next to Nick Hewer, who in turn is next to sports lawyer Mel Goldberg. On Zahavi's right is former Spurs keeper Hans Segars, alongside Ken and Suzannah Bates.

G: TV presenter Gary Newbon hands over the coveted Silver Heart. I won the Royal Variety of Great Britain's Contribution to Sports Journalism award in 2004, and there are not many dedicated football writers who can boast such an accolade. In fact there are none.

H: At the launch of my World Cup book, at the Sports Café in London with Spurs legend Martin Peters on the left, George Cohen, Jack Charlton and Gordon Banks. What a line up of the Boys from '66.

A: Harry Redknapp was one of my many guests at a series of World Cup "live" TV and radio shows. Peter Bonetti and Paul Parker are in the picture.

B: At the studios each of the guests signed pictures, and Harry was happy to oblige. (Both pictures A and B courtesy of Leonie Schwarz. 01344 841 327, 07788 728518. leonieschwartz@mac.com).

C: Simon Harris was delighted that Spurs won the Carling Cup at Wembley.

D: Ossie Ardiles and Paul Miller appeared with me on a recent Sky One show called *Off The Bar* hosted by Matt Lorenzo. Tony Gale is on the left.

E: Computer images of Spurs' swanky new ground, essential to make the club competitive financially with their rivals.

sensed here was a boy in love with the game and loving every minute of it. No one imagined he would turn into a man with such dark moods and deep personal problems.

As the years rolled by Gazza remained a favourite player of mine. I can recall telling Bobby Robson to pick him ahead of the final friendlies before Italia 90, and the England manager telling me that Gazza was "daft as a brush" suggesting he couldn't be trusted. I am convinced Bobby listened to what I had to say, and although he wouldn't admit it, he picked Gazza because of it. Gazza went on to become a star of that World Cup, and we can all recall his tears in the semi-finals and Gary Lineker's reaction.

I had many great trips to Rome to watch Gazza play, when he wasn't injured that is, for Lazio, but I never wanted him to ever leave Spurs and, despite appearances, I know how much Irving fought to keep him.

Such was Scholar's desperation that he accepted my advice to tempt Robert Maxwell, my proprietor at the *Mirror* at that time, to buy Spurs instead of the Sugar-Venables pair up that somehow I sensed would come to grief. But Gazza was so close to Venables, it was always going to be impossible to gain Gazza's support for the Maxwell move. Yet, when Maxwell made his pitch to buy Spurs, the Big Man wanted to have his picture taken with Gazza. Maxwell was a star worshipper and loved the celebrities and being in their company. He also loved the idea of owning such a big club like Spurs where Gazza was the big star.

But as Stein wrote, "On 9th September, the morning after the Derby game, the headlines were not so much about Paul's hat-trick as Robert Maxwell's bid for Tottenham. Paul's reaction was immediate, 'I'm not playing for that fat bastard. If he takes over then I'm off.' He knew the appalling way Maxwell, when owner of Derby, had treated Arthur Cox, knew that football to him was an ego trip rather than a passion, and wanted no part of it.

"Harry Harris of the *Daily Mirror* phoned me on behalf of his newspaper's proprietor to ask if there was any chance of a photo of Gazza with Maxwell if the deal went through. 'No chance,' was the reply."

As the battle for control of Spurs hotted up, it finally came down to the wire between Maxwell v Sugar. Ironic, as Maxwell was my ultimate boss, and Sugar would eventually become a close associate.

Stein wrote, "But Maxwell was still playing his own game, and whilst no formal proposal had been made, he was still using the *Mirror* to sway public opinion in his favour by its campaign to keep Gazza, as a national treasure, in the country of his birth. Harry Harris, chief football writer of the *Mirror*, was recalled from abroad."

Mel was referring to how I was summoned from Malaysia, the last port of call for a summer England tour in 1991, to help Maxwell orchestrate his final pitch to buy Spurs.

It had been a long tour; a vast amount of travelling to Australia, New Zealand and the Far East. It was hard to get motivated for the build up for a friendly against a team you knew England would hit for however many goals they felt in the mood. I had watched every England game since 1986, but this one felt like a pure waste of time, being undertaken purely for commercial reasons by the FA. It felt like one game too many. Now, it would be extremely hard to convey to any genuine football fan, who, quite rightly, believes that journalists like myself are in such a privileged position, travelling the globe to watch games at someone else's expense, in the lap of five star hotel luxury and on expenses to dine in the finest restaurants.

For so many years, it did feel just like that. A dream come true, not so much a job as a fantasy fulfilled, every football fan's ideal. But after 150 games a year, travelling out of a suitcase non stop, even the dream can sometimes turn into a nightmare. In the steamy heat of Malaysia, it somehow felt like hell. If this had been a World Cup tie, or Spurs playing for the World Club Championship, nothing would have been more attractive to me than another night in Malaysia. But, in truth, we all knew this hardly even qualified as a genuine international friendly. More like a practice match.

It was my turn to organise dinner for the Morris Men, a group of Fleet Street football writers who were often together. Neil Harman of the *Daily Mail* was a new recruit along with Steve Curry of the *Daily Express*, Colin Gibson of *The Daily Telegraph* and Stuart Jones of *The Times*. I had booked a table at an Oriental restaurant in the Malaysian hotel after arriving in that steamy city earlier in the day.

Feeling more than fed up with so long on the road, I decided it was time to stir things up with a phone call direct to Maxwell. It had all gone strangely quiet with Maxwell's interest in Spurs, while the Sugar camp seemed to be on the verge of pulling off a deal. I had called Irving Scholar for an update, and sensed it was now or never for Maxwell's bid; Scholar was on the verge of selling out with his partner Paul Bobroff. Terry Venables wanted to take control and was looking to every conceivable consortium to raise the funds without much success and a lot of controversial failed attempts. Now Sir Alan Sugar was hovering in the background and this meant business.

After winding up Maxwell about how close he was coming to losing out on the battle for control of the North London giants, to someone like Sir Alan, he immediately ordered me home to coordinate his media campaign to win over the hearts and minds of the Spurs fans and the wider public. Maxwell would also lean heavily on my inside track on events inside White Hart Lane with my close friendship with Irving Scholar and how best to keep the FA and Football League at bay because of Maxwell's son's ownership of Oxford and his own control of Derby County.

Imagine the reaction from Steve Curry and Colin Gibson when I rang them to explain I was off and couldn't make dinner. They couldn't believe it. "Surely you can come to dinner before you go in the morning?" suggested the affable Colin. "Sorry, I am actually going this minute – bye".

The guys back at the *Mirror* HQ whom I informed had to make the hastiest of hasty travel arrangements to get me back instantly. Of course all the flights had gone, there was one night flight left, and no room, apart from first class. With the seal of approval from Maxwell himself, I travelled home first class. My instructions were to report for duty to Maxwell the next morning.

It wasn't until I landed 20 or so hours later that I heard the news that Lineker had bagged four in England's predictably easy victory. But I was in the centre of the storm surrounding Spurs and that sounded far more exciting, I must confess.

It was my idea to focus on Gazza, whom Venables had lined up for a move to Lazio. And, I am sure, Maxwell's pitch to keep Gazza had resonance with Spurs fans, who were devastated that he had to be sold off to pay off the debts. It nearly worked, but Sugar won the day, which was probably for the best for all concerned in the long run given the later revelations about Maxwell's plundering of the *Mirror*'s pension funds.

I would not have pushed the Maxwell option if I didn't believe in it at the time. I would never have done anything, willingly, to harm, anything connected to Spurs. Never. Perhaps, with hindsight, it was wrong. Yet, somehow, even though it all went pear shaped with Maxwell, I know Irving would have ring fenced the club's finances around any Maxwell takeover that would not have fluctuated had any outside forces affected other parts of the Maxwell empire.

I followed the entire Gazza saga with enormous interest, both personally and professionally. Like Irving, I wanted Gazza to stay, and would have done everything in my power to assist Irving in his quest to balance the books so Gazza could stay at the Lane. It wasn't to be. But at least Gazza went out in a blaze of glory and, as one had come to accept with such a wayward talent, with excruciating pain and controversy.

Venables was a beleaguered man and badly in need of some encouragement and it continued to be supplied in just one competition, one in which Spurs had excelled over the years, the FA Cup. Spurs were drawn at home to Brian Horton's Oxford United, the club so much linked to the Maxwell family, who had already disposed of Chelsea at Stamford Bridge with a convincing 3-1 scoreline, but now they came across Gascoigne in his most irresistible mood, as he scored twice and made the other two goals in a thrilling 4-2 success. It was a performance that had Venables purring, "You cannot compare him to any player from the past. He has Dave Mackay's attitude, a hunger for the game. He has that upper-body strength that helped make Maradona a great player."

Super agent Dennis Roach, commissioned by the Spurs board on Irving's recommendation, had been busy on the Continent finding a good deal for Gazza, while Gazza was performing his mind boggling tricks. Roach's own deal was to take 1 percent of any transfer fee up to £7m and 1.5 percent for anything over that. He rang Scholar to say that Lazio of Rome were interested and a meeting was arranged. This was the start of the protracted Gazza saga, the signal that Scholar was about to lose his battle to keep the club's, indeed the country's, most talented player at the Lane. Gazza was helping to build up his own reputation as the Spurs FA Cup run continued on 16th February 1991 with another outstanding virtuoso performance against Portsmouth at Fratton Park, where another two memorable goals carried Spurs into the quarter-finals, where they would face Notts County.

Just 10 days later came the club's annual general meeting, and the speculation was building that Venables was going to front a takeover bid for the club, backed by some influential investors. But he was reluctant to elaborate on his plans. At the meeting, chaired by Nat Solomon, who had been brought in by the Midland Bank worried about their loans, the board sat at the top table, with the professional advisors seated to the right and Scholar and Venables to the left.

The meeting was held in the Chanticleer, the restaurant run by the football club where the fans would eat before the matches. There was the promise of pertinent questioning from the Tottenham Independent Supporters Association, which had been formed in the wake of the Maxwell revelations. Scholar knew he was a man under fire and that he was being fingered as the director who had led the club into crippling debt. It was only partly true, for the blame was a collective one which the board of the plc had to shoulder. That was little consolation to Scholar as he faced his inquisitors. But the reception was less hostile than he had anticipated.

Solomon handled the meeting skilfully, giving the irate fans the opportunity to present their questions, even if the answers to many of them were vague and indirect. Solomon told those who doubted his commitment to Tottenham, "I have not been a supporter of this club for the last 55 years to preside over its demise."

The board outlined the financial position; debts of £13.6m and liabilities totalling £22.9m. Solomon made it clear – money had to be found or star players sold. The Midland Bank were owed £10m and that debt could be called in at a moments notice. Solomon added, "Regarding star players, namely Gascoigne and Lineker, I would like to say very clearly that I speak for the whole board when I say we fervently hope we can find a solution to our problems that will not require them to be sold. Nevertheless, if an offer is received by the board, we will have an inescapable responsibility to look at it carefully in light of the prevailing circumstances."

Solomon confessed that discussions with three potential buyers were under way; Venables was party to one of them, the second on behalf of financial services company Baltic, and a third, unidentifiable, but not connected to Maxwell.

The shareholders were informed there had been no financial gain from the loan deal with Maxwell to pay off the Lineker transfer and that he had not cashed his dividend cheques, which had saved the club well in excess of £100,000. Although Venables and Scholar were in a state of conflict, it was recognised that Scholar did have his heart and soul in the club.

Much later it was discovered that the man behind the Venables consortium was Larry Gillick, who claimed he had the £12m needed to buy the club; the money lodged in banks in Scotland. In early March a meeting was arranged between the Spurs board, Venables, Peter Earl of Tranwood, a small merchant bank who were acting as Venables' advisor, and Gillick. It transpired that Tranwood were already in financial difficulties and eventually went into liquidation.

Scholar was highly sceptical of Gillick, describing him as resembling "an out of work gangster." Yet Gillick suggested he had almost £30m at his disposal and would buy Tottenham at 90p a share, costing £9m, plus taking on the debt of nearly £13m and would also put up a further £5m for new players.

Further investigations into the 44-year-old Gillick would reveal that his father had played for Rangers and Everton in the pre-war years. Gillick was a builder and director of the Victoria Stadium in Ayr, in which he invested £100,000 in 1980. But, after a champagne launch at the £430,000 greyhound stadium, there was never any greyhound racing, he became involved in a legal row with his "partner" Thomas McCool and the local council cancelled his lease on the stadium. Some months later the stadium was damaged by fire and re-opened several months after under new management. Six years later, McCool was jailed for five years at Edinburgh High Court for embezzlement and fraud, though there was no suggestion that these offences were linked in any way to the stadium project. Gillick resurfaced describing himself as a London property developer.

Gillick gave assurances to the Spurs board which appealed; no sale of Gazza, £5m for new players, plus buying the shares and taking on the debt. However Gillick refused to discuss his backing investors. Scholar took Gillick to one side and after asking 110p a share, settled on 95p and with Bobroff and Berry agreeing, and so accounting for 44 percent of the shares together with Scholar, a deal was done. Not so. It was not all it was cracked up to be.

It transpired that Frank Warren was behind it; had set it all up. Warren introduced Gillick to his group which also included an anonymous North London businessman who was believed to be providing the bulk of the finance. Warren subsequently withdrew, leaving Venables and Tony Berry acting as go between in the consortium with Gillick who had only been known to them for a matter of a few weeks.

Gillick dropped his bid from 95p a share to 85p, promising a banker's draft from Barclays within two days. Scholar was unhappy, but without an alternative on the table, reluctantly accepted, but warned that he would not be bullied into lowering the price again.

There had been a hint from Gillick that the money to finance the deal had come from the Middle East. In fact, it was Sheikh Tahnoon Bin Saeed Al Nahyan, the nephew of Abu Dhabi's ruler Sheikh Zayed, who was the provider, though he insisted on keeping his name secret (sounds very similar to the deal struck with Manchester City whose fans were naturally ecstatic, but it might be a sobering thought to realise that the same consortium of rich Arabs had their eye on a top English football club 16 years earlier!)

The Abu Dhabi consortium, too, felt it was wise to keep their identity secret while they tried to buy the club, since the club's large Jewish support might not have approved. However, the takeover panel, who had to be consulted in the Tottenham Hotspur purchase because it was a plc, insisted that the Sheikh's name must be made public under City rules. They refused a request for a nominee to be used for this purpose, since the Stock Exchange insist on full disclosures and would not put out an offer document which did not contain all the information available as to who was providing the funds, where they were coming from and what sort of people were going to be involved. However flawed it may have seemed this was the only offer on the table at the time. On 20th March the Spurs board met again without having any evidence that the money from the Gillick consortium existed or that he could satisfy the regulatory authorities. They had no alternative but to recommend that the offer should not be accepted. Two days later, the club's advisors told the board to issue a statement making it clear that all talks with the Venables consortium were now at an end.

But Venables had no intention of dropping his fight for control, and Gillick refused to go away. Early April saw Gillick returning with another knock down offer of 80p a share. Venables was taking the players training in the morning and then dashing off to a series of meetings in the afternoon and evening.

Scholar, though, was relaxed. He knew the Midland Bank would not call in the overdraft. If they foreclosed on Tottenham it would incur some unfortunate publicity for them and lose many customers who might have been Spurs fans.

Spurs beat Notts County, as expected, to make it to the FA Cup semi-final and a lucrative match against Arsenal was in prospect. For the first time, a semi-final was to be staged at Wembley, a controversial decision. Venables was preparing his side for that vital Derby Cup tie while simultaneously pressing forward with his bid for board room power.

The *Scottish Daily Record* had been investigating Gillick and they revealed that he had been bankrupt and only discharged three years earlier and was criticised by the chartered accountant appointed as his trustee.

Gazza recovered from a double hernia operation and had successfully come through a test on the injury against Norwich four days before the big Wembley date. With the team's form erratic, the club in crisis off the field, Arsenal were clear favourites for the final. But Venables' decision to risk Gazza was a momentous one.

Gazza's free-kick in the first few minutes remains one of the outstanding strikes seen at Wembley. He also contributed to the second, scored by Lineker. "That free-kick must be one of the best ever seen at Wembley", ventured Venables, "It is easy to bend a ball without pace or to curl it but to bend it with power and accuracy is very special, especially from 35 yards." Alan Smith pulled a goal back before half-time but Spurs were in control even though Gazza was replaced halfway through the second half by Nayim. With Arsenal taking risks Lineker was able to score the decisive second.

So the ailing giant made it to Wembley. With a month to the final could Scholar find a way out of the crisis?

Scholar had even raised the issue of a new contract for Venables. Venables had dismissed the earlier offer of a restructured deal based on performance but £25,000 less on his basic salary. Now Scholar told Venables to name his terms, but as Venables went off to celebrate nothing had been agreed.

Gillick was back with yet another master plan to acquire 29 percent of the shares, but by the end of April Venables was forced to concede that his Middle Eastern backers had withdrawn. However, he had another trick up his sleeve, a sale and leaseback deal with a company called Edennote. It would raise £11.5m with Spurs paying an annual rent of £1.5m. But part of the conditions were the non sale of Gazza. Edennote were listed at Companies House as having just two directors – Venables and Gillick.

But Lazio had a binding contract to buy Gazza while the price of the new shares was set at 70p, just over half the amount that had been offered and 21p less than the price at which they were suspended.

Just 11 days before the final there were more meetings, with a rival bid from Baltic, but with Venables pushing for a sale and leaseback deal. Scholar had also been advised it would need a package worth £2m plus salary to keep Gazza at Spurs. Scholar was highly suspicious as to whether the money really existed despite Venables' persistent assurances that it did.

In Cup final week, Venables' obsession to take control continued as he prepared his team against Brian Clough's Nottingham Forest. He wanted a deal sealed before Wembley.

Gazza's future was also on the agenda before the final. Mel Stein asked Scholar if the club was in a position to present a package to keep the player, to guarantee him a minimum £2m net after tax over the first year plus a hefty annual salary of £1.3m a year, plus extras such as bonuses and appearance-related add ons. Scholar had to at least match the Lazio signing on fee for there to be any chance of negotiations to continue. Scholar told him the chances were virtually nil. It was the eve of the final, and Scholar knew he had lost his battle to keep Gazza. Solomon was anxious for Gazza to sign for Lazio that morning in his office. Of course, he would. If Gazza was injured in the Cup final it could jeopardise the big deal that would stabilise Spurs' finances. The stakes couldn't have been higher; the drama of the entire situation could not have been more intense. Neither Scholar nor Gascoigne wanted the deal to be concluded then because they wanted him to concentrate on the most important game of his young life. Eight months earlier Scholar had made it known that if Gazza went, he would go too. Scholar said at the time, "I had tried everything to stop the transfer and, although the Gascoigne contract had been signed by Solomon at the end of April, it was only during this meeting that I finally came to terms with the fact that his sale was inevitable."

While the players were in the Royal Lancaster Hotel, the day before the final, Scholar took a call, at 4.30pm, from a mutual friend of both Venables and himself to say the Spurs manager had the money in place. Scholar made one last gesture; he said that he was prepared to deal at 80p a share... but if Venables could guarantee to keep Gascoigne he could have the club at 70p a share. Scholar was ready to drop £270,000 for his stake to keep Gazza.

The mutual friend, Sir Philip Green, went to report back to Venables at the team hotel and the lawyers and advisors got to work on preparing the agreement. Scholar came to join me and some friends for a drink while keeping in constant touch with his own solicitor, Peter Robinson.

By 10pm there was a hitch. Still no agreement. Venables was seeking "certain comforts from the Midland Bank", and as they were conditional, Venables' hopes that he would lead out his team at Wembley as the new owner of the club, could not be fulfilled.

Venables had made his own representation to Stein in an effort to keep Gazza, and to convince him to go to Italy later in his career.

While Venables' mind was in a state of turmoil, Brian Clough took the week off! His side were firm favourites with Stuart Pearce, Des Walker and Gary Charles at the back, and Roy Keane in midfield. But Spurs had Gazza, whose goals against Oxford, Portsmouth, Notts County and Arsenal, had brought troubled Spurs to within touching distance of glory on the field with the future of their star player still top of the agenda.

Clough commented, "I have not seen much of him actually, but I think he has a lot of talent and I've asked our coach driver, if he sees him in the Wembley tunnel, to run him down."

When Gazza was lining up for the presentation to the Prince and Princess of Wales and the Duke and Duchess of York, it was clear that he was once again hyped up. Perhaps more so than usual, and this surfaced in the opening minutes with a dreadful challenge on Garry Parker for which he should have been cautioned. A few minutes later, as Gary Charles supported his attack on the edge of the Spurs box, Gazza again lunged in crazily, his leg outstretched, a desperate dangerous challenge which should have brought an instant red card, but referee Roger Milford awarded a free-kick. The real damage had not been inflicted on Charles, but on Gazza himself. It was bad enough for Tottenham that Stuart Pearce then drove the free-kick beyond Erik Thorstvedt to put Forest ahead. As Spurs restarted the game from the centre spot, so Gazza collapsed and had to be stretchered off, his final finished after 15 minutes.

Gazza's enforced departure initially left the Spurs team, which was lucky not to be down to 10 men, in a depressed state. Gary Crosby missed a glorious chance to increase Forest's lead, but Eric the Viking made the save and when Lineker found himself one-on-one with Mark Crossley, he was dragged down. Penalty given. Lineker took the kick himself but Crossley flung himself to his left and touched it away for a corner.

Seven minutes into the second half, Spurs took control. A move began by Nayim and carried on by Paul Allen provided Paul Stewart with the opportunity to drive the ball across Crossley for the equaliser.

From then on Spurs revelled in the Wembley atmosphere, but couldn't find the winner. When the whistle went for the end of normal time, Venables was quickly in a circle with his players with instructions and encouragement. Clough, in contrast, never moved from his seat except to pass the time of day with a policeman. He left his coaching staff to issue the orders and this was surely an error of judgement on his part. Clough had his own unique way of going about his job, believing his aloofness scared his players and frightened them into action. This time it didn't work out. Spurs continued to hold the initiative in the extra half an hour, but the goal that won the FA Cup for them was a cruel stroke of misfortune for England's centre-half Des Walker. A Nayim corner kick, flicked on by Stewart, was heading towards Gary Mabbutt, charging in behind the Forest defenders. Walker sensed his presence, went to intercept but succeeded only in deflecting the ball past his own keeper.

Proud Tottenham lifted the FA Cup – without Gazza. For Venables, it was his first major English trophy and he admitted, "It would be an understatement to say I was thrilled by the way the lads performed to come from behind. Given the year we have just had, I would say this is my finest achievement as a manager."

While the celebrations continued that night and the next day around Haringey Town Hall, thoughts were spared for Gazza, who was undergoing surgery on his right knee, a career-threatening injury to his anterior cruciate ligament. Venables revealed at the time, "The boy is pleased for the lads but is devastated by his injury and by missing most of what was the biggest game of his life."

As it turned out, Venables was destined never to win another domestic trophy, and Gazza was destined never to be quite the player he was at his peak.

Despite the problems between them and the rift that had grown, Scholar was generous in his tribute to Venables' part in winning the FA

Cup, "I have never wanted Terry Venables to leave this club" he told the press conference afterwards, "He will be offered a new contract. That is what I want. You only need to look at what he has done for Tottenham. He has won us the FA Cup."

But even in his moment of triumph, Venables found this insincere, "I would have thought it was plain to everyone by now that unless I can get the equity, the absolute decision-making authority and the position I want within the club, I won't be staying at Tottenham. Not after all that has happened. There is no way I can continue to manage the club under the frustration I have endured for the last three years. Not only have I not heard anything about a new contract since I told the chairman some weeks ago I could not carry on as manager in the present circumstances, but the propaganda about Tottenham's offer is nothing more than a gimmick to deflect attention from the reality of the situation."

Venables came from a humble background in Dagenham, made himself a limited company at the age of 17 and, throughout his life, simply coaching a successful football team was never quite enough to fulfil his own idea of his full potential. Venables' success with the FA Cup only served to intensify the supporters' belief that he was the man who should have total control of the football club, a sentiment shared in the dressing room where Venables was highly popular and well respected.

The Wednesday after the FA Cup final, on 22nd May, the matter for discussion in the Tottenham board room was how the club could continue trading. Could and should the club sell season tickets for the 1991-92 season while it was felt the company might go into liquidation? What was now the position of Lazio in regard to the Gascoigne transfer?

While these deliberations were taking place, Venables was taking a telephone call from Sir Alan Sugar which was to give the manager the situation he had dreamed about for most of his working life... help to buy into Spurs and into the board room.

With the contest about to hot up between Maxwell and Sugar for control, Scholar felt more confident than at any other time that it might be possible to keep Gazza at Spurs. Scholar felt this opened up the possibility of Spurs forcing Gazza to honour his existing contract. Scholar recalled in his book *Behind Closed Doors*, "I had just walked into the room when Nat (Solomon) came running over to me, holding a piece of paper. He said, 'Irving, look at this'. It was a proposal by Terry Venables and Alan Sugar, but Nat was pointing to a clause in the proposal and I read it with absolute incredulity. It said that the Sugar-Venables offer was conditional on the sale of Paul for a figure of not less than £4.5m. After I had recovered from my shock I started laughing. For months now there had been any number of stories in the press as to how keen Terry was to keep Gascoigne at White Hart Lane, how if he was allowed to take over the club Gascoigne would actually remain at White Hart Lane, and he would do everything in his power to make sure he did. I was painted as the villain of the piece, the man who said he wanted to keep Gascoigne but was secretly planning to sell him. In contrast Maxwell had made it clear to Nat that he would be very unhappy if Gascoigne were sold."

In *Venables – The Inside Story*, I wrote, "At the board meeting of 6th June, Scholar recalls that Lazio's lawyers were examining an agreement produced by Ashurst Morris Crisp which would mean that Lazio would pay for Gascoigne at once and the money would remain there, with the interest going to Spurs, until Gascoigne recovered. Tottenham would have 'something like £5.3m to £5.4m in the bank'. If he did not recover, then Lazio would have the initial sum returned. Not long after, a new Venables-Sugar bid arrived, this time with no reference to Gascoigne. Scholar is certain that Venables had realised just how damaging the publicity would be if the news leaked that he had insisted on selling the player he had previously said he would try to keep."

Through my close association with Irving I believed his version of events. Although Tottenham's precarious financial position was well documented at the time, what is often overlooked is that Nat Solomon publicly stated the club did not need to be rescued once the Midland Bank had extended their loan facility for a further 12 months. In theory, at least, Gazza did not need to be sold, for the time being, if at all. However, the amount of money on offer from Lazio had become too tempting. His departure instantly turned financial uncertainty into stability, especially when combined with Sugar's wealth.

With Venables and Sugar now installed at Tottenham, Venables decided that he wanted to remove Dennis Roach from the negotiations with Lazio, breaking the contractual arrangement whereby Roach would receive his percentage. Roach could have claimed £64,400 commission on the £5.5m transfer, but instead he agreed to £27,500 as "full and final settlement". This then cleared the way for Gino Santin, a London-based restaurateur, to become the agent for the deal. He was ultimately to receive an astonishing £200,000 for his services. When Roach discovered how much Santin had been paid, he was naturally furious. It was all the more surprising considering Roach had acted for Venables when he went to Barcelona.

Santin eventually presented the new Tottenham regime with his invoice which cited work carried out by the Anglo-European market research & consultancy company regarding the transfer of Paul Gascoigne. The £200,000 requested was to be sent to a PO Box number in Zurich. The invoice was sent on 2nd September 1992 and, five days later, on the insistence of Venables, Sugar and finance director Colin Sandy signed the cheque. However, it was not long before the club issued a statement, "Mr Santin's involvement in the transfer of Paul Gascoigne is now a matter on which the board is refocusing its attention."

Sugar has always suspected Santin's role, especially as the cheque was made out to cash, guaranteed by Credit Suisse. Why was it sent to a PO Box in Switzerland and not direct to Santin's up-market restaurant in Belgravia? Curiously the address to which the cheque was sent actually belongs to another company, Commercial Treuhand, which acted as a mailing address for others. Why was part of the payment for legal advice, when Santin had no legal experience? Santin's explanation was that his accountant advised him to set it up in this format. Venables' explanation was that Santin increased the offer from £4.8m to £5.5m and was therefore worth his cut. Yet, when everything went pear shaped between Sugar and Venables and their disputes headed to the courts, a proper review of invoices threw up the intriguing possibility that Lazio had already upped their offer to £5.5m in any case! The faxed letter referring to the increased fee of £5.5m arrived the day before the takeover, and, as Venables later claimed, had not been made known to him until it was too late. The fax became one of the many details in the prolonged legal disputes, investigations and TV documentaries, in part, revolving around the Gazza transfer to Lazio.

Sugar said at the time, "I would like to say at this juncture that Tottenham has never accused anybody in relation to this Gascoigne affair of any illegal act, but Tottenham has the absolute right to demand to know what Mr Santin has done for the money that we paid him. Prior to the investigations recently carried out by us and prior to the television programme we sincerely believed Mr Venables. We have the absolute right to check into these matters... the only person that makes the suggestion that some form of impropriety has gone on is Mr Venables himself."

Venables' own interpretation of the question of the Santin invoice was, "Of course, I realise that the intention of the letter which was fed to

Panorama was to make it appear that I had lined my own pockets through Santin. The truth is that I ploughed a great deal of my own money into Tottenham and, thank heavens, I never took so much as a bag of crisps out of the social club, never mind a dodgy penny. I am convinced that there is a conspiracy against me. There has been a lot of criticism also of my financial man, Eddie Ashby, but he is nothing if not meticulously thorough. Thanks to his diligence I have copies of everything."

The chronology of the Gazza deal went as follows:

In the aftermath of the FA Cup final, Lazio dropped their price.

On 17th June, Lazio's London lawyers sent a fax to Tottenham's lawyers, Ashurst Morris Crisp, stating the fee as £4.825m. One clause agreed that Tottenham would keep the interest on the payment.

Three days later, the fax quoting a fee of £5.5m was sent.

The takeover was then completed on 21st June.

On 26th June, a party from Lazio arrived at the Hyde Park Hotel, hoping to clinch the deal and, according to Venables, there was no mention of the improved £5.5m offer, with talks revolving around £4.825m.

Venables, in Sugar's absence, threatened to call it off as he felt Spurs should get more money.

On July 5th, while Venables was on holiday, Sugar faxed Lazio director Maurizio Mancini saying that if Gascoigne was not fit by 31st May 1992, Lazio would get their £4.825m back, plus half the interest earned.

Sugar contacted Mancini again on 8th July wanting a decision by 10am the next day and stating that another club had offered £5.5m, but Mel Stein was anxious his client should go to Lazio.

On July 10th Gian Marco Calleri, Lazio president at the time, confirmed the price to be £4.825m... somehow forgetting his previous commitment of £5.5m! While on holiday, Venables contacted Sugar telling him to leave the negotiations to him and Santin.

The row over Santin intensified with claims and counter claims over the arrangement of two friendlies with Lazio and a fee to screen Gazza's Rome debut. My favourite was the notion that Venables had told Sugar that Santin would do the deal for "a drink". In reality Venables and Santin might not have actually agreed a fee for his services, and even Venables was shocked when Santin, at first, claimed a full 5 percent of the transfer fee.

Threats of writs against *Panorama*, from Venables and Santin, never seemed to materialise, at least not to my knowledge.

Given the catalogue of injuries suffered by Gazza since the 1991 FA Cup final, including a shattered knee cap after a nightclub incident, perhaps Tottenham did well to sell him when they did.

Gazza fell out with Mel Stein, but while I have had precious little to do with Gazza in recent years, my friendship with Mel has continued. Mel appeared on my TV/podcast shows during the World Cup of 2002 with a host of other guests. Mel has provided me with an insight into Gazza's state of mind; it was not an easy place to visit. Gazza has never been the most reliable particularly when drinking but nevertheless, there seems to be enormous sympathy for his plight.

I experienced his unreliability at first hand when Gazza had been commissioned by Umbro to attend a photo shoot at the *Mirror* building in Holborn along with Gary Lineker, David Seaman and Paul Parker. It was quite a coup for the *Mirror* to have such England stars turning out to model the new Umbro kit. Such a picture shoot would never happen these days, with players earning such vast fortunes, they no longer need publicity generated by newspapers and are more interested in the millions on offer from *Hello* and *OK*.

Not surprisingly, everyone turned up except Gazza. The then sports editor Keith Fisher thought it would be a laugh if I stood in for Gazza in the picture shoot, and so there I am wearing the England kit alongside Lineker, Seaman and Parker (colour page 12).

One of my favourite pictures is of Gazza and Paul Stewart in the background during one of my many meetings with Pelé (colour page 13, C). I had got to know Pelé well from my connections with Tony Signore at MasterCard, and through one of his former sponsors Umbro and their executives Martin Prothero and Simon Marsh. My interviews with Pelé included a snatched five minutes that turned into 30 minutes over breakfast in a Frankfurt hotel before Pelé was whisked off to represent Umbro at a trade fair in the City. At the fair there were giant photos of England players, Paul Gascoigne and John Barnes and it was a photo opportunity that I couldn't resist as Pelé had been discussing the virtues of both players during my breakfast interview. Pelé thought Gazza was exceptionally gifted but despaired about his lifestyle.

CHAPTER TWELVE

Gary Lineker.

As the picture shows (colour page 14, A), I interviewed Gary at Heathrow Airport before he boarded the plane for Nagoya for his first visit to the home of his "J" League club, Grampus Eight, after agreeing to a highly lucrative deal, his final contract as a footballer. Three chief football writers, myself included, through Gary's agent Jon Holmes, had arranged to accompany the striker with the bad toe to Japan and when British Airways discovered that we were being welcomed by Lineker and his agent, we were upgraded to first class by a very accommodating JAL; and it was quite an experience. The first class cabin was virtually empty apart from Lineker and his entourage which had now swelled to include the small media group.

The media had a lot of time for Lineker. He always made himself available, he was articulate, and had a charming, disarming smile. He was clearly destined to become a media star in his own right once he finished playing and indeed he has fulfilled that ambition more than he could have ever imagined. So much is down to his highly efficient and well connected agent Jon Holmes.

One of the world's greatest violinist's, Nigel Kennedy is a mad Villa fan, who stayed at the Forte Village during Italia 90, where I got to know him very well and we ended up playing doubles together against Gary Lineker and Ron Atkinson on Centre Court in front of a handful of on-lookers. Big Ron was devastating at the net, where he didn't have to run too far, but not too hot on his ground shots. Gary, being a natural athlete, was by far the best of a very average bunch and just about carried Big Ron over the victory line!

It was my investigations into Gary's manager at the Lane, Terry Venables, that led me to probe deeply into the then England striker's move to Grampus Eight. Although Lineker played on at the Lane until the end of the 1991-92 season, the move to Japan had been agreed much earlier, and was one of the main issues that led to the fall out between Sugar and Venables.

The sale of Lineker formed part of the contents of my previously mentioned book, *Venables – The Inside Story*, which I co-wrote with Steve Curry. While Steve, a close friend at the time, concentrated on the life and times of Venables the player, manager and personality of many descriptions, my part of the book focused on his transfer dealings and business enterprises mainly while at the Lane.

Let me make it perfectly plain from the outset that not at the time, nor now, am I in any way suggesting that Gary Lineker did anything untoward, or knew of anything untoward in his transfer to Grampus Eight. My investigations at the time were into the fall out between Sugar and Venables and Lineker's transfer was a catalyst for that, but I was not investigating Lineker or insinuating that he had any knowledge that his move was behind the acrimonious break down of the working relationship between chairman and chief executive.

Here is my interpretation of the Lineker sale as chronicled in the Venables book,

"England captain, superstar, Mr Clean, and still one of the world's top scorers, Gary Lineker was sold off for just £850,000! When Lineker and Gascoigne returned to Tottenham after Italia 90 after England just missed out on the World Cup final, beaten by eventual champions Germany on penalties in the semi-finals, their value on the transfer market soared. The then Spurs chairman Irving Scholar rejected a near £5m offer for Lineker from Torino; £3.5m in cash plus a Yugoslav striker valued at between £1m and £1.5m. Gascoigne was priceless. Scholar felt, even though Lineker would be 30 in November 1990, he was worth keeping – and made his views plain to Jon Holmes."

In the chapter about Lineker, Scholar was quoted as saying, "Jon Holmes went to Italy for talks and Lineker himself indicated that he would be interested in a move to Italy if the club were agreeable. I was not agreeable and, to be fair to Terry, he too was annoyed with Holmes. I told Holmes that he had no right to negotiate in Italy without the club's permission. Lineker was under contract and he would have to honour it. I have a lot of sympathy with players in this country because salaries are so vastly higher abroad, and it is hard to stand in their way. But Lineker had already made his pile from a move abroad with Barcelona, so I did not have so much sympathy. Gary and Terry were always very close, but I didn't sense that Gary turned against me because I had blocked a move to Italy. Once I had put my foot down that was the end of the matter, we never discussed it again."

Scholar and Venables did meet the Torino go-between, who was a friend of Venables, and he suggested that if they would pay £5m for Lineker that would enable him to go to Derby and get Mark Wright and Dean Saunders. Torino, however, were not prepared to bid more than £3.5m. Holmes went to Italy to speak to the club, but Scholar was adamant the deal would not go through unless he got his price.

In the book, I went on to observe, "Sugar was unaware of Lineker's valuation in 1990, only a year before an agreement was made prior to the 1991-92 season to sell him to Grampus Eight for just £850,000 at the end of the year. Venables' argument was that Lineker had reached the wrong side of 30 and had two years left on his Spurs contract at the time the deal was made. He considered it a good arrangement, but Sugar was deeply disappointed that Tottenham received such a small sum. The reason for Sugar's reaction was that in his second meeting to buy the club, his prospective partner Venables had told Sugar that Lineker would fetch £4m. Once the pair were running the club, Sugar questioned why Spurs had got only £850,000, referring to their original conversation about Lineker. Venables explained that, given Lineker's age, he was unlikely to fetch much more than £1m on the transfer market. Lineker, personally, would stand to make £4m in salary and signing on fees – but not Spurs."

The plot thickens as I continued to relate the inside track on the Lineker transfer, "Sugar describes this as one of the 'misunderstandings' that began to creep into his relationship with Venables. Sugar relied on Venables' footballing knowledge, being a novice to the game, but would no longer make such a mistake. His suspicions about Venables' ability had increased, perhaps justifiably, as £850,000 was certainly cheap for Lineker, when an earlier £2m offer from Blackburn Rovers had been rejected. Sugar was further concerned because a fee of £1m had been mentioned but Venables explained that the 'balance' was made up by Lineker waiving a cash payment of £166,666 as the final part of his signing on fee that was due on 1st August 1992. However as Lineker had asked for a move, Spurs would not have been liable to pay it anyway."

To be balanced and fair, I put forward Venables' point of view as to why it made sense to him to flog off such a star striker at what seemed such a giveaway price, "Venables was pleased with the deal he made with Japanese club Grampus Eight, because he got cash up front and kept Lineker for another year before he moved on with his age approaching 32. Indeed, had he insisted that Lineker saw out the final year of his contract, to the end of 1992-93, Tottenham would have received nothing for the sale. But, as a result of the Lineker transaction, Sugar insisted that

Venables kept him informed in the future of all major transfer dealings."

It was clear that the details of the Lineker "transaction" were beginning to leak out, as I pointed out again in my book, "Spurs intended to keep the details of the deal with the Japanese club under wraps for the entire season, no doubt not wanting to risk the wrath of the fans so soon after the departure of Gascoigne. But the news leaked to the press, and so it became public."

The Lineker issue formed part of the court hearings between Sugar and Venables. On 10th June, 1993, Venables' QC, Mr Mann, pointed out how Sugar's affidavit gave the impression that "Mr Venables' integrity has been questioned. We are, ourselves, questioning Mr Sugar's integrity."

Claim and counter claim was the throwing of mud that usually occurs in such High Court conflicts, and this time Lineker was at the centre of the storm.

Sugar mentioned in his affidavit how Venables led him to expect over £1m, but in the end the club received £850,000. Sugar wanted direct access to those in Japan who facilitated the transfer deal, and thought that would be relatively simple because of his contacts in that country through his Amstrad company which had long standing dealings with Japan. Sugar wanted to reassure himself that the full sum Grampus Eight was paying to sign Lineker was being disclosed.

As I wrote in the book, "The implication from Sugar was that some money was being paid to a third party, a suggestion that infuriated the Venables camp."

Again meticulously recording Venables' side of the story, he also pointed out at the time that Tottenham had signed Lineker for £1.2m, so "he was obviously worth considerably less aged 31. The effect of that transaction was that Tottenham were getting their money back for him. The alternative would have been to have let him serve out his contract and get nothing at the end. It is absolutely incredible that Mr Sugar should state that his faith in my business acumen has declined as a result of this purchase."

Jon Holmes backed Venables' understanding of the situation. He too, rubbished Sugar's estimate for Lineker of £4m. He also criticised Sugar's fears that the Grampus Eight agent, Christian Flood, was hiding something from Tottenham.

Like Sugar, Flood had plenty of experience in dealing with the Japanese, having negotiated tours of the country by Margaret Thatcher.

Another important fact, to justify the transfer, was that Lineker wanted to make the move and if he was kept on against his will then his motivation at Tottenham would have been sure to decline (where have we heard that one before? Oh yes... Berbatov and Keane).

Sugar's lawyer was quick to state that there was no question mark against either Lineker or Holmes in their dealings with Grampus Eight.

I concluded in the book, "That accounts for Lineker's and Holmes' positions, but not all the facts of the deal emerged in court. Flood and his Japanese partner Yoshio Aoyama were approached by Grampus Eight, backed by Toyota, and given a sum with which to negotiate a deal to sign Lineker, with the money to be split between Lineker and Tottenham. Although the precise sum is confidential, it is in the region of £5m. For concluding the deal, Flood and Aoyama received a commission of £100,000, plus the lucrative rights to market Lineker's Japanese deals in England. All payments, other than the commission, went direct from Grampus Eight to Tottenham or Lineker and his agent. It was Flood who initiated the deal because he understood how popular Lineker would be in Japan. He remains convinced that both parties got as good a deal as was possible given the sum of money available.

"Therefore, we can see how within the first few months of the Venables-

Sugar partnership being set up, there had been three big money transfer deals, involving Gascoigne, Durie and Lineker in which Venables had tried to minimise the role of Sugar in the negotiations even insisting that he did not get involved. Yet each of the deals disappointed Sugar in one way or another, giving rise to his concerns about Venables' business acumen. Had Venables involved Sugar more closely there would have been less chance for misunderstanding and suspicion."

CHAPTER THIRTEEN

Robert Maxwell And The Inside Track On How He Tried To Buy Spurs.

Because of my close relationship with Irving Scholar I was aware of the financial problems within Spurs much earlier than any other journalist. It was with great reluctance that Scholar had to concede to me how it was going, but he had no choice with leaks within the City beginning to undermine him. Scholar needed a rescue plan, and one in a hurry. My suggestion was Robert Maxwell.

Scholar and Maxwell got together and the Spurs chairman was trying to negotiate a financial package with Maxwell that would have injected £13m into the club and averted the impending problems.

For Venables it was a double edged sword. He feared that the arrival of Maxwell would take football, and more importantly Spurs, further down the line of becoming a corporate play thing, manipulated for the purpose of a new owner wanting more hands on control over the manager, as well as trying to turn a huge profit.

The big problem for Venables was that the attitude of the fans might be more powerfully in favour of someone, anyone, who would inject new funds into buying players. Venables' fear has proved correct in the modern game, where supporters are prepared to turn a blind eye to where the funds are coming from because they are thrilled with their new signings; whether it is a former Thai Prime Minister with a history of human rights issues with his assets frozen and his wife charged, or a Middle East consortium buying Robinho.

Spurs were the battle ground for one of the original contentious takeovers of global big hitters, and in the case of Maxwell, someone who turned out to be as colourful as Thaksin Shinawatra.

Venables said at the time, "The role of the manager in English football is being diminished by amateur directors who want to play at professional football and if we had Maxwell as well as Scholar we could all move one step down towards the boot room, myself included."

While Scholar was trying to save the club, Venables was giving the fans what they wanted – success on the pitch. The Venables team began the 1990-91 season with 10 games without defeat and Venables seemed to have struck a team balance that meant they had conceded four, scoring 17 in that soaring start. Venables had given David Howells a role just in front of his back four and this allowed Gascoigne the freedom to make forward runs; matching Lineker for goals, 19 apiece that season.

The club were brimming full of optimism on the field, but off it Scholar was in a panic about the £900,000 outstanding to Barcelona on the Lineker deal.

The master plan when Scholar had taken Spurs public was to invest in a diversity of areas outside of football and to utilise the profits to re-invest in the team. The chairman allayed any fears about the possible failure of these subsidiaries with the assurance that it would never affect team matters. Most of the subsidiary companies did not initially perform particularly well, but this had been buried in the accounts so that when the parent company showed a profit in 1987-88, it was mainly due to profit on football operations and the sale of the club's Cheshunt training facility, which brought in £4.5m. Two other companies, Synchro Systems, a computer-ticket operation, and the Hummel sportswear franchise deteriorated dramatically during 1989. It was a mistake to inject £3m of football club money to support it. This contradicted Scholar's belief that it was the subsidiary that should support the club. Paul Bobroff, who had been Scholar's long-time partner, took the opposite view, as he argued that Tottenham were now a public company with a responsibility to shareholders. This difference led to Bobroff's failed attempt to oust Scholar. When Bobroff discovered that the third major shareholder, Tony Berry, backed Scholar, he resigned and offered his 10 percent stake in the company up for sale. Scholar and Berry realised they could not buy this stake without having to make a similar bid to all shareholders, in accordance with Stock Exchange regulations. But then the club's merchant bankers insisted on Bobroff's reinstatement. By the summer of 1990, it was clear that two more of the Spurs subsidiaries, clothing companies Martex and Stumps, were also in serious financial difficulty.

With the problems mounting, another cash injection was urgently needed to write off the debts of the subsidiaries and to service the Midland Bank debt, which had touched £10m and was still rising. On the day of the World Cup final in Rome, Scholar spotted Robert Maxwell being driven through the streets of the Eternal City and felt it might have been an omen. For some time he had in mind that the *Mirror* Group Newspapers owner might yet be the man to rescue his ailing club from bankruptcy. He phoned Maxwell with whom he had sat on a Football League television committee in 1984, and the two men met on a Sunday morning, 25th July, in Maxwell's office.

Scholar outlined his plan to create a new share issue for the parent company while accepting that in the current financial climate the chances of City investment were small. He felt the help of a major investor would do the trick and wondered if Maxwell would underwrite a rights issue at

£1.30p a share. The shares would be offered to existing shareholders on a one-for-one basis. Scholar and some of his colleagues would not take up all their offer and Maxwell would be left with a guaranteed 26 percent of the company, possibly a good deal more if the new shares were not bought. This would have the effect of injecting £13.2m into the company, thus clearing the £12m that Scholar now assessed to be the debt. In return for an assurance that he would not sell his shares and would remain to run the club, Scholar had Maxwell's provisional agreement, providing the whole deal was kept strictly secret.

In addition there was also the outstanding debt to Barcelona, which Scholar knew would not be forthcoming from the bank. Scholar turned to Maxwell again. He asked Maxwell to loan Scholar's company, The Holborn Property Company, a sum of £1.1m which Holborn would then re-loan to Tottenham to pay out on the Lineker deal. That way, Maxwell's involvement in paying off the outstanding amount would remain secret. Maxwell, in turn, supplied the money from a private company, Headington Investments. Scholar offered a block of shops he owned in the Kings Road as security for the loan.

Scholar had to place his rescue share package before the club's directors without being able to identify the man who would underwrite it. Scholar and the club's financial director, Derek Peter, were given the go-ahead at a board meeting from which the chairman, Bobroff, was missing, having taken a holiday. Although he was unaware at the time, Scholar was now in uncharted waters and was not receiving the soundest counsel about the rules governing the conduct of public companies. The Stock Exchange would look with distaste on a company that negotiates a rights issue and loan without its chairman being present or its shareholders informed. When Bobroff discovered the plan, he felt it smacked of desperation and he immediately attempted to slow down the deal. Most of the club's shareholders were the fans who stood on the terraces and who would not normally be consulted on the running of the football club. But a public ownership should have obliged the board to inform and consult. This was to have serious repercussions on Scholar and Tottenham within weeks.

Maxwell reached agreement with Scholar on the rights issue, but was for the moment unable to proceed because of the rules of the Football League. These stated quite clearly that no individual could have a financial interest in more than one football club and had been introduced when Maxwell had tried to purchase Elton John's shares in Watford while he was still involved with Oxford United and Derby County. To proceed with the Spurs agreement, he would have to sell his interest in Derby County and when the directors there refused to buy his shares, he put the club on the market, blaming the sale on what he described as "a lamentable lack of support". He added, "They (the supporters) must realise that I do not have a license to print £50 notes". His asking price for the Baseball Ground was £8m, but he was not bowled over by the rush to buy as this was not the climate where buying a football club was seen as a common-sense investment.

It was while Maxwell was waiting for a buyer that *The Sunday Times* revealed his identity as the man who would underwrite the share issue. This story, by the paper's City editor Jeff Randall, was to send shock waves through the game at large.

Recently I spoke with Irving Scholar about the leak which effectively scuppered the Maxwell bid for Spurs. At the time Scholar suspected that Maxwell might have tipped off Randall himself, because he was getting cold feet about investing in Spurs and didn't want to let Scholar down, so thought of a clever rouse of forcing him to pull out. Scholar is now re-thinking this theory. Scholar, in a weak moment of anxiety, tells me that he confided in someone he thought would maintain discretion and keep the faith he showed in him. He now suspects he was the man who leaked the story to Randall. It may or may not be right, but Scholar has his suspicions. At the time, only Maxwell and I knew about it. Now Scholar has confessed that he also told someone else!

The Football League were still adamant that any such deal could only proceed if Maxwell sold his shares in Derby County, and that his son Kevin would need to relinquish his chairmanship of Oxford United. The PFA made comments about people who chose to use football clubs like Monopoly pieces.

Maxwell advised Scholar that the deal was off because he felt he had not been given the fullest detail of just what trouble the club was in. Scholar refused to accept he had lost his, and the club's potential saviour. Yet, it was the secrecy surrounding the deal with Maxwell that was to cause as much of a furore as the arrangement itself. Had Scholar kept his shareholders fully informed of the dire straits into which the company was sinking, he might well have evoked more sympathy and certainly prevented official action from the Stock Exchange, who launched an enquiry into the £1.1m loan from Maxwell which paid off the Lineker transfer. In legal terms, that deal should have been presented to a meeting of shareholders for their approval.

Venables was managing to shield his side from the worst of the behind the scenes manoeuvres as they embarked on a very successful early season run of results, knowing little about how perilously close they were to seeing the club's finances crumble beneath them.

A board meeting on 14th September, squeezed between victories over Derby County and Leeds, had Scholar seeking Bobroff's resignation since their destructive squabbles were threatening the Maxwell rescue package. A vote of no confidence in the company chairman was passed by four votes to one, after Bobroff refused to resign, though he could not be kicked off the board without a full shareholders vote. He insisted that he would stay to protect the interests of the smaller shareholders. Scholar threatened to call an EGM to have him removed while, in the meantime, the club's financial advisor and broker both resigned in protest at Bobroff's sacking.

At this stage, Maxwell went on David Frost's Breakfast TV programme to say that once the bickering was over he would re-start negotiations. "I am flashing a yellow card at those involved in the squabbles," Maxwell proclaimed in typical authoritarian mode, as he used his *Mirror* sports pages to try to get across his message, led by yours truly. It was riveting news coverage, almost on a daily basis, creating mayhem and animosity among our rivals, and, naturally, exclusive to our sports pages, egged on by me in the background. "It is inconceivable that I or anybody else would entertain a rights issue, or become in any way involved in a club, while some of the board are behaving like children," Maxwell declared. Privately, though, he told me, "I want Bobroff to accept me or I want him out of the way."

On October 19th, the Stock Exchange suspended shares in Tottenham Hotspur plc and would also censure Scholar for the way he had conducted his negotiations with Maxwell. When the board finally tried to explain their intentions in a letter to shareholders, several of Scholar's actions were described as "ill conceived and inappropriate". Within two weeks of the share suspension Scholar had bowed to advice that he should resign from the plc while maintaining his position as chairman of the football club.

Venables may have been shielding his players from the turmoil, but he himself was keeping a sharp eye on the various developments and sensing that this might be his own opportunity to throw his hat in the ring as the man who could lead a move to rescue Tottenham. He had made no secret from back in his QPR days that one of his ultimate ambitions was to own a football club. Here, it seemed, opportunity was beckoning, and in a big way.

Perhaps given these extraordinary off the field problems, it was not surprising that, after such a good start, results began to deteriorate. In November, Venables pointed to a squad depleted because of the shortage of money, which meant he could not rest key men and had to select others with niggling injuries. But results were not the only thing occupying Venables' mind at this time. He had been linked to a vacancy at Real Madrid following the departure of John Toshack, even though it always seemed unlikely the Spaniards would allow one British manager to follow another, even if he had once won a Championship with Barcelona. Venables was not unhappy that the story was being floated, because his own contract was due for renewal at the end of the season and he had found the new offer insulting.

Venables had clearly spotted an opening, an opportunity, and Scholar discovered through another *Sunday Times* exclusive that Frank Warren was trying to mount a takeover bid, with Venables as his chief executive and funds from overseas investors, including pension funds. Warren's profile had been a high one following the trial of Terry Marsh, the former boxing world champion, of his attempted murder in a shooting in Essex. Marsh was found not guilty.

It was all going wrong for Scholar. An indication of the financial plight came with the announcement of an increase in admission prices halfway through the season, which outraged fans, quite naturally, coupled with a slump in results. Since the beginning of November they dropped 19 points out of 30. As the team prepared for the FA Cup third round tie at Blackpool, there were humiliating revelations as Southampton threatened court action over a £20,000 sum they claimed was outstanding on items for the club shop under the old Hummel agreement. Chelsea were seeking

£45,000 over a ticket bill.

Scholar went to see businessman Ted Bull, whose company was called Landhurst Leasing. Scholar had talked to Bull previously about a scheme to raise money by creating a leasehold investment out of the boxes at Tottenham. Warren had been involved in some of those discussions. Bull was opposed to Maxwell.

Solomon had to find the finances to avert the crisis; the bank wanted a sale of assets. There was no bigger asset than Paul Gascoigne.

Scholar was unaware that the Midland Bank had made the sale of Gascoigne one of their conditions of continuing to service the £12m debt. In one of his first public statements Solomon made it clear that the sale of Gascoigne was a possibility. That news broke on the day of the Rumbelows Cup quarter-final against Chelsea. No longer could Venables protect his team and players from the board room machinations. Relations between Scholar and Venables were frosty over the Warren link, and now the impending sale of Gascoigne was the subject of red hot daily newspaper gossip, claim and counter claim.

Behind the scenes the bank were pressuring the directors over this issue, and co-director Douglas Alexiou warned Scholar that unless he complied he would have to go. Alexiou, like Scholar, wanted to find an alternative to selling Gascoigne.

Scholar said at the time, "I attended the board meeting but made it very clear I would be prepared to discuss the sale of Gascoigne only on the basis that the alternative would be putting Tottenham into administration or receivership. If it was a choice of Tottenham going broke or Gascoigne going, then I was prepared to discuss his transfer, although I was still opposed to it and would do everything to stop it."

Dennis Roach was Scholar's choice to tout Gascoigne abroad even though he had fallen out with Mel Stein over the sale of Chris Waddle to

Marseille. Scholar warned Roach that even if he found a suitable Italian club, there was no guarantee that the club would sanction the move, if they could avoid it, that is.

Scholar, though, was happy to sanction the sale of Vinny Samways to Aston Villa for £800,000, even though the "deal" was put on ice for a couple of days so the midfielder could play against Chelsea in the Cup tie. But with Villa manager Josef Venglos and his chairman Doug Ellis at the game, and after a poor display by Samways, Villa wanted to pull out of the deal. Scholar knew that Venables objected to the Villa deal as he valued Samways at £1.5m and when the manager substituted the player Scholar suspected it was to scupper the deal! Such was the paranoia behind the scenes at the time!

Venables, however, was plotting. He was linked with an offer of a huge salary to manage the US World Cup squad, and, with his connections and popularity with the press, there seemed a campaign mounted to "sort out this mess".

Spurs lost their League Cup replay at the Lane to Chelsea.

That night I was at the Lane covering the game for the *Daily Mirror*. It was a tough match report to pen. It was clear all the board room shenanigans had finally reached the dressing room, and that was hardly surprising. With the momentum growing towards the sale of their hero, Paul Gascoigne, the mood was turning nasty and Irving Scholar had become the focal point of the supporters' anger.

I sat in my seat in the press box and called "copy", and filed my report. But during my work, I received a message from one of the press box stewards. "Don't leave the ground, go to the main reception and wait in the foyer for the chairman, Mr Irving Scholar".

It was all rather unusual. Even though I was a close friend of the chairman's, I never abused that position, never hung around for him after the game, never accepted an invite to go to the board room. Strange, then, that he needed to speak to me urgently. I thought he was depressed at the result, and that he wanted someone to talk to.

When White Hart Lane was virtually deserted, he emerged from the private, director's only executive lift into the foyer and looked genuinely delighted to see me. Relieved to see me! Then I noticed, he was surrounded by police, some of them armed. Irving thanked me for hanging around, and began to tell me that he needed a police guard and that he would appreciate it if I would accompany him home in his car. Three policemen escorted the two of us to Irving's car, parked quite nearby in the director's car park. Two police cars chaperoned Irving's 4 x 4 out of the ground through the streets of North London, and all the way to his West London home.

Irving explained as he drove, that he had received a death threat, and that the police were treating it seriously. I had never seen him so shaken up. I knew from that moment that Irving would consider a potential sale of his shares, although, knowing him as well as I did, he would want to ensure the future security of "his" club.

The night before Irving Scholar finally sold out his shares to Sir Alan Sugar and Terry Venables, I sat with a very depressed and harassed Spurs chairman in the intimate surroundings of the up-market Bleeding Heart wine bar-restaurant, a watering hole down a side alley off the jewellery outlets and gold merchants, in Holborn. Linda was there with me, and we did our best to console someone who clearly was distraught at the prospect of selling his beloved Tottenham. We told him over and over again, that although he felt at the time it was right to go, it wasn't, and that he would always regret it. The whole evening was emotionally charged, with the smoke filled room, the wine and the food failing to bring any light to Irving Scholar's darkest moment in football. I knew he didn't want to sell. He didn't want me to keep on telling him precisely what he already knew.

But I was the only person who had lived through his nightmare, who experienced at first hand the night when he thought his life was threatened by some madman, and who had put up with so much for so long, that it had all brought him to his knees. Who could blame him for wanting out? I couldn't blame him for that, I told him. Surely, it made sense to sell, get out of the mad house, and let someone else have a go? He knew his time was up, and he couldn't come to terms with it.

I reminded him of the battle to acquire the club in the first place, how he had out thought, out manoeuvred the old board, to buy up shareholders' voting rights, to ensure he had a foot hold in the club. No one would have more heart and soul in the club, no matter who bought it now or in the future.

Irving desperately wanted me to tell him, it was the right thing to do. Eventually, I did. Just to console him. But deep down, I knew he could turn it around if he had the energy and or the inclination. I could sense he had neither. He was drained, and he feared the club he loved so much was drowning. He no longer felt he was the man to pull them out of the mire with the determination to take it forward. It had been such a hard slog to get to this point. He knew it might be years ahead of struggle, and it was tough. A really tough call.

Irving will never concede that I was right. What he didn't know at the time, was that his associate and former friend, Paul Bobroff, was under financial pressure to sell his shares. Bobroff was made personally bankrupt in 2006, having failed in a number of subsequent ventures.

More significantly, to this day, Irving tells me the truth about what really happened behind the scenes during that contentious period, and he swears that the extent of the crisis was greatly exaggerated. He was deeply hurt by what he describes as "lies" that the club was on the precipice of going bust. He never believed that was the case, or that the problems were so insurmountable. He argues very formidably that the facts didn't support the "spin" put about by his enemies.

What a shame that such a genuine football man was hounded out. Many people who get involved in football, often from afar, think that it's easy; it isn't. Irving is living proof that even a deep affection for the club doesn't guarantee it will all go smoothly.

But it was all fairly straight forward for Irving. He understood a manager's mind set and their problems. He shared their desire for a successful team, as the priority for the club. He shared the supporters' desire for a winning, successful team that could bring back the glory, glory days. His heart was in the right place. Now, you cannot say that about some of the game's owners, can you?

The will-he-won't he sell Paul Gascoigne scenario alienated his basic support, but the fans didn't know the truth, and it's my hope that detailing much of what really went on behind the scenes will make them understand where Irving was coming from, and where he was going.

In an exclusive interview for *Down Memory Lane*, Irving Scholar recalls how he tried to tip off Sir Alan Sugar that Venables had no intention of remaining as manager; that he was plotting to quit the dug out for a more lofty position of attempting to control the board room. Sugar was convinced he was unfit to do this and Sugar was equally adamant that he would not allow Venables to move into the board room.

Scholar now reveals that had he known Venables would have been allowed to become chief executive he would not have sold out to Sugar!

Scholar told me, "Just prior to the takeover I spoke with Alan Sugar on the phone and we agreed to meet one to one and I was going to warn him what TV (Terry Venables) was like. The day of the meeting I got a message from a friend that TV had found out and was going to be there. I rang Sugar and told him it was off but wanted his confirmation about what TV's role was going to be should he take over. He assured me that he would continue as manager and came out with the phrase that caused trouble when *Behind Closed Doors* was published, 'TV thinks he's an entrepreneur but I don't'. Had I known that TV was leaving the dressing room, I would never have sold to Sugar and TV would have known that. I wanted him to continue as manager, because that was what the fans wanted, I knew he would have lasted maybe another season; two maximum if I had stayed with him, but the fans believed in him. He's too clever by half and knew that in the end, all managers reach their sell by date unlike CEO's or directors.

"In September 1994 I watched Spurs at Leicester and sat next to Nat Solomon in the director's box. In 1991 he had been completely seduced and won over by TV and was totally convinced that he was vital going forwards. At Leicester he said to me during the game 'I am sorry Irving, but had I known what he was really like, I would never have made that decision. I apologise'. At least he was honest at making a bad judgment.

"When I met Sugar in the South of France in the summer of 1993 just before the court case, I asked him what he would have done about TV had Spurs won the FA Cup the season before, instead of losing to Arsenal in the semi-final at Wembley. 'I think I've got big balls, but they ain't that big' and that from the supposed hard man in the board room! So football IS all about results after all, even morality takes a back seat."

It took Irving some time to recover from the traumas of Spurs and being forced to walk away from the one thing above all else he treasured the most. Irving tried his hand at football club ownership again, consulting me, before he took the plunge with Nottingham Forest. He missed the day to day involvement with football, but it was always destined to end in tears at Forest, as any club would always be second best for a man who had, and still has, Spurs in his blood.

He had his moments at Forest, appointing Dave Bassett, who got the relegated club straight back into the Premiership, and then appointing Paul Hart to revamp the youth policy. Ironically, Spurs bought three players from Forest, Michael Dawson, Andy Reid, and Jermaine Jenas, who benefited from that policy. Irving also revitalised the Spurs youth system in his time at the North London club, bringing through Sol Campbell and Nicky Barmby, by giving Keith Burkinshaw a totally unexpected £250,000-a-year budget.

He was wrongly accused of wanting to cash in on players like Gazza and Waddle. Instead he should long be remembered as the chairman who fought passionately to bring the best players to Tottenham like Gary Lineker, Gazza and Waddle in one of the most entertaining eras in the club's history and for persuading Glenn Hoddle to sign the longest contract of his professional career; four years.

But Irving Scholar's great claim to fame, was that he was one of the architects of the Premier League and the advent of the modern game with all its sky high TV revenues. He was the chairman of Spurs when it was part of the Big Five of English football, and he plotted with the elite the threatened break away from the Football League, until it eventually turned into the Premiership.

He was a leading light in the development of the modern game, when, along with his close friend David Dein at Arsenal, he helped to smash the TV cartel which had artificially held back revenues in the game.

Irving Scholar was the first to take a football club to the Stock Exchange, he was the first to have TV advertising for his games, he was the first to look at more global merchandising, and appointed the architect Bill Jenkins to prepare the master plan of the modern White Hart Lane.

And on a Saturday you would even find him in the Spurs shop selling the products himself in an effort to make his ideas work, and to make money for the club. He was a real football man, who put his beloved Spurs before himself. His encyclopaedic knowledge of the game is legendary and he always loved a quiz because invariably he would win it.

Yet, perversely, he was also something of a traditionalist. He loved to reminisce, especially with his idol Bill Nicholson, the man he called the Greatest Spur of all after leading the team to the 20th century's first League and Cup Double in 1961. Bill had an empathy with Irving, who loved to talk about the old days.

Bill, who passed away in 2004, would occasionally pop into the board room on a match day and, if Irving was there, he would always seek him out and sit next to him for a good old chin wag, something Bill wasn't noted for.

CHAPTER FOURTEEN

Glenn Hoddle, King Of White Hart Lane… And A Good Friend.

How wonderfully gratifying to read the then Sunderland manager, Roy Keane's remarks regarding Glenn Hoddle, on the eve of the early season encounter with Tottenham at White Hart Lane. As it was pointed out, for most boys growing up in Cork during the 1970s and 1980s, the Irish enclave was a natural hot bed of interest in football geared around the likes of Liverpool, Manchester United and Celtic; yet there was also a lingering love-affair with Tottenham Hotspur. Hoddle was Roy Keane's inspiration, "I've got a soft spot for Spurs", confessed the hard man of Manchester United converted into highly promising management material by invitation of former Arsenal centre-forward Niall Quinn at the Stadium of Light who then walked out after a succession of defeats. Keane added (about the team under Juande Ramos at the time), "I like the way they play football and the attacking players they've got." Keane certainly had a hankering to snatch as many Spurs players as he could for the new campaign, bidding for five and landing three in Steed Malbranque, Teemu Tainio and Pascal Chimbonda. But the magic was beginning to disappear more with the departure of Robbie Keane to Anfield and the impending removal of Dimitar Berbatov from Spurs' front line. As it was, Berbatov was left out of the squad for the opening home game of the season with Ramos citing psychological problems, a euphemism for the player not wanting to play with his mind on Old Trafford and a £30m move that had stalled.

As Roy Keane plundered all three points, and Spurs slumped to successive defeats at the start of a new season reminiscent of the old one under Martin Jol, all Spurs fans, myself included, could be forgiven for burying their heads in the sands of past glories, none more so than those of Hoddle and his ilk.

For me Glenn Hoddle epitomises everything about Spurs and every reason why anyone with purity about the game should be a Spurs fan.

Brought up on the Double team of Blanchflower, White, Mackay and Jones, the push and run, pass and move ethic from the Arthur Rowe team of the 1950s that included Bill Nicholson as its full-back, there had not been a higher level of football attained at the Lane.

Ruud Gullit called it sexy football, Pelé, the beautiful game, but whatever criteria you might use, it is the brand of football that can take your breath away, a touch of magic from Maradona or Ricky Villa. The kind of touch you will always associate with George Best or Johan Cruyff or one of the world's masters of the art of performing something that you thought you might never see.

So, how gratifying for me that my true claim to fame is not my big news breaking exclusives and all the awards as a reward for them, but that I got Glenn Hoddle into the Tottenham team!

On the *Tottenham Weekly Herald*, it was my duty to cover the Spurs youth and reserve teams as well as the senior side, and having set the precedent with Bill Nicholson, I would attend a Monday morning briefing each week with the managerial incumbent. On this occasion it was Terry Neill, who had succeeded Nicholson. Having spoken to the Spurs reserve manager week after week, and on the odd occasion actually watching the team, it soon became apparent that a kid called Glenn Hoddle, at the age of just 17, was already first team material.

I am convinced that Terry Neill had never seen him play, when one Monday during my regular weekly briefing with the manager, enquired when we could all expect the latest youngster from the Spurs conveyor belt of local talent to be playing in the first team. Terry looked at me blankly, but never one to be lost for words, waltzed around my question with relative ease, talking about never rushing kids and his time will come and so on and so on, but it was clear to me he didn't know anything about the kid.

The next week though, to my surprise, Glenn Hoddle was named as a substitute for the senior team, and he came on, and kept his place in the team the week after that for his full debut against Stoke City when he scored a spectacular cross shot goal.

During the many lunches Glenn and I have shared over the years, I never tire of reminding him about that story, which always brings a chuckle. I keep repeating it in the hope that Glenn will one day actually believe it. I know, it is hard to believe.

Of course Hoddle would have eventually made it to the first team with or without my prompting. He was just too good.

Brian Clough tried often enough to sign him for Nottingham Forest. Cloughie was a committed Hoddle fan. He once said, "You don't have to bare your false teeth to prove you're a real he-man in football. Some people are morally brave and Hoddle is one of them. I've heard him criticised for non involvement, but I'm not sure what that means. If you can compensate with more skill in one foot than most players have in their whole body, then that is compensation enough."

Back in 1987, I "ghosted" Glenn's autobiography *Spurred To Success*, in which he personally subscribed this touching note "To Harry – Thanks for your support – over many, many! years." Not content with that, I got him to sign another copy at the book launch, in which he wrote "God bless. Great working with yer!"

The club is riddled with actual "fans" behind the scenes including the club's executive director Paul Barber, who used to be an executive at the Football Association. Paul recalls his first Spurs game and the first time he saw Hoddle...

"It was August 1975. I was eight years old. I had spent the previous three nights unable to sleep as my dad, a lifelong Spurs fan, had told me we would be going to see Spurs play Norwich at White Hart Lane – my first ever game. I remember the day itself being warm and sunny – just as well as I wore full Spurs kit, shorts and all! The thrill of seeing the pitch for the first time was unforgettable as we secured a good spot in the Enclosure in the old West Stand. My dad's family, keen watchers of reserve team football too, had been raving about a curly-haired youngster called Glenn Hoddle. As luck would have it, the gangly youth also made his debut at the Lane that day coming on as substitute as we battled for a 2-2 draw. The player who was to become the most outstanding midfield player of his generation made an immediate impression rescuing a poor ball with exquisite chest control and spraying a 50 yard pass – later to become his trademark – cross-field to feet. The mood in the Enclosure audibly lifted. 'This boy will be a star', said dad, and murmurs of strong agreement spread from those long-time Spurs watchers all around us. The rest, as they say, is history!"

Hoddle was capable of such magical moments; his chip against Watford, his sideways angled volley or an 80 yard pass of perfection. In the introduction to Hoddle's autobiography, I wrote at that time, "He has been described as the 'White Pelé'; he has Diego Maradona among his admirers; yet despite his rare gift for inspirational skills, he has remained English soccer's greatest enigma for more than a decade. Glenn Hoddle provokes almost violent debate among fans, managers and football journalists alike. Some say he is a genius – others condemn him as gutless. Managers at the highest level are divided on the question of whether they would choose Hoddle for their team. The 'Hoddle Argument' is more fundamental than a simple assessment of an individual performer – it highlights the deep and often disturbing morality of the English game. Are we too dependent on workers and runners? Should we develop the more complex artists? Can we afford to 'carry' the play-maker who does not bear the responsibility of defensive duty?"

I raised the point that those questions had haunted Hoddle for his entire career since the time he scored a wonder-goal by inventing an unorthodox side-foot drive from outside the box to score on his England debut against Bulgaria at Wembley at the age of 22.

"Hod", as they affectionately called him in the Tottenham camp, won two FA Cup medals, a UEFA Cup medal and a Little World Cup medal with the England youth team. But the league title eluded him, and that hurt.

It is often cited that Hoddle should have won far more than his 53 England caps; that he should have been one of the elite England Centurions, and he would have been if more England managers had trusted in his skills. Instead, Hoddle was hardly given the chance of two successive internationals until Bobby Robson persevered with him a year before the World Cup finals in Mexico.

Never blessed with blistering pace, he made up for it with the kind of creativity that raised Spurs to a team you wouldn't want to miss watching. And at times, this was shown in his international games.

Again I can only call it a privilege to have been the chief football writer on the *Daily Mirror* covering the Mexico World Cup finals, the 13th La

Copa del Mundo. Ineffective, together with all of his team-mates, against Portugal, in a terrible and controversial opening game, Glenn began to shine against Poland when he was involved in all three Gary Lineker goals. Hoddle really turned on the magic against Paraguay, creating all three England goals, two more for Lineker and one for Peter Beardsley.

The turning point for Hoddle in the World Cup was a mixture of farce and fortune. Ray Wilkins managed to get himself sent off in a fit of pique and frustration shortly before half-time against Morocco and strangely that worked in Hoddle's favour, almost decreed by the fate upon which Hoddle placed so much store in his personal beliefs. Immediately England reorganised, Hoddle assuming his familiar central midfield role, and his flair for the creative long ball began to become evident in the second half against the African team that was hailed the surprise of the World Cup. With Peter Reid installed as Wilkins' replacement against Poland, Hoddle had more freedom in the next two games, but unfortunately he was vastly overshadowed by Maradona in the quarter-final tie when, in the Azteca Stadium in Mexico City, Hoddle was unable to achieve such heights one more time against Argentina. Had he done so, then Hoddle would have been spoken about in terms of one of the world's greatest ever. Instead it was Maradona who took the game by storm, with Hoddle missing his midfield dynamo Bryan Robson to protect him and Peter Reid, who had been such a great foil for Hoddle in the earlier games, was no match for stopping the mighty mouse of Argentinean football.

Thanks to the generosity of Irving Scholar, Hoddle was promised that he could pursue his ambition to play on the Continent, and the Spurs chairman granted that wish when he allowed his star player to move on to Monaco, where under Arsene Wenger, Hoddle was allowed the kind of freedom he was never granted in English football. Hoddle blossomed and also forged a close relationship with Wenger, and the pair remained close when they were both rival managers.

I had been in Toulon with a group of football reporting colleagues from the rival papers covering the under-20 tournament when we heard that Hoddle was being transferred from his beloved Spurs. Bob Harris from the *Today* newspaper told us all confidently that Hoddle was going to Paris St Germain, but I knew differently. Yes, Bob was right to an extent, it looked as though a deal with PSG had been fixed up, but there was a last minute change of heart and dramatic change of direction. I had spoken to Glenn direct and knew he was on his way to Monte Carlo. I left the media hotel with a couple of other journalists to head for Monte Carlo, while Bob and two others he had convinced Glenn was signing for PSG, were heading off to Paris.

When we reached our destination and checked into the Beach Plaza, we bumped into Glenn and Mark Hateley who were both signing for Monaco with the same agent, Dennis Roach, orchestrating the double signing.

It might have been a journalistic coup to be at the right place at the right time, but in many ways it was sad that Hoddle was leaving Spurs at the age of 29.

One journalist, Rob Shepherd, was sure Bob Harris was right, and was planning to go with him to Paris, but as my taxi was pulling away from the hotel the following morning, "Shep" was rushing down the stairs to the lobby with his suitcase hastily packed, with a shirt or two hanging out the sides, to join us on the trek to Monte Carlo. It was a good change of mind for Shep.

I have known Pelé, Maradona, Cruyff and Best, not just from the stands as a fan mesmerised by their unique skills, but have met each one of those world icons, and have gone much further and become so close to them that I have been privileged to have written their life stories. I have written George Best's last book, Pelé's life story, met Cruyff in the offices of Robert Maxwell in the *Mirror* building at Holborn, and written Glenn Hoddle's autobiography.

In fact, I've even played football with Hoddle! Well, I've got the pictures to prove I had a bit of a kick around with him (colour page 15, E). It was an invitation from the FA for a charity event when a few journalists challenged Hoddle in a test of accuracy. Needless to say Glenn won with ease.

It was as England manager that Hoddle reached the heights in his coaching career, but it was also in charge of the national side that he suffered his biggest heartbreak in football, while the shock, premature death of his brother Carl, no doubt was the real tragedy in his life.

The day Glenn was sacked as England coach I shared the entire day of apprehension, followed by anger at the delay of the final decision on whether he would go, and then the pain when the axe did finally fall. Together with his then agent Dennis Roach, the three of us paced up and down a little used London terraced town house Hoddle owned in Queen's Gate, Kensington. Naturally, it was a stressful time for all of us as we awaited the news from the FA. When the decision to sack Hoddle was transmitted to him via a telephone call from David Davies, he was visibly shaken, absolutely devastated. The catalyst for Hoddle's demise had been a concerted media campaign against him.

He returned a hero from the 1998 World Cup finals in France, where David Beckham had been sent off against Argentina and 10-men England had put up a courageous fight in their second round match, but had gone out on penalties. However, a poor start in the following European Championship campaign saw the anti-Hoddle faction get to work. Hoddle was savaged for the "audacity" to publish a World Cup diary, as if he had been giving away some sort of state secrets, when, in reality, all the previous England managers had brought out similar books, and never incurred such wrath from the media. In fact, dear old Sir Bobby Robson brought out a whole library of books, giving away the World Cup secrets of two tournaments, let alone Hoddle's one! The big difference was that Sir Bobby was extremely popular with the media. Hoddle was far too aloof for their liking. The irony of the World Cup diary that helped to bring down the England manager was that it was co-written by the FA's own head of communications, David Davies, the former BBC sports correspondent. Hoddle hadn't divulged very much more than was already known about his well published confrontation with Paul Gascoigne when he left Gazza out of the World Cup squad.

Gazza's wife Sheryl first sold the story within an hour of being told of what happened in Hoddle's hotel room when Gazza phoned home with the news. Later Gazza gave his version of events by selling his story to a newspaper but somehow many sections of the media condemned Hoddle for giving his full and most explicit version in his book.

Ten days before Hoddle's enforced exit, I had organised an informal off the record lunch with the England manager and half a dozen senior football writers, who, as yet, were not committed to forcing the FA's hand into pushing Hoddle through the exit door. We gathered at Scalini's restaurant in Walton Street, the up-market Italian restaurant where pictures of famous football stars adorn the wall, and the waiters are all mad keen football fans, where I advised Glenn to be circumspect with his interviews.

There was a trust between Glenn and myself that had gone way back to his early days at Tottenham and I was in a unique position to tell him afterwards that he had taken the wrong advice when he agreed to be interviewed in *The Times*. A chance remark about the disabled made enormous impact and proved the final straw and his undoing at the FA.

David Davies wrote in his recently published book *FA Confidential*,

"Glenn was formally announced as Terry's successor on May 2nd 1996. The change of tone between Venables and Hoddle could hardly have been greater. Terry liked a good laugh but all the jolly japes were left at the training ground gate. Terry really controlled training. So did Glenn, but less sympathetically in the players' eyes.

'Training is so bloody serious,' one of the players confided to me. 'It's not much fun. It's like he's trying to distance himself from us,' I was told. 'He played against some of us.' It was during Glenn's reign that I made the biggest mistake of my 12 years at the FA – accepting our young manager's offer to write a book with him on France 98 – the infamous *Glenn Hoddle: My 1998 World Cup Story*. When it came out, many columnists vilified us, even accusing Glenn of taking his eye off the World Cup because he was distracted by the book. What rubbish. Even during a full-on tournament, the England manager was allowed a few hours spare time. On reflection, though, writing the book was wrong. No ifs, no buts. Wrong. Wrong. Wrong. 'I'm angry with myself,' I told Susan. 'I let personal ambition to do a book, and my own journalistic instincts of what makes a good story, run over my sense of what was right and wrong. If the England players pummel me, I really will think about leaving.' Some were certainly unimpressed. Graeme Le Saux was very critical. So was Gary Neville. Both were players I counted as friends. 'The book shouldn't have been written,' Gary told me. Yet the players knew Glenn and I were writing it. Not one of them came up during France 98 to complain about what we were doing. Within Lancaster Gate, some people called for my resignation. Paid to see the downside of everything I hadn't with the book. I was probably saved from the sack by the fact that I had permission from Graham Kelly.

"In the build-up to a game with France on February 10th, Glenn talked over the phone to Matt Dickinson, then chief football correspondent of

The Times. The interview appeared on January 30th and caused carnage. It was all about the disabled paying for their sins in a former life. 'I've been misinterpreted,' said Glenn. Somehow a football interview turned into a discussion about reincarnation. 'I thought it was off the record,' Glenn added. How on earth could I put this fire out? The moment *The Times*' first edition dropped at 11pm, all hell broke loose. At 2am, my phone was still ringing with reporters from other papers seeking reaction. 'We have a serious problem,' I told Susan. I encouraged Glenn to make lunchtime television appearances but the incoming tide of revulsion over his comments quickened. I knew Glenn was doomed when I tuned into *Richard & Judy* and heard the Prime Minister, Tony Blair, being asked, 'If Glenn Hoddle has said what he is reported to have said, should he go?' 'Yes,' replied the PM."

I have known David Davis for many years, and believe him to be a decent enough chap. But I have told Glenn on many occasions that he was ill advised to have cooperated with *The Times* over an interview set up by Davis. Hoddle's grievance about the circumstances of his England sacking will live with him forever, and I am sure he would like to return to the England post sometime in the future. But I am equally sure that isn't going to happen.

To a large extent Glenn has now managed to put the past behind him, moving on to his new project in Spain where he plans to regenerate wasted young talent, a highly commendable project as well as a commercially based one. I still enjoy lunches with him whenever we can arrange them in and around Sunningdale, usually at Café Fego where Sky presenter Richard Keys, Kirsty Gallagher and Gary Lineker can often be spotted.

CHAPTER FIFTEEN

The Day Spurs "Signed" Diego Maradona.

Ossie was panicking. Diego was fast asleep and Ossie was pacing up and down the hotel lobby. "Typical Diego" moaned Ossie, shaking his head and fretting like I had never seen him before. Always super cool, this was the one time I had ever seen Ossie Ardiles lose his cool. "Always asleep, sleep, sleep, sleep, he loves to sleep, and he's always late, late, late and he's late now..." But this was an important assignment; it was Ossie's testimonial for Spurs at White Hart Lane that night.

I was there to witness all the behind the scenes drama in getting Maradona to London in the first place, to get him and his substantial entourage from Heathrow to the airport, and then to awaken Diego from his slumbers so as not to miss the big kick off.

Because of my great friendship with Ossie, and also with Glenn, Ossie had brought me with him to the hotel for a pre-arranged exclusive interview with Diego himself. What a coup. The *Mirror* were absolutely enthralled by the prospect, and the sports editor had put aside the back page and a two page spread inside for the big interview.

Now I was beginning to catch the Ossie bug, the nerves, the fear he would sleep through it all. Worse still, my interview was looking increasingly like it would be aborted. The plan, put into place meticulously by Ossie, was that as Diego would have arrived early that day, there would be plenty of time and opportunity long before Maradona left the central

London hotel for North London, that I would be able to sit down for a relaxed interview. So, chat with Diego, with Ossie interpreting, stay at the hotel to file the wad of copy to the office by phone, and then I could take my time getting to the game and watch it having already filed the story. There would even be time for the two Argentineans to catch up on old times. Not a chance. When Diego eventually emerged from the lift with his entourage crammed in behind him, there was barely enough time to make it to the ground in time for kick off. Diego might have thought it was still early, but Ossie knew the peculiarities of the Seven Sisters Road.

Ossie suggested that I accompanied them to the ground, and there was just enough time for a quick photograph with myself, Diego, his wife at the time, and Ossie outside of the hotel, on the way to the car. At least it was worth the photographer's long and patient wait. He then hurried off with his precious pic to the office. The photograph of Maradona, Ardiles, and myself currently adorns my wall, alongside some signed shirts from Pelé, David Beckham, Ruud Gullit and a signed copy of George Best's European Cup winning shirt – not a bad collection.

The day was still full of surprises, as Ossie said he would personally drive the three of us to the game, with me in the back seat, and Diego in the front passenger seat alongside our driver.

I sat there armed with my notebook and pen. Diego's entourage and wife followed in a couple of limos. I asked the questions and Ossie translated as he drove.

Diego was just a kid when he first got into the national side and Ossie looked after him, almost like a father figure, giving him advice and helping him to settle in. Diego never forgot how much support he had from Ossie. Because of the strength of that relationship, I knew Diego would be as honest as he could be under the circumstances, when I eventually got round to the pertinent question about his Hand of God goal against England, the one I was there to witness in the Azteca Stadium. He confessed, for the first time, that he accepted that it was indeed handball, but he refused to back down from his belief that it was divine intervention because he hadn't actually intended to handle it and had jumped to try to head the ball. At least he had gone part of the way to confessing it was handball, and that was sufficient for my story, and for the headline writers back at the *Mirror* headquarters.

I also asked Diego if he would one day like to play in English football and he was very positive that he would, and if he did he would like to follow Ossie to Spurs. I know the club made some attempt to see if it was possible, but it never really came close to coming off. Still, it was headline news for me that Diego wanted to play in England.

More recently the BBC invited me to a hotel in Covent Garden where they were filming for a documentary on Diego fronted by Gary Lineker, which in itself made headline news as Gary also asked him about the handball. There was much media criticism that Diego had been paid £50,000 for this particular interview. The BBC executives I spoke to said it was much, much less, but no doubt it came close with all the travelling and expenditure involved.

All I can say is that it cost the *Daily Mirror* absolutely nothing for their red hot exclusive on Diego Maradona and the truth about the Hand of God.

I caught up with Ossie Ardiles and Paul Miller in December 2008, for a Sky One show called *Off The Bar*, hosted by Matt Lorenzo. We all met up in an up market pub Botanist on the Green, in Kew Green, Kew, for the filming. After recording the show which just happened to coincide with the day Roy Keane quit as Sunderland manager, Ossie, Paul and myself enjoyed a quiet meal chewing over old times, and chatting about the day Maradona came to town to play in Ossie's big game.

The memories flooded back as if it were yesterday. Ossie recalled, "The game had to be delayed for 15 minutes because it took us so long to get there! Even so, it was worth waiting for. Everyone wanted to see Diego who was still then the best player in the world. That's why the ground was bursting to capacity."

Paul chipped in, "That was some game, Diego in a Spurs shirt playing for us and Liam Brady playing for Inter Milan. The brochure from Ossie's testimonial was some prize, particularly if it was signed by Diego. I sat in the dressing room and got Diego to sign a hundred copies! He was absolutely delighted to do so. My mum has got one somewhere, I gave a lot of them away. Here was the best player in our lifetime sitting next to us and signing our match programmes. He embraced us quite well I thought for someone so important in the game.

"And make no mistake, this was no testimonial. We were playing Inter, and we had Diego in our side. We wanted to win, and win badly. Me and Robbo (Graham Roberts) were kicking shit out of them, Pat Jennings came on and played for Spurs in the second half and Chippie Brady scored against him, did him with 'the eyes' from a free-kick, but we won 2-1."

As you can see "Maxie" Miller took no prisoners as a player, and now he is just as uncompromising in his new life as an entrepreneur.

With his City connections, he actually launched a bid to buy Spurs from Sir Alan Sugar.

He told me over lunch, "Backed by the Bank of Luxembourg and a consortium of four private investors I tried to buy Spurs from Sugar. I offered 85p a share at the time when they were trading at 80p a share but Sugar wouldn't entertain the bid. In fact he told me that I wasn't welcome at the club anymore. I bit my tongue, never said anything against him or the club. However I did tell Sugar, 'This will always be my club, it will never be your club.' No, I don't like him. But I have always kept my silence about what happened."

Ossie listened intently to his former team-mate, but declined to join in the anti-Sugar lobby – even though Sugar sacked him. Ossie explained, "I don't have a fucking problem with anybody! Managing Tottenham was my dream job of course it was, but I did a crap job, of course I did. I couldn't do the job the way I wanted to do and that is my deepest, biggest, regret in football. I cannot blame Alan Sugar if I got it wrong. For me the circumstances are different to what happened to Paul.

"For many the dream job would be Real Madrid or Barcelona, but not for me, it was always Tottenham. I put so much into it..."

In those days the *Daily Mirror* had an awful lot of clout, particularly at a club such as Tottenham. The players knew I was close to the chairman and owners, and Max added, "Monte Fresco was the photographer at the *Mirror* at that time, and he was a big Spurs fan and a lovely fellow. The *Mirror* was 'our' paper."

Maxie did not score too many goals in his Spurs career but the header he powered into the Anderlecht net in the first leg of the 1984 UEFA Cup was pivotal in the club's history. He understandably looks back on that tie with great satisfaction, having played such a major role in that triumph. But he had his doubts in that first leg as the team missed chance after chance. Miller praises the strength shown on the night by his co-defenders Graham Roberts, Chris Hughton and Danny Thomas which provided the platform for ultimate victory. "Looking back, it was a wonderful evening," said Maxie. "We had fantastic support from the Spurs fans behind the goal who made it feel like a home game for us... if we had won 3-0 Anderlecht could not have complained."

CHAPTER SIXTEEN

Gary Mabbutt, Jurgen Klinsmann, And... Dennis Bergkamp.

There doesn't at first glance seem to be any kind of symmetry between Spurs icons Gary Mabbutt, Jurgen Klinsmann, and... Dennis Bergkamp.

I have written books about Mabbutt and Klinsmann, and as I got to know them, I would say they are poles apart in the way I look upon them.

Mabbutt is an extremely warm personality and I have got to know him well beyond his playing days at the club. Klinsmann I found very self centred and calculating. So, in many ways, the German former ace goalscorer would have made a superb manager for Spurs, but not, I fear for say Chelsea, or indeed Bayern Munich which became his first club managerial call.

I will return to Mabbutt and Klinsmann, but first let me explain the intrigue surrounding Bergkamp, and the inside story of how one of English football's greatest ever imports ended up at the wrong club...

The flying Dutchman should have been a Spurs player and had he been, I am convinced that Spurs would have taken off, rather than Arsenal. The signing of Bergkamp in the wrong sector of North London has defined the recent history of both clubs.

A close friend of mine, Marcel van der Kraan, a journalist in Holland, rang me to say that Dennis wanted to quit Italy, where he had not been enjoying his football with Inter Milan and had not scored a goal in open play all season, having netted just once from the penalty spot. Marcel, who I trusted implicitly, told me Dennis wanted to try his luck in England, had always been a Spurs fan because of his boyhood hero worship of Glenn Hoddle, and asked if Spurs would be interested. I knew Marcel had a close affinity with some of the leading Dutch players and he did know Dennis extremely well, clearly well enough for the player to confide in him, and seek his help in trying to set up a move to the Lane.

I rang Sir Alan and asked him if he would like the opportunity to sign Dennis Bergkamp. "Dennis Who?" came the instant reply. "Dennis Bergkamp", I repeated, assuming everyone had heard of him, but, of course, while Sir Alan loved his football, he was no expert and didn't know the European scene that well.

I explained to Sir Alan, the pedigree of this player. "He's a fantastic footballer, can score goals, create goals, has such wonderful vision he can pick out some delightful passes, he has that silky skill that Spurs fans love – they will love him at the club, and he will be a brilliant signing for Spurs and I am told he will be reasonably priced, something like £3m, perhaps no higher than £5m."

Sir Alan asked me to hold on for a second, and I could here him shout across the room to his son Daniel. "Here, Daniel, I've got Harry on the line, he says he has a great player for me called Dennis Bergkamp. Have you heard of him?"

I have no idea what Daniel told his father, but Daniel did know his football, so I could imagine he was positive about it. "Well, Harold (he liked to call me Harold at times like these!) Daniel knows him and thinks he is a good player, so I shall come back to you."

Sir Alan said he would make some enquiries with his then manager Gerry Francis, and see what transpired. I didn't hear anything the next day, so I called back the day after. Sir Alan was extremely polite and told me that he was very thankful for my help and all the effort I had put in, but that I should tell whoever I was talking to that Spurs were not interested. He then sounded quite indignant, as if I was trying to pass him off a dud. The Spurs chairman went on to explain that his manager didn't fancy Bergkamp at all and thought of him more of a midfield playmaker these days whereas Gerry Francis wanted an out and out striker. Gerry went on to sign Chris Armstrong from Crystal Palace.

Mel Goldberg, who has been a close friend over the years, and who is an avid Arsenal fan and specialist sports lawyer, also offered me the chance to place Bergkamp at Spurs because he was experiencing difficulties dealing with the power brokers at Arsenal.

The Gunners were keen on taking Bergkamp, but were intent on cutting Goldberg out of any potential deal. Goldberg was shocked to discover how the price had suddenly escalated to £7.5m. But that's another story and due to legal reasons I will decline to detail it here.

Of course it didn't take long for the Dutchman to make his mark in English football. He was signed when Bruce Rioch was manager, but because Rioch only survived one season, the beneficiary of Bergkamp's presence within the team was the new manager, Arsene Wenger.

Wenger and Bergkamp together completely overhauled a club of diminishing resources and dwindling influence as a European power. It shows you what can be done if you can pick the right manager and have the perfect player as a catalyst for that team. Arsenal got it right on both accounts and the rest is history at Highbury with Bergkamp making most of it.

Unfortunately Spurs went in the opposite direction. Sir Alan could never quite get it right in his selection of managers, and in turn the managers could never quite get to grips with buying the right player to ignite the team for any length of time.

So that brings me back to Klinsmann, a player that had the ability to inspire a much needed Spurs revolution, who, like Bergkamp had failed in Italy and then with Monaco, and was an inspiration when he first arrived at Spurs.

When Jurgen was the golden boy of German football, I and a handful of other English journalists from all the main papers, interviewed him ahead of England's epic clash in the semi-finals of the 1990 World Cup. The small group of English reporters had turned up at the German team hotel before one of English football's biggest ever games. When he emerged from the lift, to conduct the interview agreed by him and set up through the German FA communications department, he wanted to know which of the English writers was from the *Mirror*. He looked me straight in the eye and said, "Ah, you're the one I am supposed to worry about!" It was hard to tell whether he was deadly serious or taking the mickey. "Not at all", I told him but he didn't seem to look assured. Someone had obviously tipped him off about me and the *Mirror*. But then he broke into a wry smile. He was certainly as reassured off the pitch as he was on it, dealing with the English media with a stylish delivery of perfect English, interlaced with some wise cracking and some more smiles. He had charmed us all. You came away warming to him even more.

Years later when he turned up on Sir Alan Sugar's yacht and ended up signing for Spurs, I thought it was a tremendous coup, not just for the North London club, but for English football in general, even though he had been experiencing a goal-drought during his spell at Monaco. I still considered Klinsmann to be one of the most charismatic goalscorers in world football at that time and a wonderful addition to the growing list of category A players beginning to turn up in English football.

Klinsmann was such a captivating new addition to the Premiership scene that I decided to write a diary of his first season at White Hart Lane, detailing every aspect of life on and off the field that surrounded his high profile first season. It was certainly an uplifting experience, even if somewhat unexpected for a German to sign for a predominately Jewish club, with Jewish chairman, and a high percentage of Jewish support. A certain section of the fans do, after all, call themselves "Yids."

Jurgen showed he had a sense of humour when he "dived" in a unique goalscoring celebration that captivated the nation and ended up being copied by virtually everyone for a while, and still remains one of the stereotype goal celebrations. It was Jurgen's way of mocking the critics who for years had taunted him as a player who dived. Compared to some in the English game at the moment, that accusation now looks laughable.

However, I saw a darker side to Jurgen's character. All my efforts to seek his approval for the book, maybe for him to endorse it in some way, perhaps write a foreword, came to nothing. In frustration I opted for the direct approach and the next time I was at White Hart Lane, I hung around the entrance area where the players pass by from the dressing rooms to the stairway taking them to the players lounge. It's the perfect vantage point for reporters hoping for a quote or two, if one of the players was prepared to take a few minutes of his time to stop and chat. Most suspected the reporters by this time, and even if they did stop to be interviewed, were cautious about what they said.

I asked Jurgen if he would stop for a chat, and he was happy to do so while he thought it was an interview for a newspaper which would provide him with an opportunity to project his image. Jurgen was one of the few footballers of his generation who knew that any publicity was good publicity and that if you cooperated with the media and made sure you were in control with your answers, that the vast majority of the time he would be generating positive publicity for himself. However, he was most reluctant to continue the conversation as soon as I mentioned the book, even though I explained that the publishers were happy to make a contribution to one of his favourite charities and for him to see it before it went to print, to show him that it was going to be an upbeat celebration of his first season with Spurs.

Only later did it dawn on me that one of the reasons for his reticence was that he didn't plan to hang around too long and had known that he might be heading off to a bigger club for more money. I don't know, maybe I had misjudged him. Perhaps he was protective of his own image and was not interested in any unauthorised book. However, my gut instinct told me, judging by my conversation, that his annoyance was because he was not in control of something that was a commercial issue using his image, even though an aspect of it was for a charitable cause.

As I have always said, as a journalist it is imperative to try to keep your personal allegiance to a club distinct from your working environment, in other words to be unbiased. I didn't hold it against Klinsmann being difficult with my book about him as I voted for him as Footballer of the Year, an honour which he won. But just before he received the award at the prestigious Football Writers Association annual dinner at the Royal Lancaster Hotel, it was announced that he was quitting Spurs and heading off to another country.

No wonder Sir Alan threw his Klinsmann shirt in the bin – in a very high profile fit of pique by performing this act of disgust on TV.

Sir Alan told me the inside story of how he had been misled by Klinsmann and his entourage. He told me how Jurgen and his agent had been in his Chigwell home discussing how best to persuade the star striker and now Spurs talisman to stay on, but it became clear that even though the player told the chairman he was happy at the club, he would be invoking a clause in his contract which gave him a way out if he wasn't... well, happy!

Sugar felt bitterly let down. In his desperation to lure Klinsmann to Tottenham in the first place, he had given away far too much in the contract details. A "happy" clause was something that was far too weighted in the player's direction.

Sugar could have contested it, but there's no point keeping a player who wants to go, and Sugar was not in the mood to make him too much of an extravagant offer to persuade him to stay, considering he felt the player owed him because he had rescued him from his gloom in French football and Spurs had become the launch pad which had resurrected his career. Yet, remarkably a year later when Spurs were in desperate trouble and in danger of relegation Jurgen came back to the rescue. Klinsmann was earmarked to become a future Spurs manager, and I still wouldn't rule that out.

When I first joined the *Tottenham Weekly Herald*, I got to know the club's physiotherapist Mike Varney well and soon wrote a book with him called *The Treatment of Football Injuries*. I have initiated other projects to do with Spurs because I wanted to write the life stories of the people I knew, liked or who had fascinated me for a variety of reasons. However, it is not always easy to convince publishers about your ideas, and even harder to win commissions from them, as they have such a wide selection of options.

So, Irving Scholar came up with the novel idea of producing his own publishing company, calling it, appropriately Cockerel Books Ltd, the company's address listed at his own business premises in Maddox Street, off Oxford Street. One of the first and, indeed, one of the few Cockerel Books was *Against All Odds*, the Gary Mabbutt autobiography, published in 1989, which I had the privilege to write for one of the players I admired most in the game.

There were two forewords to the Mabbutt book, one from the player's consultant in diabetes at St Bartholomew's Hospital, E A M Gale MA,

FRCP, in which he wrote, "I think the word that best sums up Gary Mabbutt is commitment. Everyone knows how hard it is to get to the top as a professional footballer. What only a few people know – or perhaps not so few, since diabetes affects one person in a hundred in this country – is the commitment it takes to make a success of a life with diabetes. To combine top class football with diabetes takes a very special sort of person. Gary's performance on the football pitch has given pleasure to fans all over the world, but I wonder how many have paused to think of the very special meaning it holds for those, particularly the young, who themselves have diabetes. Gary has provided hope and inspiration for countless thousands by showing in the most practical way possible that if you can learn how to live with diabetes, the sky really is the limit.

"I would not care to count the number of times I have turned to someone with diabetes and said 'if Gary Mabbutt can do it, so can you.' The message of this book is simple: you really can."

This was one of the least commercial books I have been involved in, but, by far, the most important, and I can only applaud Irving for insisting the project went ahead, and my admiration and respect for Gary multiplied after sifting through the inside story of his life with diabetes.

The England manager at the time, Bobby Robson, also put his name to a second foreword in the book, in which he wrote, "There is no doubt in my mind that I have never come across any player like Gary Mabbutt. Injury is an every day hazard for the professional footballer; diabetes is not. Any manager will tell you, there are certain players who use their injuries to escape responsibility. Because of it, some of them never reach their full potential – they simply will not deliver the goods when it matters. What do you say, then, about a 17-year-old who discovers he is diabetic but, instead of giving up, learns how to cope with it, gets back into training within two weeks, captains the England youth team, becomes a star with and captain of one of the country's top teams and goes on to represent his country at under-21, 'B' and full international levels? You have to say that he is something special and, as far as I am concerned, Gary Mabbutt certainly is.

"His adaptability, his skills, his athleticism and work-rate would be remarkable in a young man enjoying perfect health. In a lad who has to cope daily with the problems of a debilitating illness, these attributes are astounding. Yet I have never known Gary Mabbutt to look for sympathy or make a fuss about his diabetes. The nearest he gets to advertising the fact is the bottle of Lucozade that he brings with him to every training session. Also, from time to time, on a long flight, Gary will quietly get up from his seat, put on his jacket and stroll off to the toilet. Very few of his fellow passengers will realise that he has slipped quietly off to give himself one of the self-injections that he needs on a regular basis to keep his metabolism in balance. The thought of it fills me with horror – Gary takes it calmly in his stride.

"It is the same air of quiet authority which brought him the captaincy of Spurs and which led me to pick him for my very first Wembley international, when I became England manager in 1982."

Robson went on to talk about Gary in glowing terms about his commitment to the England cause, but his final paragraph summed up the player and the man the best, "For me, Gary is the original Bionic Man. I wish him every success with this book, which I am sure will prove an inspiration to many youngsters facing a setback in their lives, and with the rest of his career in football."

The book did prove an inspiration, and to this day Gary remains a major figure in the campaign to help youngsters come to terms with diabetes.

The real shock for me was to hear the horrible truth about how

Gary's life was often threatened by his condition. One of the most serious incidents occurred when Gary was preparing for a midweek Littlewoods Cup tie with Barnsley. He told me this story which appeared in his book, "Part of my routine, and most footballers' come to that, is to sleep in the afternoon prior to the game. I had now switched from my earlier schedule of two injections a day to four and also had a compact blood testing machine. This machine accurately reads the blood sugar level. I would have six to eight tests a day to work out the exact amount of insulin I would need. We trained in the morning, then I had lunch – a gammon steak – taking a blood test before the meal. I was surprised that the test showed quite high levels of sugar in my blood; after all, I was about to eat, I hadn't just had my meal! It was pretty unusual. The reading on the machine was 18. A normal reading would show levels of between five and nine, so to compensate I injected twice the amount of insulin I would normally need for lunch. This sort of thing had happened before, I had worked out the right amounts and everything had been fine.

"I had my injection, then my lunch and went to bed at 1.30pm. All I know from my side is waking up in hospital at 2.00am the following morning. I've missed the Cup tie. I haven't a clue what has happened. Everything else is a complete blank.

"I have only managed to piece the rest of the story together accurately through information given to me by other people. I've been told that I did not wake up, I did not turn up for the match at White Hart Lane and that at 6.30pm, just an hour before kick off, the management, staff and players in the team began to worry about me.

"The team meeting went ahead as usual, but obviously without me. Everyone thought there must be a logical explanation. Was I perhaps held up in traffic? Generally, I'm a punctual sort of person; I'm hardly ever late for training, let alone for an important Cup tie. One or two people became frantic, knowing me well and knowing how unlike me it was to be so late. Some players are always late and they are continually being fined, but not usually me. As it got closer and closer to kick off time people started to wonder whether something really serious had happened. They knew that if there had been an accident I would have phoned in, or at least the police would have notified the club.

"At 6.45pm Ossie Ardiles, one of my closest friends at the club, got really worried and thought it was about time to do something – to find out if I was ok. From the dressing rooms, with now just 35 minutes before he was due to trot out with the team in readiness for the Cup tie, Ossie rang up one of Tottenham's former players, centre-half John Lacy, who lived two doors away from me. 'Can you go and see if Gary is alright? Have a look if there is a light on or see if his car is there', Ossie asked.

"Big John Lacy was only too happy to help out and became concerned when he looked out of his window and couldn't see any lights on where I lived. He went round and looked in the garage, where my car was still parked. Fortunately, I had kept the back door open to let my Afghan Hound walk in and out to the garden. John came in through the back door and started calling my name. When he came through the door to my bedroom the sight that greeted him must have led him to think that I had been attacked. The entire room was turned upside down and I was lying naked on the floor, unconscious.

"There was blood all over my body, face, arms, legs – all over the bed, behind the bed, on the walls, on the curtains. I had cut myself all over. What had happened was that I had tried to give myself a blood test, and was so 'low' that I was unable to do so, and kept cutting myself.

"I was out cold. John could get no sense out of me but he noticed that I once opened my eyes, although all there was was a glazed look. It must have been frightening for him, and he couldn't be sure what had happened. He snapped to his senses and remembered that amongst our neighbours there was a couple, both of whom were doctors. He rushed over and the wife was there, the husband was out on his calls.

"Knowing that I was a diabetic she tried to give me some sugar, but I was in no condition to take it. Her husband soon arrived on the scene. They decided to give me a glucose injection straight into my veins... I still didn't come round. That was the point where they both began to worry. It is normal to come round after the sugar level in the blood is restored. An ambulance was called and I was rushed to Queen Elizabeth Hospital in Welwyn Garden City. It was felt that once they got me to hospital I would be alright – although that was what they had thought once I was found and given the sugar! When I finally woke up there I had two drips in my arm feeding me glucose intravenously. Just imagine how I felt. I didn't know where I was or how I'd got there. I saw two nurses and asked them, 'What's happened?' They started to explain that I had fallen into a deep diabetic coma.

"The next thing I thought about was the game. I was supposed to have been playing against Barnsley. 'How did Spurs get on?' I asked the nurses. They didn't have a clue. Perhaps I should have been more concerned with the fact that I was lucky to be alive, rather than that I had missed the game. But my main reaction was sheer shock. What had happened? I just couldn't work out what had gone wrong. I had always gone for an afternoon nap before a game, and if ever I was going 'low' that would normally be a good wake up call!

"Remarkably, the next morning when John Lacy walked into the hospital to visit, I was fine, absolutely nothing wrong! I'd even got up out of bed. Of course I looked terrible, unshaven, no clothes, but I was ready to go. John had kindly brought me one of my tracksuits and drove me straight round to White Hart Lane. I began training! I was running round the track by myself as good as new. The manager, David Pleat, asked me how I felt and I said, 'Absolutely fine'. He looked unsure, was no doubt still concerned, and said he would take advice before considering whether to play me that weekend. As it turned out I got the all-clear, travelled up to Liverpool on the Friday with the team and played at Anfield – I was delighted that I had a good game. Thursday I was in hospital, Saturday I was playing. That shows you just how quickly it can all change."

It was, naturally, in the club's and Gary's best interest for the full gory facts to be kept out of the media, so very little was given away at the time about why Mabbutt missed the Cup tie.

Gary also told me how he had once lost consciousness at the wheel of his car, and ended up in a ditch, but that was one of the stories that we decided at the time would be best kept out of the book. Gary was still involved in the game as a player and it would not have helped his cause, so the episode remained confidential.

I experienced at first hand the kind of problems that Gary has suffered all of his life. It was frightening. Once, when I invited Gary to the *Mirror* and he was sitting with me in the sports editor's office, his blood sugar levels fell drastically. At first he rambled, then became incoherent and then virtually passed out before we called "medical". Fortunately we had a medical department within the building. A bar of chocolate was the miracle cure to raise the sugar content of his blood, and within seconds he was fine.

There was never a sign of any mood swings or anger at his condition even. Gary is one of the nicest guys you are ever likely to meet.

Gary is also the only man in the history of the FA Cup to score twice – one at each end! The 1987 FA Cup final, the first final the club had ever lost, was the only final settled by an own goal. Although it was a dire day for the club and their fans losing to unfancied Coventry, the Duchess of

Kent, as she handed him his loser's medal, praised him for all his good work on behalf of diabetes.

As Spurs fans we had become spoilt by success in the FA Cup. Far too often dubbed a Cup team, as the league always seemed to elude even some of the best teams, it was with enormous pride that the club notched up FA Cup triumphs at record levels. But defeat against Coventry was really hard to take.

Gary Stevens was another Spurs player who was articulate and who tried his hand in the media. I liked Gary a lot, and can recall playing in a match at the Lane which I had helped to organise, a Media XI against the Spurs staff, in which Peter Shreeve played and Gary did too, making a long awaited comeback after injury. Peter asked our team before the game to take it easy on Gary because of the problems he had suffered, and he was looking for a gentle reintroduction to match play, "so try not to tackle him", cautioned the Spurs coach. One or two of the media footballing team got a touch too fired up but Gary managed to ride one nasty looking challenge.

I actually came on as a substitute, and I cannot tell you how much of a thrill it was to play at Spurs wearing the Spurs kit. I got a bit too excited and made a charging run from the left-back position to get inside the penalty area in time for a Trevor Brooking cross. However, I wasn't quite quick enough; I was around a yard short of making a very ambitious flying header to connect in front of goal from Trevor's very tempting cross. Instead, I landed face down in the mud, and both legs seized up with cramp. The cramp was so bad that I was carried off on a stretcher.

I also played in the same media side as Peter Shreeve back in the 1980s on the Queens Park Rangers plastic pitch. That day I played up front alongside Malcolm MacDonald, the former Newcastle and Arsenal centre-forward. But one of the games greatest ever No 9s turned round and was heard to say to me, "I have seen players who can't kick with their right foot, I've seen players who can't kick with their left foot, but until now I have never played alongside someone who can't kick with either foot!"

After that put down I stopped kidding myself about my footballing prowess, or lack of it.

CHAPTER SEVENTEEN

Sir Alan Sugar... The Prime Minister, Sol Campbell And The Dud Managers.

Former Prime Minister, Tony Blair was charming, inquired about the state of the game, and has a genuine affection for football as I discovered when my wife Linda and I were introduced to him at Sir Alan Sugar's 50th birthday bash.

As you would expect from the Sugar's, it was a grand affair organised by Sir Alan's lovely wife Anne, his family and his trusted aid and PR guru Nick Hewer. The venue was the rather swanky Reform Club in the West End, and although Tony Blair didn't stay for dinner, no doubt with affairs of state to concern him, he did put in an impressive appearance during the lavish evening of festivities.

The event had been a closely guarded secret, kept from Sir Alan to maximise the impact of a red book style *This is Your Life* presentation. It was wonderful theatre and a packed audience of close family and friends to enjoy it. Michael Aspel was there to present the *This is Your Life* red book to Sir Alan, and apparently, Michael was ticked off by his TV bosses for taking part in the stunt. But it went down well, if not with the powers that be at Television Centre.

Sir Alan enjoyed enormous profile as Spurs chairman but with it came grief in equal measures to any pleasure he might have got from, say winning the League Cup at Wembley. If anything the downside was far more turbulent, and I always felt that he was relieved to have got out of the game after a relatively short period in it.

Apart from the blindingly obvious nightmare scenario of taking on Terry Venables, of continually switching managers, and his personal conflict with numerous players, Sir Alan was always needled by the accusation that he was a skin flint and never put his hands in his pockets for player purchases. Rodney Marsh was a thorn in Sir Alan's side. Rodney was on Sky TV, until he was kicked off after making a distasteful joke about the tsunami on their programme *You're On Sky Sports*, as well as writing in his *Daily Star* column at the time. Sir Alan felt Rodney was not fully conversant with all the facts and misunderstood his motives. To be fair, Rodney showed the kind of attitude that the majority of Tottenham fans shared during Sir Alan's reign; a deep suspicion that their chairman could have spent more in the transfer market than he did.

My advice to Sir Alan was not to sue Rodney, as he threatened to do, but to fight back with some juicy quotes in my column. He always suspected that I had an ulterior motive, which, of course, was true. But equally, I never let down a good friend or contact, and would always try to advise them on the best course of action. It never pays to sue, as it often takes a year to get to court, by which time the issues are long forgotten, and Sir Alan, for example, has then failed to get his point across when he needed to most.

The only problem was that Sir Alan was a stickler for getting his comments precisely as he wanted them. It was hard work to get the article I wanted into the paper's pages. He would like to paw over his comments, so I would fax him the article, he would then "go into one" blasting down the phone that I was crap at my job and hadn't written it the way he wanted, and had changed his comments, put them in a different place. Phew, it was time consuming to get it the way he wanted it, in return for a hard hitting article that would make people sit up and take notice the following morning, the "piece" which would often be quoted in the morning on TV and radio for maximum impact. That was the way to hit back, and invariably it worked a treat.

It is only since Sir Alan sold up, that the Spurs faithful have come to appreciate him more and to recognise the contribution he made to stabilising the finances. In fact, under Sugar, Spurs' level of expenditure on player purchases were far higher than most people were prepared to give him credit for – including Rodney.

Rodney Marsh, however, was little more than an irritant, compared to the main event; the court room battles with Terry Venables.

When Venables first lured Sugar into buying Spurs, the battle lines were drawn in the PR arena, with Venables convincing Sugar that I should be persona non grata for a variety of reasons. Venables had clearly put the knife in, and that was no huge surprise, knowing how close I had been to Irving Scholar when Venables was plain old "manager" of the club, and how much he had to be careful when it came to his personal views about me. No longer. He was off the leash, and anxious for revenge. He took it alright, and as quickly as he could.

So Sir Alan Sugar had a preconceived idea about me, provided by his new ally Venables.

Then, when they fell out big time, I was the journalist Sir Alan Sugar came to for help.

Sir Alan invited me and my *Daily Mirror* sports editor Keith Fisher to his Chigwell home accompanied by Nick Hewer. I made the initial approach through Nick and Sir Alan was persuaded to give me the interview. But, it seemed, I wasn't to be trusted on my own, and so Nick suggested that my sports editor should attend the meeting so that Sir Alan could set the parameters of the interview and the head of department would be on the spot to agree them. This, of course, suited me, because the worst case scenario would be for me to agree something with Sir Alan, only to be overruled by the sports editor, and that would have been a recipe for disaster. I had been nagging Nick Hewer for some time saying that I thought it would be in Sir Alan's best interests to comment on Terry Venables, after his enforced exit from Spurs for financial dodgy dealings. In the midst of the storm caused by my revelations, the club was threatened with having 12 league points deducted and being banned from the following season's FA Cup, although in the end most penalties were merely suspended. As the supporters' anger grew, Sir Alan, as chairman, took enormous flak as Venables had been hugely popular with the fans, at the time at least, due largely to the style of play he had brought to the team as manager.

Of course it was also in my best interests to pull off such an exclusive interview. What a coup that turned out to be. But there was no point in trying it on with someone as streetwise and astute as Sir Alan Sugar or his vastly experienced media advisor, Nick. So, it was a genuinely mutually beneficial exercise to get together. Nick Hewer could see it. So he took the risk and organised it.

Sir Alan took us into his vast office at his home and the interview turned out just as Keith and I thought it would – wall to wall sensationalism. Keith, although an avid Arsenal fan, knew the newsworthiness of this interview, and could hardly contain himself as we left for the nearest pub to plan the day's paper. Keith contacted the office and instructed his back room team to clear the decks for his back three pages. No mobiles or computers in those days. Just my notebook and pen, and the wall mounted phone in the pub. If anyone wanted to use the phone, of course, we had to let them. Keith decided which stories he wanted and I got onto the phone, went through to copy takers to ad lib the lot.

The *Mirror*'s sports pages inside spread headline was "I Feel Like The Man Who Killed Bambi" as Sir Alan explained why he had no choice other than to rid the club of Venables and why he was painted as the ogre, even though he knew he was taking the correct course of action. In fact, he was left with no other choice, apart from an elaborate cover up, which he wasn't prepared to do, even if it had been suggested to him, which, of course, it had not; it would have got short shrift indeed.

The back page was an even bigger exclusive about how he planned to hire the popular Ossie Ardiles as the new Spurs manager. The impact was enormous, the tone of the articles met with Sir Alan's approval, even though he was worried about the quote about Bambi, which I promised him would go down well. In fact, it has become a classic, one of his best.

Due to the way it turned out, Sir Alan and Nick trusted me in the future and our relationship grew and we socialised regularly throughout his reign at Spurs. He was a generous host and every season, when Spurs were at home to Chelsea he invited my wife, Linda, and her dad to the director's box for a lavish lunch and the best seats in the house while I slummed it down below in the press box!

Sir Alan's Chigwell mansion was pretty impressive, and not too long after the infamous Bambi epic I was invited on to his yacht for a follow up article. The instructions were to turn up outside La Cantina, a landmark restaurant, on Butler's Wharf, near the Tower of London, where someone would greet me and take me to the yacht. I turned up on time, it was at the right venue, but where was the yacht? I walked round to the opposite side of the dock, still no damn boat. I wandered about for half an hour and couldn't make it out. I knew Sir Alan liked punctuality, in fact, he was a stickler for it, and didn't take too kindly to being kept waiting, so I thought this wasn't going to make much of a good impression. Suddenly I heard this guy yelling at me. I looked down towards the river, and there was a very smart young man all decked out in a perfectly ironed white uniform. "Where have you been?" he inquired politely.

"I've been here all the time, for the past three-quarters of an hour, looking for Alan and his yacht." I explained. "Couldn't you see Mr Sugar's yacht?" he asked, sounding as if he was discussing the issue with some kind of simpleton, as he pointed to this huge boat, one that you couldn't miss unless you were totally blind. It was the biggest boat you had ever seen. But it was so big I had hardly given it a second glance. No way, could that be anyone's yacht. "That's not a yacht", I thought. "That's a ship!"

Onboard I explained that I hadn't imagined it would be that big. He gave me a guided tour, the dining room had a ballroom annex, and each of the bedrooms were en suite, the master bedroom was bigger than my entire Chelsea flat.

When Sir Alan first hooked up with Venables, he had been told that I was a journalist to avoid, not to be trusted, so I had absolutely zero contact with him. But whatever Venables had been telling him, Sir Alan Sugar had ample opportunity to find out for himself. Sir Alan told me that Venables had put the poison in about me, and that it had taken him a little time to adjust to the truth. Then again he found out a great deal that Venables had told him, didn't actually turn out to be very accurate.

Sir Alan Sugar had his run ins with many of the players who were loyal to Venables, but he also had his conflict with one of the nicest guys in football, Darren Anderton. Cruelly called Sicknote, Anderton defied the image of being on the treatment table by playing on until his late 30s, retiring recently at Bournemouth. Darren hated the nickname Sicknote. "It came about because I was struggling with injuries for pretty much the whole season before Euro 96, and the same thing happened before the 1998 World Cup, so my problems were highlighted because of the intensity of the media coverage. It was something fans called me, not players."

Darren recalls how Sugar used me to ridicule him in the press. Darren laughed when he told me, "Yes, I can recall the time when Alan Sugar picked up the phone to you at the *Daily Mirror* and slagged me off. He had the hump because the injuries started just after I'd signed a new deal. I don't hold it against you, you were doing your job, but it was the way he went about it, that sticks in my throat."

Anderton recalls another encounter with Sugar when he was being wooed by Manchester United. "Alex Ferguson had called and I said I'd see him, but then I went to see the chairman and he wouldn't let me leave the room until I signed a new deal. To be fair, he was passionate about Tottenham and I didn't want to go anyway. I was only 23. But in hindsight, once I did start picking up injuries, I maybe could have got different care somewhere else. The care could have been better at Tottenham."

In 2004 his career at White Hart Lane came to an abrupt end. "I'd had a verbal offer of a new contract, but I'd been out for a couple of months struggling with my Achilles and I was in America seeing a specialist when I got a fax from the secretary. One line. 'We won't be renewing your contract.' Perfect. I spoke to the chairman (which by then was Daniel Levy) and told him what I thought of that. It turned out that they'd decided to choose between me and Jamie Redknapp. The chairman's excuse was that Jamie and (his wife) Louise were settled in the area. I said 'I've been at the club for 12 years. I think I'm pretty settled'. But that was it. I went to Birmingham, which I enjoyed, and later to Wolves, which I didn't. I'm proud of the career I've had. I'm proud of my 30 England caps, because the first 28 were all starts, which means that I was first choice for all that time. People get caps for coming on for five minutes, but I preferred to get them my way."

Who were the Top Five he played with or against whose talent was in a different league to his own? "Zidane, who I played against a couple of times. He was unbelievable. Gazza. Klinsmann. Scholes. And Teddy. He was so clever, and he made other players look good with his movement. As centre-forward he played quite deep but he still scored 30-odd a year, and he could score any sort of goal."

One of the most contentious internal squabbles Sugar had during his time at the club was over the defection of Sol Campbell to Arsenal on a free transfer. I have known Sol since he was a boy at Spurs, where I always admired his determination, speed and solid defending, and I got to know him better whenever the England squads assembled for major tournaments.

Sky Andrew, his agent, wanted some balanced media coverage at the time of Sol's contentious move to Arsenal, as his client was going through a torrid time with the Tottenham fans, which was hardly surprising. I was only too willing to help. Sky is one of the few agents who I trust unequivocally. Equally, he trusts me. He knows he can confide in me and I won't let him down.

Sol really wanted to move from Spurs to better himself, something that he could hardly say in public, as Spurs fans would have wanted to crucify him. As it was, they hated him for moving to their bitter rivals but he desperately wanted to play Champions League football, to test himself at the highest level, and with all due respect to Spurs, he couldn't have done that at White Hart Lane. Now, that is hard to take, and that is what made genuine Spurs fans angry. Angry with the way the club was going, rather than angry with Sol. But for Sol, the Judas chants, and the hatred, was something I was surprised he was prepared to put up with. Equally, no one is irreplaceable, not even the mighty Sol, and there were such huge hopes for Ledley King. Ledley has all the attributes to become as good as Sol, perhaps even better, for both club and indeed country, so what a shame he has been held back by a succession of serious injuries.

Regrettably Sol still has to suffer some intolerable insults as there remains lingering resentment against him. But what occurred recently at Portsmouth is strictly off limits and was widely condemned and has to be stamped upon by the authorities.

It was bad enough that one of Tottenham's best ever defenders defected to the bitter rivals across North London, but it was another issue that Sir Alan opted to hire a former Gooner manager – now that was about the worst moment of all.

Yes, George Graham. George was known as "Stroller" as a player and had a reputation as a ladies man and a rebel, who was once sent home by his Chelsea manager for misbehaving along with a group of the stars of that era. Ironically Graham the manager was the archetypal disciplinarian, who fell from grace at Arsenal when he was sacked for his part in the 1990s bung scandal.

When Graham later popped up as Spurs manager, I felt it was a bizarre choice for Sir Alan, and told him so at the time. I had the effrontery to disagree with him and this is an important point. Steve Perryman says in his extremely hard hitting foreword to this book that he felt Sugar had surrounded himself with "Yes" men and that he felt "his" club was crying out for someone with Sugar's ear to tell him when he was getting it wrong. Steve thought I had sufficient influence to be in that position. For many years Perryman had harboured the belief that I was one of Sugar's "Yes" men, when, in reality, it was the opposite.

When Sir Alan rang me to tell me he had definitely appointed Graham as his manager, I was sitting in the press box in Monte Carlo watching a

Super Cup final, and I told the Spurs chairman that he had appointed an outstanding manager, one of the finest of his generation, but he was the wrong man for this club. I made the point that he was appointing a man who would never be taken to the hearts of the Spurs supporters and it would all end in tears. If he won the league title, which he wouldn't, then I might reconsider my opinion. But the warning was made right from the start, and I never wavered in that view point. Sir Alan, as is his nature, became very defensive about it (as defensive as Graham's Arsenal back five), and, although to a degree, he shared my reservations deep down, he explained how he had left it to the so-called professionals on his board and the overwhelming recommendation had been to go for Graham.

Of course, Graham did win Sir Alan his sole trophy as Spurs chairman, the League Cup in 1999, but eventually, inevitably Graham was on his way out.

And, naturally, as usual I got the blame for Graham's sacking.

As it turned out, I did play a major role in Graham's dismissal, but purely an unwitting one as I was merely doing my job in pursuit of a good story.

I noticed Graham on the ITV local 6 o'clock news programme *London Tonight* complaining about his budget, or rather lack of it, and the fact that he couldn't spend as much money in the transfer market as he had wanted on the new players he was telling the world were so necessary to take the team and the club forward.

Now, this was like a red rag to a bull to Sir Alan. No one at the time, maybe apart from the big three or four clubs, were spending more than Sugar's club, and yet the Spurs chairman had been savagely criticised by the Spurs fans, and in turn by the media, for not spending enough. I knew it would hit a raw nerve and pursued the matter, tracking down David Buchler, the club's executive vice-chairman, for an official club reaction.

It proved to be a pretty damn powerful one – and was clearly the prelude to a confrontation between George and the board that was always going to see only one winner – the board. And only one conclusion – exit George.

Buchler might never have responded publicly so quickly, perhaps not at all, if I hadn't been successful in tracking him down. An article in *The Sunday Telegraph*, analysing how Graham came to get the sack, reported at the time in graphic detail. Colin Malam's spot on analysis of how Graham came to be sacked included a section devoted to my involvement in the affair as he wrote, "The strangest thing about the whole affair is the rather implausible explanation Buchler gave for the appearance in the *Mirror* on Friday – the day every other newspaper eagerly carried Graham's complaint about a 'limited budget' – of an exclusive story quoting the executive vice-chairman as telling the manager to shut up.

According to Buchler, it came about quite by chance...

"It so happened that when I came out of a meeting on Thursday night at about 6pm", he explained, "I put my phone on to ring my wife. I pressed the green button and, instead of getting my wife, Harry Harris, the *Mirror*'s chief football writer, had just phoned in. He asked me if I knew about Graham's remarks. I said 'no' and added that it was not the sort of thing I wanted to have discussed in the press. I really didn't think that the press should know about the intricacies of a meeting."

That didn't just happen by coincidence. I must have rung Buchler's mobile number a hundred times that evening, maybe even more, determined that I would get hold of him, knowing the fragile position of Graham at that time, and the extreme sensitivity of his remarks. Colin Malam pointed out that to publicly express concern about having a limited transfer budget is an old managerial trick to prise more cash out of the board, but not at Tottenham, and not at that time. Graham knew the score, it was as if he was pressing the self-destruct button. If he was taking some kind of calculated risk, then it backfired on him spectacularly.

So just three weeks before the 2001 FA Cup semi-final against Arsenal, Graham was sacked when Buchler called him in the next day for an explanation of his comments.

Did I play a part in Graham's sacking? Colin Malam seems to think so, and I am not going to argue with such an esteemed football writer.

CHAPTER EIGHTEEN

Gerry Francis Takes His Own Trip Down Memory Lane To Reveal The Truth About His Reign As Manager And His Relationship With Sir Alan Sugar.

Fate intervened as I heard a shout outside of Waitrose. "Harry!" In the front seat of the parked car, was Gerry Francis.

Gerry had a break before heading back off to Stoke to continue his coaching regime, where the newly promoted team were having such a profound impact on the Premiership, and, naturally, he enquired about what I was up to. When I told him I was in the advance stages of writing *Down Memory Lane*, we agreed to have a further, more detailed chat.

Gerry wanted to take his own trip down memory lane, to put into perspective his fascinating, if brief, reign as Spurs manager. But, first, he revealed his deep rooted affiliation to Spurs, dating back to the early 1960s and memories of the great traditions and the glory days under Bill Nicholson.

He told me, "As a kid my earliest memories were watching Spurs on the old black and white television when they played Dukla Prague in the snow. The two teams making the most impact in the 1960s were Spurs and Burnley and I was fascinated by both the clubs, but more so with Spurs and they were the team for me at that early age, I could rattle off all the names then, and still can today; Jones, White, Mackay, Marchi when he came into the team, Maurice Norman, Smith, Dyson, Baker, Brown, Blanchflower... and then Jimmy Greaves coming to the club and replacing Les Allen.

"If I had to pick a player out of that lot, the one I admired most as a kid, it would have to be Cliff Jones, and those diving headers, I was in awe of such a small winger able to gain such heights and power with those far post headers. Jones on one wing, Dyson on the other, it was a wonderfully attacking team.

"Whenever I watched England my boyhood hero was Bobby Charlton, I looked up to him maybe because I was a midfield player.

"I got to know Dave Mackay quite well later on, as a manager against him, and it was such a privilege to have so many discussions with Bill Nicholson and Alf Ramsey.

"My dad played professionally for Brentford, so Brentford and QPR were also teams that I followed, but Tottenham and Burnley were the two teams that I took on, they were always in the news. Spurs were winning the FA Cup two years in a row and I supported Spurs because of what was going on at the time, while Brentford were in the Third Division South, and it wasn't quite the same compared with Spurs who, at that time, were one of the best teams in Europe.

"So in the early 1960s, Spurs thrilled me, then England won the World Cup in 1966, and not long after that I was being called up into the England team by Alf Ramsey and I am playing in the same team as Gordon Banks and Nobby Stiles, and am still in awe of them.

"Then I go on to manage Spurs, and get to meet the great Bill Nicholson and to work with him..."

So, we come onto the three year reign of Gerry Francis as Spurs manager.

I remember that period well. I was reporting on the *Daily Mirror*, Sir Alan Sugar was the chairman, the politics of the club had taken over from the football. And I had an inside track into the thought process of the chairman and what he thought of Gerry. Sugar actually liked him a lot but the fans never quite took to Gerry.

Maybe at the time, the supporters wanted someone else in charge of their team, the desire for more flamboyant football, greater emphasis on individuals, but the mind can play tricks, because it was nowhere near as bad as you might have thought at the time. And history has proved it was much better than what was to follow.

The last time Tottenham Hotspur finished above Arsenal in the league was in 1995 when Gerry was the manager. Robson & Jerome's *Unchained Melody* was No 1 in the pop charts and Oasis and Blur fought to be kings of Britpop. George Graham was dismissed as Arsenal manager in February of that season and Stewart Houston, put in temporary charge, was replaced by Bruce Rioch in the summer. A year later, Arsene Wenger was appointed manager at Highbury. The Tottenham stars were: Ian Walker, Dean Austin, Colin Calderwood, Gary Mabbutt, Justin Edinburgh, Ronnie Rosenthal, Darren Anderton, David Howells, Nick Barmby, Jurgen Klinsmann and Teddy Sheringham. From one of the world's greatest goalscorers to one of the most injury prone.

When Francis took over from Ossie Ardiles as manager in November 1994, Tottenham were effectively in the bottom four of the Premiership because of a points deduction for financial irregularities and were banned from the FA Cup. By April they had been reprieved, had brushed aside the eventual champions, Blackburn Rovers, in exhilarating style, but lost in the Cup semi-final and finished seventh in the league.

The same points tally they achieved in Francis' first two seasons (62, 61) would have secured Champions League football the previous season.

Sir Alan Sugar's highly successful TV series *The Apprentice* has the well known catch phrase "You're Fired" and when chairman of Spurs, he had a reputation for firing his managers.

Gerry tells me, "I wanted to talk to you about my time at Spurs because it does rile me when I still see some articles saying that I was sacked at Tottenham. I was never sacked, and that is a poor indictment of Alan Sugar to suggest that he sacked me as he spent a lot of time trying to talk me out of leaving. We actually got on very well.

"There are two sides to Alan Sugar, the side everyone sees and the side you're not able to see, but I was able to see it. He is one of the best chairmen I have worked with. He would make decisions, and make them quickly, it was a simple 'yes' or 'no', very little messing around, but at least you knew where you were with him. Yes, of course we had our rows, arguments, and disagreements, but we worked together."

Why did he walk out? "Lot's of reasons. It's quite complicated. Spurs, at that time, were very much a political club. There was still the Terry verses Alan, the media sided with either Venables or Sugar. Terry was the England manager, there was the points deduction, the ban from the FA Cup, the Jurgen situation. No money to spend in the first year. Perhaps one of the big reasons was that, after what I did for the club, I didn't think I was appreciated. I always felt sometimes, had I been at any other club in the country, I would be treated like a God for what I achieved. Sometimes I felt I was under pressure not only to win, but to win in a certain style, and it is not always possible. That has been one of the reasons why they have never been able to sustain a really good league run.

"Yet, I'm the only manager to have finished as top London club in the Premiership with two different teams (Tottenham and Queens Park Rangers). The Premier League wrote to me a year ago to point out that record, as they were compiling some sort of quiz. I managed the best two league positions in over a decade until Martin Jol finished twice in the top five. I had the best record in the first 50 games going back to Arthur Rowe in 1949.

"The biggest problem with doing well is to reproduce it when you are under pressure. The expectation becomes tough and people were causing the team a lot of problems."

Francis, considered one of the brightest young managers in England at the time, was more pragmatic. "I would hear things on the radio, that it was boring to win 1-0. They said, 'We would rather have lost 4-3', which was the case with Ossie. Tottenham used to say, 'Well it's not our day today, we will try next week'. I wanted (my team) to roll our sleeves up, because they can't stop us working and fighting for a result. But 1-0 was a result, a good result for a coach, but it was not reflected in the minds of the fans who sometimes weren't that impressed with four wins on the trot if it was 1-0 wins, they wanted more goals, more excitement, to win with style and that is not always possible, not even Manchester United and Chelsea can do that all the time."

From a promising beginning, the team's progress stalled and things turned sour. Come the summer, Jurgen Klinsmann left for Germany, Nick Barmby fled north and Gheorghe Popescu moved to Barcelona. And some supporters, for whom panache remained as valuable as points, became more demanding, yearning for the kamikaze style adopted by Ardiles, who had installed Klinsmann as the star of the fondly-remembered "famous five" attacking diamond (the others were Teddy Sheringham, Barmby, Ilie Dumitrescu and Darren Anderton).

Gerry recalls, "We had our moments, though. An FA Cup quarter-final at Anfield where we won 2-1 and I am convinced that, had I had Sol Campbell, Darren Anderton and Justin Edinburgh, we would have won the semi-final against Everton, who, mind you, went on to beat Manchester United in the final. I had beaten Manchester at Old Trafford 4-1 when I was manager at QPR and on New Year's Day we beat Manchester United when they were third and we were fourth in the league. We had such a good run up until Christmas that we hardly conceded a goal.

"But after that first year, they all seemed to go; Jurgen, Dumitrescu, Barmby. I didn't know Jurgen had a clause in his contract that allowed him to walk away. That summer I had to build a completely new team. We bought Chris Armstrong, who in the end cost £4.5m."

A lot has been made about Spurs turning their backs on Dennis Bergkamp, the one player above all others, who transformed a dour Arsenal under Graham, the authentic 1-0 specialists, into the prototype side under Wenger.

Gerry tells me his side of the Bergkamp saga, "I had Jurgen and Teddy a fantastic partnership and then Chris and Teddy, and I believe Chris and Teddy scored more goals than Jurgen and Teddy. You know Chris Armstrong and Teddy formed a great partnership and it was such a shame for Chris that he broke his ankle and he was never quite the same player. I don't believe for one minute that Alan Sugar would have spent the amount of money Arsenal did on Bergkamp, we would have struggled financially to have pulled off that deal. But I had Teddy Sheringham and Bergkamp was identical, they played in exactly the same position and performed the same function within the team. They both liked to drop off into that 'hole' behind the striker. Yes Dennis was an exceptional player but so too was Teddy and Teddy scored more Premier League goals. How would I have accommodated both of them in the same team? Alan Sugar made a statement at the time, shortly after Arsenal signed Bergkamp, that they had paid a ludicrous amount of money for him. Yes, Alan was saying what everybody else was thinking, but it didn't do me any favours, it only put me under more pressure."

Three years after taking charge, Francis stepped down after a 4-0 defeat away to Liverpool. He doubted that it was the right decision and Sir Alan Sugar implored him to change his mind. "I never finished below halfway, my worst position was 10th and that was mainly because we had such a lot of injuries that season. But for the first two seasons we were as good as anybody outside the top four, and as I said, finished top London club for two years. I went to Spurs without signing any contract, I only shook hands, and that was good enough for me. People said I was mad, but contracts didn't worry me at the time and never have done, but in the last year I was there I did actually sign a contract. I didn't get a pay off because I wasn't sacked."

Francis did, though, sign Ledley King, the present Tottenham captain, as a teenager. "We had to be on our strictest behaviour because of previous financial activities and had lost quite a few good kids. Alan rung me up and said, 'You have to sign Ledley'. I called him later and said that Ledley had gone to Manchester United. He went mad, and I said, 'It's ok, we signed him'. Ledley was talented, quick, strong, good on the ball. He reminded me of Sol Campbell."

Francis lost to Arsenal just once in seven Derbies, winning 1-0 against George Graham's side at White Hart Lane early in his Spurs reign. "My first taste of the Derby was electric, a frenetic game, a feeling that you never want to finish. We were mentally strong, and it's getting that psychological strength that Tottenham need to adopt now. Like Arsene Wenger, George Graham was winning things. I didn't have the luxury of the money that Martin Jol had available.

"Tottenham's consistency has always been their inconsistency since 1961."

Teddy Sheringham formally requested to leave Tottenham on Francis' wedding day. On the first day of his honeymoon he flew back to Heathrow to try to sign Eyal Berkovic, only for the deal to collapse. Sugar put a fax machine in Francis' honeymoon suite so he could keep in touch. Klinsmann still calls Francis about once a month and sometimes Francis offers the Germany coach advice.

When pressure from fans and media drove Francis to resign as Tottenham boss in October 1997, a disappointed Sugar bitterly quipped that, what with fancy-dan foreign coaches suddenly being all the rage, his manager would have had a much fairer public hearing if he'd changed his name to Geraldo Francisco.

That theory, though, was disproved. For though Francis faced flak, it was never as fierce as that fired at his Swiss replacement, Christian Gross, who from the moment he arrived at White Hart Lane was targeted for abuse and ridiculed in the press for nothing more than his broken English.

Before Sugar hired Gross I was so convinced that Sven Goran Eriksson was the right manager, at the right time for Spurs, that I almost begged Sir Alan to take him.

After his season with Manchester City some might argue it was a blessing in disguise that the move that I initiated fell through. However, the City fans mounted a campaign to keep Sven, and after the debacle of Steve McClaren, and the failure to qualify for the European Championships, the England reign of Sven doesn't look so bad – he qualified in all three tournaments, and reached the last eight in them all. But at the time I recommended Sven to Sir Alan, the Swede was at the peak of his powers, and his reputation within European circles was at its height.

I was waiting outside the gates of England's training ground at

Bisham Abbey with the rest of the media pack awaiting entry to the usual format of events prior to an England match – open training session/press conference – when my mobile rang. It was an old friend Bryan King, whose wife comes from Scandinavia, where he lived and worked and had become somewhat of an expert on football in that part of Europe. He wondered how Spurs were getting on in their search for a new coach and I told him, that they couldn't find the right candidate, and that Sugar was at a loss.

"How about Sven Goran Eriksson?" ventured Bryan. What a great idea, I thought, but didn't think for one moment that Eriksson would come to England. I was sure he had much bigger fish swimming around him in Europe to want to consider England. Sven had been highly successful in Sweden, Portugal and Italy, and although he had only managed to win the Championship once, he had rather unfairly been dubbed the "nearly man". Instead of the negativity that came with him from Italian football, all I had heard was glowing, positiveness surrounding his laid back management style.

When I suggested to Bryan there was little to no chance of luring Eriksson to Spurs, he quickly put me right. "Oh yes, he would be tempted", continued Bryan, "I know him well, and I have spoken to him recently and he would love to come to England. Do you think Spurs would be keen?"

Immediately I contacted Sir Alan. Naturally enough, the Spurs chairman hadn't heard of him. Sir Alan suggested he would make some enquiries about Eriksson and his CV and come back to me.

The next day Sir Alan called back and told me that he had consulted with people at his club and elsewhere and that Eriksson was not for Spurs.

So instead Spurs fans were treated to the unique management style of Christian Gross, who arrived in London at Heathrow airport, and who took the tube, waving his underground ticket for the photographers. It wasn't long before it was suggested that everyone hoped he had taken the precaution of buying a return ticket.

The campaign was so sustained throughout his 10-month tenure that "Christian Gross" became synonymous with "clueless continental". If an English club hires an unknown coach from overseas, fans will mutter, "let's hope he doesn't turn out to be another Christian Gross". Dismissed in September 1998, Gross did a respectable job at Spurs despite being regularly undermined. He has had subsequent success at Basel – where he's won three Swiss titles and masterminded European defeats of Liverpool, Celtic, Deportivo and Juventus.

Des Bulpin was on Gerry Francis' coaching staff at Tottenham and Peter Crouch was struggling as a first-year YTS trainee, all finesse and no brawn, when Bulpin told Crouch that one day he would play up front for England. Tottenham would allow him to leave in 2000, not convinced that he would make the grade. He stood by Crouch throughout his growing pains and when he left QPR with Francis for Tottenham in 1994, he encouraged his new club to take the youngster across London. "When we first got Peter at QPR, he was outstanding on the floor, he had a brain and technique but he just couldn't run," said Bulpin. "But I knew that once Peter got strength, he would be good in the air and become a player. People make mistakes with kids by letting them go before they develop physically. At 17, the weak boy can become just as strong as the others." Bulpin recalls the taunts that Crouch endured. The other boys would call him "Stick" and Crouch, introverted and conscious of his height, would hunch himself over in an attempt to blend in. Having taken him to Tottenham, the efforts to bulk him up began in earnest. "I gave him a load of milk, yoghurt, porridge, currants and raisins, told him to put it all in a blender and drink it wherever he went," said Bulpin. "I don't think he liked it. Then, there was the weights programme we put him on."

When Crouch left Spurs, Francis and Bulpin took him back to QPR in a £60,000 deal, where he scored 12 goals in 2000-01. Global recognition has since followed. Bulpin recalls, "A lot of people were talking about Defoe at the time; I think he was at Charlton, it was just before he moved to West Ham and people were talking about him like they had done with Michael Owen. I'd seen Defoe play and he was very quick, a perfect foil for Peter, in a little-and-large partnership."

Maybe now that Harry Redknapp has arrived, he might bring Crouch back to the Lane like he has done with Defoe. Who knows?

CHAPTER NINETEEN

Daniel Levy And How I Persuaded Him To Buy Spurs.

I had some business related dealings with Daniel long before he became Spurs chairman, and maybe I can take the credit of pushing him towards making a big investment in the North London club.

Together with Alan Green, the chief football commentator at Radio 5 Live for many years, I had dinner with Daniel to discuss an internet project that Alan and I had started up called Voice of Football. We dined at an Italian restaurant that clearly Daniel frequented quite close to his offices. Over dinner I tried to persuade Daniel to increase ENIC's portfolio of European football clubs with the purchase of Spurs. I was persistent, if nothing else, in trying to convince him that it would prove to be the right move. He wasn't too keen at the time, but I must have sowed the seed, as he eventually made Sir Alan Sugar an offer he couldn't refuse.

Daniel Levy, though, was not the only potential owner of Spurs with whom I had discussions. Surprisingly, one of them was a fellow journalist, the *Daily Mail*'s columnist Richard Littlejohn. He's a lifelong Spurs fan and I know he was more than interested in mounting a consortium to buy out Sir Alan Sugar at the time. I know Patrick Barclay thought he would have made an interesting independent chairman of the Football Association before the appointment of Lord Triesman of Tottenham, so why not a journalist as part owner of a football club?

Another potential owner of Spurs would have been Robert Earl, but he chose to help out his old pal Bill Kenwright at Everton. The London born owner of Planet Hollywood was once tipped to buy Spurs, before Sir Alan Sugar took control. I met Robert at the Sofitel Hotel in London recently and after a long chat know his allegiance to Spurs remains intact, but he is also totally committed to the Everton cause.

Sir Philip Green, boss of Arcadia, and one of the country's richest men, has been a go-between in some of football's biggest deals. His behind the scenes activities are known to only a handful of insiders in the game. Sir Philip helped out Kenwright by bringing Earl onboard at Goodison Park as an investor, at a time when Kenwright was experiencing great difficulties with his former shareholder at the club. With Green's prompting, Earl bought out the previous shareholder and between them they own 51 percent of the club. He acted as a go-between in arranging Wayne Rooney's transfer from Everton to Manchester United, where he is well connected with his relationship with Sir Alex Ferguson and his trusted agent Pini Zahavi. If Spurs are seeking a benefactor then Sir Philip Green, a big Spurs fan, would be ideal, but Sir Philip is far too wise to throw his hand directly into football, knowing there is only a downside to his peace of mind and lifestyle; he just doesn't need all the hassle that goes with it. The combination of Green and Earl would take the club forward, of that I have no doubt.

Rumours of an impending Spurs sale have been going on for some time. I recall writing about a "done deal" almost a year ago, which was not denied by the club, nor was it corroborated mind you.

Spurs fans might wonder what happened to this "done deal", well my sources tell me the guy who had settled on a price with Joe Lewis had an operation – and died!

Having said that Levy has unveiled ambitious plans for the new 60,000 seater super sleek stadium with all its additional income that it can generate and has recruited Harry Redknapp who is making an effort to turn around fortunes on the pitch in the wake of the acrimonious departure of Berbatov and the latest managerial upheaval with the removal of Juande Ramos.

Glenn Hoddle would not have tolerated the Berbatov saga that dragged on all summer before the Bulgarian eventually signed, inevitably, for Manchester United for £32m. Berbatov's desire to leave was the main talking point throughout the close season. Hoddle said, "You can't have that happening. What I would have done is set a deadline of three weeks before the window closes. The later it gets, the harder it is to replace the player who has gone. You are almost left with what you can get."

Berbatov reportedly refused to play against Sunderland in the opening home game of the new season and Hoddle said, "If that was the case, it would never have happened with an English player in this league. One would never refuse to play."

Hoddle pinpointed the frequent managerial upheavals at the club as the root cause of Spurs' failure to establish themselves among the elite. He has no doubt about what the biggest problem has been at his former club in recent years.

"There has been a lack of continuity at Tottenham," said Hoddle. "They have not built. When you are building a house, you start with strong foundations and Tottenham have not done that. That has been the case for the last six years. I thought Martin Jol was going to get that time you need but that wasn't to be, for whatever reason. Hoddle thought that Ramos should have been given the chance to finish the job. Hoddle pointed out wisely, just before Ramos was sacked, "These are difficult times for a football manager. Look what happened to Avram Grant. His team were up there challenging for the title right until the end and Chelsea were a lick of paint away from winning the Champions League. But under Luiz Felipe Scolari I think the owner Roman Abramovich will get what he wants; success with flair."

Daniel Levy believes the club could have been relegated had they stuck with Jol as manager. Levy, speaking after taking some testing questions from Spurs shareholders at the club's first Extraordinary General Meeting after the Jol sacking, claimed Spurs were on a downward spiral under Jol who had "lost the confidence" of his squad. Levy said, "We wanted Martin to succeed. The outside publicity was unfortunate but, in the end, it comes down to results. You can't have a situation where everybody is talking about finishing in the top four and then being in the bottom three. You cannot afford to take the risk that you may end up in a very, very bad situation. No club is too big to be relegated. We just weren't winning at all and you could look at the players, and there was a point when I think Martin had lost the confidence of the players. That happens in football." Levy refused to apologise for the way he sacked Jol, insisting the Dutchman never said sorry to him for applying for other jobs behind his back. Levy has gone on record for the first time to confirm that Jol spoke to Newcastle and Ajax, while he was in charge of Spurs. Levy said, "People say I should apologise, but I don't hear anyone talking about Martin going for two jobs while he was here. No one has had a go at him. Have I got an apology? We are in the football business and I completely understand that he went to talk to club X while he was still here, that's just the way it is."

So, out with Jol, and in with Ramos. Yet, after all the fuss and bad publicity in prising Ramos from Seville, it wasn't destined to last very long. Ramos is now coach at Real Madrid, would you believe, and Levy has ditched his beloved Continental system in favour of the old fashioned managerial role model in Redknapp.

CHAPTER TWENTY

The Fans' Cup Final.

Carling did their best to make the League Cup final, the fans' final, and I can only applaud them for it. Their motives are right, their marketing strategy spot on. The problem is that the game has headed off towards the corporate sector, slowly at first, and rapidly over the past few years. Like it or not, and Roy Keane has never liked it, the prawn sandwich brigade are here to stay. That's not to say that Carling, more earthly and grass roots, shouldn't attempt to address that situation. It's all credit to their marketing department and PR advisors Hill and Knowlton, who inundated me with their innovative ideas to make it more of a fans' final.

For a start, more ordinary tickets are designated to the club's supporters for the League Cup than the FA Cup, and that's how it should be. But the FA have a much more global problem in trying to keep everyone connected with their vast organisation sweet. There is less of that problem for the Football League.

Paradoxically, my wife Linda and myself were in the exclusive hospitality area designated for the Football League dignitaries, and some selected media.

The corporate sector at Wembley has taken some deserved stick for preferring to continue with their food and drink at half-time rather than taking their seats, leaving gaping holes in the stands which have been caught out on TV. Quite right. This is not conducive to persuading everyone that this is still the people's game.

I have seen the gradual change over the years, and more recently the lightning change towards the corporate sector throughout the game, not just at Wembley. This is one of the reasons Spurs need to move out of White Hart Lane to build a brand new stadium that can cater for more executive boxes and corporate areas.

Just because I took up Carling's invitation via Hill and Knowlton doesn't necessarily make me an elitist football fan. How can it, given my upbringing? But let's face it as you get older and wiser, who would turn down the comfort and luxury that goes with being on such a grade A guest list?

While the dress code suggested was smart casual, many of those in the official sector wore the shirts and scarves of their team, supposedly such attire was off limits. But it showed a degree of flexibility, and there was no hardship to discover such a partisan section of the hospitality group.

Of course it was tough for me to celebrate too strongly, as my delight at Spurs' success, came at a cost; Linda's misery. My son Simon and his Spurs supporting friend attended, courtesy of morc strings pulled to obtain the tickets, and they were delighted when we met up with them afterwards outside of the stadium in the North London drizzle.

Full circle, I suppose. My mad mum managed to pull whatever few strings at her disposal, so why not me doing it for Simon?

Anyway, let's hand it to Carling for coming up with the novel idea of a group of Chelsea and Spurs fans enjoying the ultimate armchair football experience after Carling decided to bring Wembley to their front room. With the final hugely over-subscribed as usual, Carling treated two lucky sets of supporters to a Wembley makeover featuring club legend, Graham Roberts who played for both clubs. The "Sponsors Lounge" saw fans from both clubs experience the excitement and traditions of the game from the comfort of their armchairs. A Chelsea legend and a Spurs legend each provided commentary on the game from their respective fans' lounge and a marching band kept the fans and their mates entertained ahead of kick off as they performed in their street. An opera singer even performed the national anthem live in their lounge at 2.50pm. The fans' lounges were given a stadium-like feel as the sponsors constructed life-size Carling perimeter boards in the lounges, handed out official match day programmes hot off the press and gave the fans the official match ball to boot. Hot-dogs were served at half-time, alongside chilled Carling, so the fan and their mates enjoyed the game in style and didn't have to battle in the half-time queues. Carling Cup marketing manager Richard Smith said, "If they can't make it to Wembley we thought we'd bring Wembley to them. We've got over 3,000 teams signed up to our pub football community – most of them play on a Sunday so will miss the final as they don't want to let their team-mates down. With this in mind it seemed like a good idea to offer them the chance to have a unique Carling Cup final experience at home. Although nothing can replace being in the stadium and watching the big match live, getting all your mates around to your house and having a beer on Carling is a pretty good second. The idea is that each lounge will look and feel as much like the Cup final day as possible – capturing the great traditions of a showpiece final and the fantastic atmosphere which goes with it."

Dimitar Berbatov and Robbie Keane looked so happy on that day, but were even happier to quit the club. Daniel Levy urged the Premier League to review the transfer system following the departures of strikers Berbatov and Keane to Manchester United and Liverpool respectively. United were linked to Berbatov for some time and he signed at Old Trafford, despite a higher bid from Manchester City. Levy was bitterly unhappy at the manner of the exit; it was "further evidence of the need for the Premier League to review the system". Tottenham also lost Keane to Liverpool in July, with the 28-year-old Republic of Ireland striker joining the club he supported as a boy. Levy added, "We found ourselves having to deal with the unexpected challenge of both our leading goalscorers making it clear they wished to leave the club. I have already stated my opinion on the manner in which our players were approached and the nature of the negotiations surrounding Robbie Keane and Dimitar Berbatov. I have also previously said that we had no need to sell players on long contracts – this no longer remains practical. The decisions we took to allow the transfers of Berbatov and Keane were made after close discussions with the coaching staff."

Berbatov joined United on transfer deadline day in a deal worth £30.75m. United striker Frazier Campbell, 20, moved in the other direction on a season-long loan deal and Spurs decided not to pursue their complaint to the Premier League accusing United of chasing Berbatov. The 27-year-old had been left out of the Tottenham team for recent games because Ramos felt the Bulgarian was too distracted by United's interest in him. Levy said, "Juandc was clear, and I believe correct, in not wishing to embrace any player within the dressing room that had no desire to play for the badge of this club and for his team-mates. Under these circumstances we had no option but to sell these players."

Spurs' victory over Chelsea at Wembley sent expectations soaring, but little has gone right for the club since that day. A £77m summer spending spree yielded only two points from their first five Premier League matches, leaving Spurs bottom of the table after their worst start to a campaign since 1955.

Chris Waddle, who scored 38 goals in 176 games for Spurs from 1985-89, worried that the Carling Cup triumph raised hopes to an unrealistic level. The former England winger observed, "The Carling Cup came too soon for Spurs, because it meant that expectations grew out of proportion. Spurs have always been a great Cup side, but the fans see other teams challenging for the title or a Champions League place, and think that is where Spurs should be. Cup competitions are the best bet for the clubs. It is not easy to get into the top four". Waddle made his observation just before Ramos was sacked and thought that the manager should have been judged at the end of the season.

Ex-Spurs defender Chris Hughton was in temporary charge on Tyneside at this time. Hughton spent 13 years as a player and 14 as a coach at Spurs, and had been No 2 to Ramos' predecessor Martin Jol before he was sacked along with the Dutchman. Hughton was in charge of first team affairs immediately after Keegan left Newcastle, with the club's hugely unpopular owner desperate to sell up after seeing the fans turn on him.

Hughton was working alongside Jol when Spurs signed Jenas from the Magpies, and the England midfielder admits he was surprised by Tottenham's lack of progress since their Carling Cup win. Jenas said, "The Carling Cup was a benchmark for us, and we wanted to take that into the new season, but it hasn't happened. We definitely didn't envisage being bottom of the league after five games. Some very influential players have left, like Keane and Berbatov, but it is a matter of us gelling. Going forward, we just don't seem to be clicking."

For all the wheeling and dealing it was a dreadfully depressing start to the new season especially for all the new recruits. But in the Cup tie Spurs won at St James' Park with rumours of a comeback for... El Tel!

I was due to discuss the possibility of Venables becoming the new boss on BBC Newcastle radio, but the whole debate had become defunct overnight.

The next day Mike Ashley called for Joe Kinnear appointing the 61-year-old as interim manager after failing in a bid to persuade Venables to take over on a temporary basis. With typical Kinnear humour he said, "I am being linked with the 'Cockney mafia' – they forget I was born in

Ireland and played for Ireland all my life. So be it. I have come here to do the best I possibly can because I know it's a short contract, I know what is stored around the corner for me, if you like. But sod it, so what? If I can come and do a really good job here, who knows where it is going to lead?" Kinnear had not managed a club since resigning as Nottingham Forest boss in December 2004. He made his name at Wimbledon until he was forced to take two years out of the game after suffering a heart attack in 1999.

The Dubliner started his career at Tottenham and stayed at White Hart Lane for a decade. He joined Spurs as an amateur in 1965 and went on to make more than 200 appearances. He made his Spurs debut at right-back against West Ham in April 1966, and his international debut a year later against Turkey. He played 26 times for his country up until 1975. Joe played in the 2-1 FA Cup final win over Chelsea, and was part of the team that beat Aston Villa 2-0 to land the League Cup in 1971. Joe won a UEFA Cup medal when Spurs beat Wolves over two legs in 1972, and a year later Spurs won the League Cup again beating Norwich 1-0. In 1975 Joe left Spurs for Brighton and retired as a player aged 30 in 1976.

After five years abroad managing in Dubai with former Spurs team-mate Dave Mackay and heading India's national side, he rejoined Mackay at Doncaster in 1977. He became manager when Mackay switched to Birmingham, but a takeover saw him lose his job to Billy Bremner. Bobby Gould recommended him for a job as reserve team coach at Wimbledon for £15,000 a year. Dons owner Sam Hamman later said he liked him so much when he first met him he gave him an instant £2,000 pay rise when he joined in 1991.

Jermain Defoe put Pompey ahead when he drove in a penalty after Jenas needlessly handled a Glen Little free-kick. Spurs lacked a goal threat but were denied a penalty after a Lennon cross struck Diarra's arm. Peter

Crouch nodded in Pompey's second before Diarra was sent off late on for two bookable offences. It left Spurs with just two points from six top flight games and, while it was early in the season, the club had made their worst start for 53 years.

Ramos was the target of some anger from Spurs fans during his side's 2-0 defeat by Portsmouth. Asked if he had the confidence of his chairman and board, Spaniard Ramos said, "Absolutely. We speak regularly and everyone is aware of our delicate position." Some Spurs supporters were unhappy with Ramos when he substituted Pavlyuchenko with Darren Bent after 73 minutes. The move kept the visitors with just one recognised striker on the pitch, despite having to chase the game having gone 2-0 behind. "Whether I survive is something for the chairman and the board to decide but I'm not hurt (by the fans' abuse)," added Ramos. "What hurts is not winning matches."

Spurs were then the only club without a Premier League victory. They had twice as many points at the same stage the previous season, yet that got Martin Jol the sack and led to the appointment of Ramos. To add to Ramos' discomfort, Jol was now in charge at Hamburg, who led the German Bundesliga.

The manner of Tottenham's defeat heaped humiliation on Ramos. Portsmouth had conceded 10 goals in their previous two matches but eased to victory with goals from Jermain Defoe and Peter Crouch. Defoe later left Spurs because the London club thought Ramos did not need him. The England striker converted a penalty and was applauded by Spurs fans for not celebrating. Then, when he was substituted two minutes from the end, the away supporters joined in the ovation for him. But they taunted Spaniard Ramos with "You don't know what you're doing" for playing with only one forward.

Spurs drew in Poland and scraped into the group stages of the UEFA

Cup but ahead of their Sunday match at the Lane with Hull City, the *News of the World* carried the story of a return to the Lane for... none other than Terry Venables.

Coincidently I had been booked by Radio 5 Live for a morning review of the Sunday papers and a look ahead to the fixtures, more Premiership games than had been the previous day. Naturally reference was made to the writing of this book and the content it might contain about Venables. I suggested on air that if Venables did make it back to the Lane, then there was no chance of this book being sold in the Spurs shop! Part of the review of the press was Martin Jol's comments in *The Sunday Times* that the club had lost its identity, and it was a point that was sure to raise a fascinating debate about not just Spurs but a number of other clubs.

The point I made on Radio 5, was that, for Spurs fans, a heavy dose of nostalgia would help ease the pain of the present predicament.

Well, could it get worse? It sure did. Spurs lost at home to Hull that afternoon to register the club's worst start since 1912... the year the *Titanic* went down. At least Joe Kinnear's side, two down at Goodison Park, fought back for a valiant enough and unexpected draw. It left Spurs well and truly rooted to the foot of the Premier League with just two points from the opening seven games with Ramos coming up to his first year at the club.

My Spurs supporting pal Barry sent me a flood of texts with the latest Spurs jokes, all revolving around three points and not being able to beat anyone. "I know people are having a laugh at the fact we are bottom of the league at the moment but it's up to everyone at the club to stop the jokes," said Bentley. "We're not happy with what has been happening. You cannot hide from the situation but what we need are a team of leaders who take responsibility. We have to grow as people. We have more than enough good players at Tottenham to get us out of this situation and I give my word that we will." Bentley blamed Ramos for him missing out on the current England squad for not playing him often enough and playing him out of position. The winger, who moved to White Hart Lane from Blackburn in the summer of 2008 for £15m, does not regret the switch to North London. "I still love being at Spurs and I don't regret joining the club for one second. I know I haven't been at my best but I haven't become a bad player in a fortnight. The manager believes in me."

Jol was sacked after making a poor start, but feels Spurs should not make the same mistake. "They've changed the team but have done it with good intentions as they want to be better. They need to get good results, but it will take time, and unfortunately in England you don't get time. I was unhappy to leave Spurs. It wasn't to be and I've moved on. Yes, they won the Carling Cup after I left, but that was my team and my players. Now the team is different. I did well for a couple of seasons, the sun was always shining, it was a great atmosphere at the club and the players did well. The only person who was always complaining was Berbatov. They said to me he wants to leave because of you, but I don't think it was because of me. He proved me right and left anyway. I wish them all the best as they are a big club with over a million supporters and they were great to me. The fans are the best in England."

Could it possibly get any worse? Of course not. Oh yes it could. Bale saw red for a foul on Soares and Higginbotham scored the penalty before Bent poked home an equaliser for 10-men Spurs at Stoke. But after the break Spurs' fight back disintegrated as Delap tapped in to make it 2-1 before Fuller struck both posts with a penalty and Delap hit the bar. Dawson was sent off for a tackle on Sidibe and Fuller hit the post in 11 minutes of injury time, which came after Corluka was badly hurt. The Croatian was caught by the knee of his own keeper, Heurelho Gomes, fell on his chin and required medical attention on the pitch. He left the field on a stretcher wearing an oxygen mask and was taken to hospital. Two points separated the teams at the start of the game, but Spurs were left three points adrift at the foot of the table after falling to their sixth league defeat of the season.

No team with two points from their first eight league games had ever survived relegation.

This was the worst start in Spurs' formidable history.

CHAPTER TWENTY-ONE

The Arrival Of Harry Houdini.

It was one of those How Dare You moments.

Live on air, on Radio 5 Live actually, I was asked about my reaction to the sacking of Juande Ramos. "Predictable", I replied "and, Harry Redknapp is the new manager of Spurs!"

The show was broadcast from Manchester, rather than London for some strange reason I am still not quite sure about, and the presenter, who was unfamiliar to me, was indignant that I should be so confidently suggesting that Redknapp had been appointed the new manager. "Who have you been talking to? What are your sources? How can you be sure?"

Usually, during my multi-media interviews, whether on TV or radio, I have been circumspect about what I have said, because my newspaper column would be appearing the next day. But, since I have left the *Express*, my appearances have increased on TV and radio because I am more available. Also, I am less restricted in what I can say. So, it must have come as a shock that I was not holding back and radio was the recipient of one of my "exclusives".

While I declined to reveal my sources on air, despite being challenged to do so, I did then mention the fact that I was writing this book (everyone who knows me, knows how I do like to plug my books on air), and that events at the Lane had become so predictable. Having prolonged the agony of Martin Jol as a "dead man walking", it was transparent that Ramos was dead in the water a week after the humiliating defeat at Stoke, followed by the loss in the UEFA Cup in Italy. According to my sources the Spurs board felt the performance against Udinese was the final straw, that the manager's run-ins with players such as David Bentley and the comments about a losing mentality from Jonathan Woodgate, caused a dramatic U-turn in the attitude of the players which was showing up on the pitch – the players no longer were playing for their manager, was the feedback I had received. My Spurs insider told me, "In that European tie you could see that the players were going through the motions; that they no longer were playing for the manager, and once that happens there is no way back."

The call immediately went out to Harry Redknapp. Harry opted to get out of Pompey before the club was sold and he might be replaced by new owners seeking another foreign option, and it was clear he would not say no to Spurs as he had when he was offered the job after Jol.

In the days and even hours leading up to the sacking of Ramos the club's legends lined up to give their views. One of the most pertinent came from Perryman, who lifted the FA Cup twice as Spurs captain and played a record 854 games for them. Perryman was going through agonies watching their relegation battle unfold. So even in retrospect it is worth recording Steve's opinion as he was actually skipper the last time the club dropped out of the top flight in 1977. Spurs seriously damaged their UEFA Cup hopes as they crashed 2-0 to Udinese, but it was their Premier League status that worried ex-Spurs players who were voicing their fears, such as Gary Stevens who talked about the players being more concerned with their hairstyles. The pressure was building up on Levy to act.

Perryman blamed the Spurs board for the management structure they imposed on Ramos, with sporting director Comolli having a huge say in player recruitment. Perryman said, "When I was a player at Spurs there was a base of home-grown people there. What the club stands for now is increasingly difficult to see. Everyone seems to be just passing through.

Tottenham is not the same club I knew. It's Hollywood. It's not real. We were not passing through. I did 19 years at Spurs. We had a depth of feeling about the place. We had our cobblers kicked by the supporters when we did badly, we were lifted on their shoulders when we did well." Perryman's Spurs lifted the FA Cup in 1981, 1982 and the UEFA Cup in 1984; the club's last real sustained spell of success. Comolli was expected to be relieved of his duties, when the former Tottenham midfielder believed the damage had already been done. Any club that devalues the power of the manager is walking on thin ice. I don't know if the manager is going to be good enough or not. That has not been proven either way yet. But you have to appoint a manager you believe in, and follow it up. Don't water him down or attack him from above. I saw all that go on when Ossie Ardiles was undermined as manager. I've been through all that crap. Bill Nicholson was the right man. You could not possibly question him. Get the right manager and then back him.

Perryman is director of football at League Two Exeter and at the age of 56, he is no threat to manager Paul Tisdale. "I just help the manager. I am not a threat. That is the only way it can be. The manager has to be the man. The success must be the manager's, the failure, his. That's why he picks the team, that's why he buys the players, he makes the substitutions. Fighting relegation is dark. They were dark days in 1977. There is never any let-up. You are depressed, you are down, negative, not confident. You are expecting bad things to happen. You need strong people to drive through it and we did not have them then. I hope there is integrity at Tottenham to do the right thing. The right thing might mean making the hard decision to get rid of someone. Or it might mean to keep them. You can never say they are too good to go down. We went down in 1977. It happens."

So the inevitable happened. The Tottenham squad, staying at the Radisson Hotel in Canary Wharf in preparation for their Bolton home game the next day, were told to go downstairs for a meeting with Levy. The chairman informed the players of the management change. Levy had overnight averted the fans planned protests! Ramos, Comolli and first team coaches Marcos Alvarez and Gus Poyet were all sacked. It came just a day before the anniversary of Martin Jol's exit.

Spurs had a shocking two points from their first eight league games, leaving them four points adrift at the bottom of the table. Levy said "At this stage where Tottenham is, we need a fighter. We need someone who has inspiration. I'm a Spurs fan and it's a sickening feeling seeing Spurs where they are and we need to get back up where we belong, which is near the top." While Levy refused to blame any individuals, he did reveal that he had become uncertain about the player recommendations he was receiving. "We have spent about £175m on new players over the last three years. The purchasing of new players is a critical aspect of our club. Given our current position, it is essential that we go into the January transfer window with absolute confidence being offered to the board. Following a meeting of the directors and a full review of our football management structure... Damien will not be directly replaced. In Harry, we are also accepting with his appointment that now is the right time for us to move back to a more traditional style of football management at our club."

Ramos has not escaped criticism and his training methods have been questioned, as well as his admission that he barely looks at the opposition before a game. Levy added that the decision was "not something I have undertaken lightly" but that "significant change was necessary as a matter of urgency".

Redknapp admitted he couldn't turn down the opportunity. Shrewdly, Redknapp laced his comments with a touch of Tottenham's traditions, references to Bill Nicholson, and icons of their real glory days. "It's a big opportunity to manage a big club before I retire. I am a big follower of the history of the game and Tottenham have been a great club over the years. I followed Tottenham, I trained there as a kid so I know the history of the club. People think I was a West Ham fan as a kid because I love that club, but it was Spurs I used to go and watch, they were the team I supported. Now I've been given an opportunity that I've waited for all my life. Since I started as a manager, I've always craved working for a big club, a club with heritage and style, that's what Spurs have got. I want to put them back where they belong, up there with Arsenal. I'll be at White Hart Lane of course I will. I'll go into the dressing room before the match and say, "Hey, fellas, let's go out there and win a football match." It's all about confidence. I want to put that back in the players and give them the chance to show what they can do. There are fantastic players here and they deserve the opportunity. I'll do the job on my terms. If we're going to survive, then I'll do it as the manager. I've always wanted to be in charge. If I sign rubbish players then I'll get the stick for it but they will be my players, not some director of football's".

Redknapp recalled telling Bill Nicholson that he was a right-winger who did not score goals when he came for a trial at the age of 11. Nicholson replied that Stanley Matthews was similar, but that Redknapp probably didn't have the same ability. Redknapp said, "He was one of the all-time great managers." Nothing would endear him more to the Spurs fans than the belief he was returning to his roots, even if they were really only partial roots. He went on, "It is a big, big, club. It is a club that has massively underachieved this year – to be sitting there with two points and, let's be honest, in a real desperate situation, a relegation battle. There's a lot of quality players there that obviously haven't done as well as they should have done. You don't end up with two points from eight games if you're doing what you should be doing. So they need to start performing as I know they can. Whether it's confidence or whatever, it's up to me to go in and try to get the best out of them players."

Portsmouth established themselves in the Premier League and won the FA Cup but Redknapp admitted, "I had a great time at Portsmouth and we had an unbelievably, successful time over the six years I was there. But Tottenham made a fantastic offer to Portsmouth and it was difficult. It was a lot of money – I think £5m, crazy money really". Harry added, "Of course it's tough to turn my back on Pompey because I love it there and I'm leaving behind some great friends. But how often do you get the chance to manage Spurs? When anybody says Spurs, I think of Bill Nicholson and the great Double winning team of the 1960s. They played with style and that's what I want to bring back. It was a hard decision but Portsmouth have picked up £5m in compensation and I reckon that's a world record transfer fee for a manager. I hope that helps heal a bit of the pain they'll be feeling and I think they'll understand my reasons for leaving. I spoke to Clive Allen, who is Spurs through and through, and he just said, 'Harry, go for it, it's what you've been waiting for all your life.' And he's dead right, a fantastic club with a magnificent history, how could I say no? Yes, I've got a great life down in Dorset but that's not the be-all-and-end-all. I'll be moving back up to London because I want to devote everything to this job. Listen, I'm 61 years old, this probably won't come around again. When I turned Newcastle down, I thought I'd be at Pompey for life. I feel sorry for Juande Ramos, he did the best job he could do but it didn't work out for him. It's tough on the fella but it's happened to me in the past and you just have to accept it and move on. I know Spurs are in a dire position but I wouldn't be taking the job if I wasn't confident of turning things around. If I don't get it right and we're relegated, then I'll walk away. I'll hold my hands up and admit I wasn't up to the job, I won't hang around. But I don't think that's going to happen, there are too many good players for that."

Portsmouth's owner Alexandre Gaydamak denied reports that he was looking to sell Pompey because of escalating debts, but of course, not long afterwards he was confessing that the club were up for sale! Redknapp knew what was going on and it was the right time to get out.

Redknapp instantly delivered what Tottenham wanted all season – a victory, 2-0 over Bolton. Pavlyuchenko and Bent grabbed the goals at the Lane. They were still bottom of the table but made up ground with other strugglers and crucially had a morale-boosting first league win of the season, at the ninth attempt.

Ramos' hasty departure came too quick for the club to change the match day programme, so fans were given a chance to read the Spaniard's final notes.

"If you believed everything that was being speculated on then your perception of the club would be far removed from the reality," he wrote!

The reality was Ramos heading back to Spain (incredibly pitching up at Real Madrid a few months later) and Redknapp was in the dressing room and dugout, even though reserve team coach Clive Allen picked the team.

Redknapp was unveiled to the Spurs fans before kick off. The encouraging sign for Redknapp was skipper Ledley King being available, four days after playing in the defeat to Udinese. It was the first time he had been ready for games in such quick succession for 10 months. As expected of a team with a new manager, there was an extra zip. Luka Modric struggled to make an impact since his £16.5m signing, but he was given a free role behind the striker and resembled a new player. Bentley was back in the team after being dropped for Ramos' final game following an outspoken assessment on Spurs' start to the season.

"Harry Redknapp's white and blue army," sang the Spurs fans after watching two players who struggled under Ramos combine for the opening strike.

Redknapp remarked, "I've taken over clubs before where I look at it and think how do we get out of this one, but there is real quality in this group of players. You look through and there are international players. You look at the quality and they shouldn't be where they are, but two points in eight games is an amazingly bad start. We have to start working as hard as we did today for each other, picking up points, playing as we did. They passed the ball with real quality which I was really impressed with." Although Redknapp did not pick the team, he was keen to get involved. "I met the players at the hotel today, came in on the coach with them and got in the dressing room with Clive Allen. I can't afford to be up in the stands sitting back and saying 'well if they got beat it was Clive's fault and if they had won it was me who picked the team'. Clive picked the team, but I got involved straight away. He did a good job but I like to think I had some influence as well."

Redknapp insisted he alone will pick which players come to the Lane. "I wouldn't let anyone else pick my players. I will pick the players we sign and if the chairman can deliver them, then great. I'm not going to ask him to buy Ronaldo for me. There'll be some players out there in January who we'll bring in. I'll just deal with the chairman. There will be no sporting director or director of football. The last word on players has to be with the manager. At Portsmouth, Peter Storrie did all the deals but it was my choice on picking the players. If people are giving you players you do not fancy, it is impossible." Tottenham fans made it clear they would welcome Defoe back by chanting his name within 10 minutes of Redknapp's first game.

Redknapp would never have forgiven himself if he had not taken the Spurs job. "I could have come maybe 18 months ago, in all honesty. I nearly came here when Martin Jol was manager, but things happened.

Tottenham is a big club, whether they're languishing at the bottom of the league or not. I nearly went to Newcastle and people said I didn't want the challenge of a big club. I took Portsmouth to seventh in the league with a fantastic group of players, but things are a bit tight financially and I would have regretted it for the rest of my life if I hadn't come here. Kevin Bond is a terrific coach and there are a couple of ex-Tottenham players who have great futures in the game and I'll try to talk to them. I don't know about Jamie, *Sky Sports* probably pay him too much!"

Jamie Redknapp said, "When I was growing up, Spurs used to be the golden ticket in London. Arsenal were pragmatic, Chelsea had long left behind the heady days of the 1970s and Tottenham played football on the deck, with a style and swagger. I captained the club when I left Liverpool, but my fitness never allowed me to make the impact I hoped for. The club was sliding and subsequent years have not been kind. Are they a big club? Like Newcastle, they can be. And that is surely why people must understand Harry's reasons for taking this job. My dad has taken over a team low on confidence and morale, but the players are already showing they are inspired by his arrival. 'What's his secret?' I am often asked. It's really very simple. He makes a player feel special. When I was a boy playing for him at Bournemouth, if I played well he would tell me. 'Different class today,' in front of the dressing room. The flip side is that he will tell you when the performance isn't good enough. He is clear and precise with his instructions and he wants players to perform with expression and flair. Attacking football is his favoured way. Another player spoke to me after the game, when I went into the dressing room. He complained about the training under the previous manager and the style of football. Players will always look for excuses, but they also need to look at themselves after their start this season. It can't all be down to Juande Ramos. I was surprised that Ramos used Ledley

King in the UEFA Cup, though. King is struggling with a knee injury, but the priority has to be the Premier League. I don't want to criticise the previous regime at Spurs too much, nor the appointment of a coach who could not speak English when he arrived, but so much of football is about communication. It's not what you say sometimes, but how you say it to a dressing room of established internationals. The point or the moment can be lost in translation. Our clubs now have a worldwide appeal and some have investment from faraway lands, but we have to trust home-grown coaches and managers in key positions. Hopefully, having managers such as my dad and Manchester City's Mark Hughes in high-profile roles will help buck the trend. Now Tottenham have a manager who talks their language and plays their football."

King admitted Redknapp's arrival rejuvenated a Tottenham dressing room that was falling apart under Ramos. "The players seem to have a weight off their shoulders. They played with freedom, and it was more like the old Tottenham. Harry has been there before with teams and produced his magic, and I'm very confident he can do it with us. It is brilliant to have an English manager. It has been a while and I am looking forward to the relationship. Harry spoke to us for the first time on the morning of the game, and he gave us confidence. He said we had brilliant players in the team, and that he believed we could get out of this situation."

Ramos released a short statement on his website that read "Results are what count in football. Now we have to see if this decision is the best one for the team to recover and have a good season." But two days later Ramos criticised Tottenham's transfer policy under Comolli and insisted he was not given enough experience in his squad. "In the summer we experienced a difficult pre-season due to the changes in the squad, which prevented us from working with the tranquillity that the summer preparation needs," Ramos said in an open letter on his personal website,

"Furthermore the young age of some of the signings, despite their quality, means they needed some time to adapt and mature, which because of the urgency of the competitions they have not been given. Also the departures of Robbie Keane and Berbatov, important players in the team for their technical and human qualities and their scoring abilities, were too hard a blow for the squad. All this triggered a situation which I hope will be turned around as soon as possible because the club and fans deserve it."

Jol wanted a left-sided midfielder in the summer before his departure but Comolli never found the right man. Comolli's failure has been highlighted by Levy scrapping the continental structure Ramos was working under. Ramos added, "After almost 20 years in the game I know the unwritten rules of football and that's why I accept the decision taken by the leaders of Tottenham. We arrived with the highest hopes to a team in the relegation zone, in a situation similar to that which is found at these moments, and we had a good start which saw us get to the middle of the table. Furthermore, we were able to qualify for Europe when it seemed almost impossible. We achieved it with a great effort on the part of all the team despite the enormous difficulties that we had. We also achieved the difficult challenge of lifting a title, which after nine years without tasting success was an enormous joy for the club and the fans. For this we can catalogue last season as tremendously successful."

Redknapp was settling in with his first major press conference. Bentley, Woodgate, Huddlestone and Dawson all dropped out of England contention and Jenas had fallen behind Barry in Capello's pecking order. But, having revived the England careers of James, Defoe and Crouch at Portsmouth, Redknapp wanted to rescue his new Spurs players. Even injury-plagued King should not give up hope of playing for his country again. "If you look at David Bentley, four months ago he was David Beckham's successor," said Redknapp. "Now he's had a little dicky spell and found himself out of the England team. We know what a good player he is and we've got to get him playing like he was at Blackburn. We've got to do the same with some of the others. Jenas is an international player. We've got to get them back to what they should be." Redknapp was willing to lighten his load in training to get him through games and, unlike Ramos, will keep the captain back for Premier League clashes. "When Ledley's fit he is a fantastic centre-half," said Redknapp. "He's got strength, he's good in the air and good on the ball. He's an England player. He will train when he feels right to train. He's got his own fitness regime and if I can get him out on the pitch Saturday to Saturday I'll be delighted. For me the league games are going to be more important than playing in the Cup games."

Redknapp was by no means concentrating his efforts solely on Spurs' English contingent and is particularly excited by Croatia playmaker Modric and Welsh international Bale. "It's about getting the best out of everybody – and confidence. Life is about confidence. Whatever you do, if you are not confident you don't perform. It's up to me to get the confidence running through the players and if I can get that instilled you'll see a team that really plays."

Redknapp's own confidence was sky-high. His immediate target may be modest but his long term aim is one few Spurs managers before him have achieved. First up, survival. Then he wants to match Arsenal!

A victory over Bolton had not deluded Redknapp, "Long term, the aim is to get Tottenham up there challenging for a top four position, but the first goal is to make sure we stay in the Premier League. It is realistic for Tottenham to try to catch Arsenal, though, yeah. They're both big clubs with similar crowd potential. If we had a 50,000 or 60,000 stadium, then we'd be filling it because that's the support Tottenham have. Financially, there would be nothing between the clubs, it's about what you do on the pitch. Without a doubt Arsenal are ahead of us and it's going to take time. They've moved away this season and there is a fair gap, but with hard work it can be closed. They are both major clubs and it is up to us to get Tottenham back to where we should be. You've only got to walk around Tottenham to feel it is a club that is really geared for the big time. It's had the big time. I know the history of the club, the early 1960s with Dave Mackay."

Redknapp had let it slip that Spurs approached him in the summer of 2007 after a shocking run of results had put Jol's job on the line. Levy had to react when he said, "I can't give details but I'm sorry that, for whatever reason, we didn't appoint Harry then. It would be unfair of me to give details on the historical discussions with Harry. Perhaps we wouldn't be in this position if we had. I hope he can be a top four manager but he has never managed a top four club so you are never going to know until, hopefully, we get there. We have confidence Harry has every chance to get us there. We went for what we considered to be the best manager but other people may disagree."

On the eve of the match at the Emirates, Wenger said, "Only time will tell whether Harry Redknapp will be a success. What is important is how well we will play, not who sits on the Spurs bench. If there is one game that is special for Tottenham, no matter who sits on the bench, it is Spurs against Arsenal. So I don't think that (a new manager) will change a lot. We have a very strong united spirit in the dressing room."

Redknapp hailed his side's "never-say-die attitude" after two injury-time goals earned them an amazing 4-4 draw at Arsenal. "It was a real old-fashioned slugging match. We went for it and then they went for it. We conceded sloppy goals but we never gave up, we showed a never-say-die attitude and came back brilliantly. It was a fantastic performance and a great result in the end." The extraordinary display at the Emirates provided further encouragement. Redknapp even suggested he had never experienced a match like it in his entire 25-year coaching career, "It's been a difficult week, leaving home at 5.30 in the morning and not getting home until nine, but this makes it all worth it. It really was an amazing game of football to be involved in. We gave away some bad goals, from set-pieces too, even though we worked hard on that in training. We need to stop giving away goals like that, especially as one of them was straight after we pulled it back to 3-2. But the boys have been fantastic, there's a real spirit there, a determination. They are jumping for joy in the dressing room."

Spurs opened the scoring in the 13th minute with former Gunner David Bentley beating Almunia with a superb 40-yard volleyed lob. Surely, goal of the season! Jenas, who scored Spurs' third goal, hailed the impact Redknapp had already made since his arrival. "Harry is great motivationally. The lads have done him a favour by reacting to it. It showed complete team spirit and togetherness. We always believed. We just showed that never-give-in spirit. Any team who comes to the Emirates and gets a result has done well but given the circumstances, this is just brilliant."

Stand-in skipper Jenas insisted his team-mates still had to pour their "heart and soul" into every game. "Harry has brought togetherness to the whole squad. Even the players who aren't in the team seem to be happy. It's his demeanour, the person he is. You can sense his presence and belief when you're on the pitch and when you're in the dressing room. I don't want to undermine what Juande Ramos did but Harry is famous for his man-management skills. We have a lot of young players at Tottenham who need a bit of help and an arm around the shoulder every now and again. Harry is just the man for that. He hasn't had much time to find his feet yet but he has still managed to find the time to have a little chat with every player. It's just the type of guy he is. He puts himself around and makes himself a part of the dressing room."

Tottenham confirmed their intention to build a new 60,000-capacity stadium near their current White Hart Lane ground. Spurs announced the Northumberland Development Project at the same time as their financial results, June 2008. The development will include leisure facilities, public space and housing. "The scheme includes the current site and adjoining land, with the stadium sited to the north of the existing one," said Levy. For the year ending 30th June turnover was up 11 percent and the building of a new training centre is expected to start. Revenue was up from £103m to £114.8m with net debt of £14.6m though that figure includes property acquisitions.

Speaking about the need to sell naming rights, Levy said, "Unfortunately it's a function of modern day finance – absolutely there will have to be naming rights on the stadium. It's going to be a new stadium so it won't be White Hart Lane. If we want things to progress, things have to change." Levy insisted paying for the new stadium will not stop Redknapp from recruiting players, "The stadium has no impact on our transfer policy. When Harry took the job we had a conversation about the current squad and we agreed we have the talent here. One or two small changes maybe but generally we have the talent here. Harry's confident and I'm confident that we can move up the table."

The Tottenham board pushed ahead with proposals for a larger stadium with a season ticket waiting list of about 22,000 but were conscious of the importance of remaining in the Haringey area. "With a waiting list for season tickets of over 22,000 and club membership levels of over 70,000, our need for an increased capacity stadium has been clear for all to see for some time," said Levy. "Having reviewed our stadium options it was clear that there were a limited number of alternative sites to our current location. Following discussions with council bodies, the London Development Agency, Transport for London and local and central government officials, redeveloping the existing site emerged as the most viable route. We have spent five years buying and taking options over property around the current stadium site to enable us to either develop locally or to gain the critical mass to achieve a substantial site sale as a contribution to relocation. To date this includes almost 60 separate property transactions, including 40 residential and potentially 160 commercial properties at a commitment of £44m. The public consultation period will now begin and we would hope to submit a planning application in 2009. I am personally delighted that we have been able to put forward a viable option which we know to be the fans' favourite – remaining at the club's spiritual home."

Redknapp ingratiated himself immediately to the players by putting tomato ketchup back on the tables of the dining room at the Tottenham training complex! In addition to his salary of a basic £3m, he agreed a very lucrative bonus system, close to £1m for maintaining the White Hart Lane outfit's Premier League status, and will earn an extra £250,000 if he retains the Carling Cup and double that amount if he wins the FA Cup. He will pocket a similar amount should he miraculously send Spurs soaring into the Champions League. Levy commented, "Champions League football is obviously something this club strives for eventually but it is very difficult to break into the Big Four. The hope is that Harry is here for the long term and will help us achieve it. In Harry, I believe we now have the right manager and one the players do respect. Now the players have to show the club and the fans what they can do. Can we make a Big Four become a Big Five? That is certainly possible."

While, as a listed company, Spurs are always subject to rumours of potential takeovers, Levy insisted the club is definitely NOT for sale.

"None of us have a crystal ball but I very much hope I'm still here when the new stadium is built. I'm a fighter. I don't give up." However, if the price was right, Levy has a duty to put the bid to shareholders.

Redknapp recruited Tim Sherwood and Les Ferdinand to his ex-Spurs legends think tank. Sherwood, just 39 and a close friend of Jamie, confirmed, "I will be here in some capacity. I'm pleased to have the opportunity to be involved at such a great football club. I'm not sure how I'm going to be involved. It's only going to be part-time because the club won't be in my mind 100 percent of the time. It's a fantastic football club. If someone would have asked me where I wanted to get back into football then I would have said Tottenham Hotspur. I don't know what the plans are. This is a great club."

Redknapp, who managed Sherwood at Portsmouth, said, "I would like to get Tim involved. It's about time we got the younger guys involved. People like him and Les Ferdinand have a lot to offer. Get him in a couple of days a week. Tim's got a terrific football brain. I'd like to tap in to that and get him on the coaching ladder and see if he likes it. Les, what a great fellow to have around. We've got to have English coaches coming in coaching at the top of the Premier League." Redknapp was excited by the news of a proposed new stadium for Tottenham, even though it was unlikely to be completed for six years, "I hope I'll be here to see it. If I'm doing a good job I'd love to stay long term but it's a results business and if you do get them you'll stay around. You never know."

Admitting that he and his team-mates are far happier under their new coach, Pavlyuchenko joked that, on match days, Redknapp is so excitable that it seems as though he has walked straight out of the local pub, and into the changing room. "The atmosphere in the dressing room has changed completely. Everyone is more optimistic, we now smile and make jokes much more. We feel more at ease. It is because Redknapp is a very colourful person, to be honest, we joke that he looks as if he comes to the stadium straight from the pub." Pavlyuchenko insisted that his recent form is down to the manager giving him an identity within a team he never previously looked to have settled into. "Redknapp told me, 'Your position is in the box, you finish attacks, you don't start them'. Now I feel very much part of my new team. Harry is cheerful with me. Each day he asks me how I am, how my English lessons are going." As for the departure of Ramos, Pavlyuchenko regrets the decision the club had to take, but that recent performances can only back up the fact that it was a good one. "I haven't seen or talked to Ramos since he was sacked. It's a pity he had to go, he is not a bad manager but we couldn't get decent results under him. You couldn't recognise how much the team has changed since."

Without a win all season under Ramos, Redknapp transformed the atmosphere, "They're good lads, they've worked hard and trained well since I came here. It's only a start. But it's got us off the bottom of the league, which is good. It's been a tough week but to take seven points is a fantastic return. It's a difficult one to balance the team here. But there are options."

After such an exhilarating start Redknapp warned the fans that he is no "miracle worker" and in no way bears comparison to Bill Nicholson. Redknapp made the best start to a managerial reign at Spurs for 110 years but he laughed off comparisons with Nicholson. "I'm certainly not the best boss in 110 years for Tottenham", said Redknapp. "I couldn't lace Bill Nicholson's boots. There is a long way to go. Of course I'm not a miracle worker. No one is."

He was right. The bubble burst as Spurs crashed at Fulham and Redknapp axed the goalkeeping coach and brought in Tony Parks to help calamity keeper Heurelho Gomes who made yet another error. Parks, whose penalty save in the 1984 UEFA Cup final against Anderlecht enshrined his place in Spurs legend, replaced Austrian Hans Leitert as specialist goalkeeping coach. Redknapp said, "I needed to bring in somebody who knows the English game a bit more. Tony's a terrific personality and everyone at Tottenham remembers him for his UEFA Cup final penalty save. I spoke to Trevor Brooking about him, and he said Parks is highly regarded at the FA, where he's been looking after goalkeepers taking their coaching badges. Tony's a talker, he's enthusiastic about his job and I think he will be a big help to Gomes in terms of rebuilding his confidence. They've worked together for a couple of days this week and already have a good relationship. Tony has been genuinely impressed with him. He's a real character and it's important he is able to project his personality because our goalkeeper is a quiet man, and he needed someone to work with him on the things he's got to do in England. He's been putting him under pressure, getting him used to coming out for crosses with lots of bodies in the way, and he's working on him being more vocal. It's important he's able to relay information to his defenders all the time and he has to be able to boss the game, pulling people into position and talking to them. Communication is so important, as we saw with the mix-up between John Terry and Scott Carson in Germany. The keeper should really have been telling John to stick it into touch. There aren't many talkers left in the game, not even among English players. Where are the players like John Terry and Tony Adams who boss others around on the pitch? Most players now seem to concentrate on their own game and it's a dying art. Maybe it's because there are more foreign players and not everyone speaks the same language, I don't know. We all saw what happened at Fulham last week, but there isn't a keeper in the world who has never made a mistake. Great players like David James and Petr Cech have days where it doesn't go right for them. Hopefully Gomes will show us that whoever was responsible for bringing him here was right to spend

£10m and let Paul Robinson leave. You don't pay that kind of money if he's no good. But he has to learn to trust his centre-halves as they're strong in the air and they can deal with crosses into our box."

Redknapp believes there are similarities between Gomes and David James, whose career he revitalised at Portsmouth, but added, "I'm not going to try to buy Jamo in January. Hopefully Gomes will prove to be the top keeper we need."

Redknapp told the club's annual meeting that they must spend big to challenge the top four. Redknapp, addressing 200 supporters at White Hart Lane, said, "I can't tell lies. We are getting the best out of the squad we have. We need proper players and a proper team who can take us to where we want to go. If we are talking about finishing fifth the squad are well short of that. They're not as good as Aston Villa or the top teams up there."

In a remarkable speech, Redknapp ruled out qualifying for Europe on league position and admitted the priority is still Premier League survival. Yet he is determined to build a team who are the envy of Europe before he eventually retires. He said, "You are never too good to go down, but we want to build a team that everyone can be proud of. We have a group of players who are honest, but there is no magic formula. We try to get people playing in their right positions. It is amazing how many managers don't actually do that. If people don't perform I tell them. There are 13 teams stuck in a relegation battle. All the clubs with 23 points or less are in it. Anyone can have a bad run and slip into it. Everybody is scrapping for their lives and looking over their shoulders. I can't stand here and honestly say we are looking to get into Europe. When I came here it was clear that staying up was our main objective. We have enough to get out of it, but we have to keep looking over our shoulder until we are well clear. We want to build a team that everyone is proud of. Then I can bow out in a few years' time and leave you all with a team in the top four."

Tottenham were 15th following their 0-0 draw against Manchester United, and Redknapp told Levy he needs players and is determined to recruit a central-defender. King is unable to play more than one game a week and Woodgate, who damaged his back again, is also troubled by nagging injuries.

When Redknapp took the job he immediately said with typical cheeky Cockney humour, "I thought it was a wind-up at first", when approached about the job. Not since Terry Venables has Spurs had an English boss with quick witted one-liners, a wickedly cheeky smile and a way with the media.

But *Down Memory Lane* went in search of the real Harry Redknapp, and found him open and remarkably candid in an exclusive interview...

CHAPTER TWENTY-TWO

When Harry Met Harry. An Exclusive Interview.

Associated so intrinsically with West Ham, it was refreshing for Spurs fans to appreciate how much the club are in his blood. As a kid he trained with Spurs, met the club's greatest legend, Bill Nicholson, and rubbed shoulders with the likes of Dave Mackay, John White, Danny Blanchflower and Cliff Jones. Perhaps, he's even half Jewish! Who knows?

But then Harry Redknapp went and spoilt it all when he confessed, "I'm an Arsenal fan!" Oh no, can't be. Well, no need to panic. The good news for Spurs fans is that he truly has a deep and meaningful relationship with the Tottenham traditions.

Of course, there's Hammers in his soul, after all he played for the East London club and managed them too. Arsenal are in his heart, because his dad supported the Gunners and took him to Highbury as a kid but Spurs formed much of the fabric of an impressionable young footballer.

Harry Redknapp is passionate about everything he has done and plans to do in football. And, oh yes, he has the three Lions on his mind as he wants to be England manager.

"My dad was Arsenal mad", recalls Harry as he takes his own trip down memory lane, "and as a mad Arsenal fan he took me along to watch Arsenal, so Arsenal were the team I supported as a kid.

"But when I was 11, and playing for East London Schools, Spurs scout Dickie Walker spotted me playing at the Old Den against Wandsworth

Boys, came over to my dad and said, 'Hello, I'm Dickie Walker the Spurs scout, your son has what it takes.'

"Dickie Walker asked to see my dad for a chat and I ended up the next four years at Spurs training on Tuesdays and Thursdays. Tony Marchi took the kids and Bill Nicholson had time for us boys and that's where I first met him. During the school holidays I would train at Cheshunt where I first came into contact with the likes of Dave Mackay and Danny Blanchflower. I ended up following all their games, especially the European midweek ties which were something special in those days when Spurs played against sides like Gornick and Bobby Smith terrorised opposing goalkeepers the only way Bobby Smith could.

"I ended up at West Ham and people think they are my club and in many ways they are when I played there with Bobby Moore at the age of 15, but now Spurs are 1000 percent my club."

Harry Redknapp nearly took the Newcastle United job, but opted out at the last minute, and has found his way to the Lane, potentially his first really giant club, although everyone appreciates they are one of those Newcastle type of sleeping giants, albeit with the occasional trophy whereas silverware sort of eludes St James' Park.

Spurs also provides Redknapp with a platform that could, finally, elevate him to be a candidate for the England job – providing he makes a big success of turning around Spurs' fortunes. All Spurs fans hope he can do that.

Redknapp was in the frame as England manager when Steve McClaren was sacked. Personally, I never thought he was on the FA's shortlist. My FA contacts assured me that he wasn't. Redknapp is not convinced either, despite the media hype at the time. However, there was a momentum growing in the media, where the Portsmouth boss was hugely popular – just like Terry Venables. Redknapp felt his arrest by the City of London police at that time scuppered any chance he might have had of fulfilling that particular dream.

The City of London police came knocking at Redknapp's door just after 6am on 28th November 2007, fractionally under a year before his appointment as Spurs boss. After fraud officers investigating alleged corruption in football raided his Dorset retreat, the then Portsmouth manager condemned the heavy-handed approach. His wife, Sandra, was described as "absolutely petrified".

At the time Ladbrokes had put Redknapp at 9/2 to succeed McClaren as England manager. The night after the raids, he had slipped to 10/1.

He tells me now, "I didn't really see myself getting that job, anyway. I thought that after what happened to Steve McClaren that the FA would go for a big name foreign manager. It was inevitable. They hired Capello and that was the right choice, everyone can see that he has done a fantastic job."

But perceptions about Redknapp can change. He is convinced that moving to Spurs will help. He explains, "You never know about the England job in the future. For sure I would love to be England manager one day. I am definitely not ruling it out. It depends on if I'm doing a good enough job at Spurs, and I plan to do a good job here.

"There is no doubt that Capello will move on, probably sooner rather than later. I don't see him here for ever. But I am 61 and once my job is done here at Spurs I still think I would have time left to be England manager. If that opportunity should ever arrive – fantastic. It would have meant that I would have taken this club forward."

Redknapp is passionate about the England team and the necessity for an English coach in the Wembley dressing room. "Of course we should have an English England manager. We produce so many great players, and so many great coaches, surely there is somebody out there good enough to do the job from our country? It's crazy to think that at the moment there isn't. It doesn't make sense to me. We definitely have enough capable coaches from which to select an English England manager; for sure we do."

Redknapp confessed to me that he does suffer from an image complex but he feels that Spurs can be the perfect rehabilitation centre.

It seems to be more a question of style over substance. Image over fact. Whispers over hard evidence. Whether it has been *Panorama*, Lord Stevens, the City of London police or the FA, absolutely nothing has been proven and, in this country you're innocent until proven guilty.

Not the easiest question to field; the topic of bad publicity about his image. Yet, Redknapp refused to even shirk the question. He responded, "Yeah, you're right, I do have an image problem but that's because people don't know me.

"They think I'm Jack the lad, but that image couldn't be further from the truth. I have been married 40 years, and Sandra and I just love the quiet life. There is nothing flash about me, even though people think I live in a big house on Sandbanks, but I spend every spare minute of my life with the wife, or walking the dogs on the beach. People think I spend all my life ducking and diving, but that couldn't be further from the truth. I live a very quiet, probably even boring life."

Harry doesn't seem to have any deep lying psychological hang up about being overlooked for the England job, or even that he is wrongly perceived to be something he is sure is not the real him. Maybe he does regret, though, his association with football agent Willie McKay.

Lord Stevens' team of investigators raised concerns about Redknapp's relationship with the ubiquitous football agent, who was involved in five of the deals highlighted in Quest's lengthy inquiry. McKay told the inquiry team that he registered a racehorse in Redknapp's name, and while Lord

Stevens found no evidence that the deal was linked to a specific transfer, he recommended "inquiries into this matter should continue". The Lord Stevens report stated "Harry Redknapp has confirmed that this could well have happened, though it was a very unsuccessful horse that resulted in no material gain or reward for him." Redknapp, an owner of several thoroughbred horses, said McKay's registering of a horse in his name was "purely a PR exercise". He added, "Trainer Dandy Nicholls wanted people from the world of football involved to gain publicity for his yard but I have never even seen the horse run and have never gained a penny out of it or contributed to any training fees." Nicholls supported Redknapp's version of events.

Redknapp tells me, "I don't know why everyone looks at me, I really don't know. Perhaps it is because of my association with Willie McKay. He got me Freddie Kanoute at West Ham and then Paolo Di Canio, and they were terrific players but then everyone thought that I only did deals with Willie McKay, which, of course, is just not true."

Redknapp held a press conference after his release on bail. He said he believed he had only been arrested because he was a "high-profile" figure. However, police strongly denied that they had tipped off the media, and the judges rejected Redknapp's complaints about the circumstances of his arrest and release on bail.

As a specialist investigative journalist, Redknapp and I go way back. I scrutinised the peculiar betting patterns when he returned to Fratton Park from arch rivals Southampton. The FA investigated, but apart from indicting a minor player, nothing much came of it. Redknapp called me once at home for a long chat. He wanted to get it off his chest, he wanted to let me know that he was innocent and felt he was victimised. It was an impassioned 30-minute conversation. I have got to hand it to Redknapp, he was never abusive, he never accused me of victimising him, but he felt that my *Daily Express* column at that time was concentrating far too much on this aspect. Perhaps, he had a point, I told him. I had a meaningful chat with my then sports editor Bill Bradshaw, a seasoned campaigner, who himself was Sports Journalist of the Year at the *Sunday People* for his investigations into Swindon Town. We both felt that my column had made its point. We called a truce. And, again, to be fair to Redknapp, he agreed to appear on my World Cup TV and radio shows during the 2006 tournament in Germany. His appearance was facilitated by his agents Jon and Phil Smith who wisely wanted to end hostilities. Unfortunately, four months later, Redknapp was pictured outside of Soho Square by *The Sun* newspaper where he was being questioned for a sccond time about the betting patterns on him returning to Pompey. Bill Bradshaw called. With Redknapp back in the headlines, my sports editor wanted an update. I rang Redknapp's private mobile line several times, and left several apologetic messages, my point being that I had to break our agreement to no longer mention him in my column because he had suddenly become newsworthy again.

Yet, when he became Spurs manager, by chance, in dealing with Barratt Southern Division, one of the builder's directors Julian Jones, had been in touch with Redknapp. I suggested to Julian that it might be worth mentioning my involvement with Barratt and whether Harry Redknapp might want to renew acquaintances. Could he forgive and forget for one more time? To my astonishment, Harry agreed to take my call. I asked him why? He said, "You know me, I never hold a grudge, life is too short." Harry accepted that I was doing my job, and, in reality, I had never actually accused him of anything. I was reporting the accusations being made by others.

I told him I hoped he would succeed in managing "my club", and asked him if he would cooperate with the *Down Memory Lane* project, which he agreed to do.

While with Harry Redknapp in charge Spurs fans are beginning to feel more optimistic for the future, this book, in the main, looks back with pride at Spurs' glories of the past and I look forward with hope. Hope that very soon my son Simon will see a Spurs team he can be proud of the way I have been in the past. It is with great pride that my Simon has taken on the inheritance of being a Spurs fan. There was a stage, though, that I worried about Simon's judgement. Well, he was only small, and at that time all the kids favoured Liverpool. They were the most dominant team in the country for such a long time. I took him to meet Kenny Dalglish, and Irving Scholar arranged, through his close friends at Anfield, for me to take Simon into the director's box for a match. He loved it. There was little to nothing I could do to change his mind, so I made no effort to persuade him to follow Spurs, a club in the doldrums. But it all changed when Simon grew up. I've no idea why. Perhaps, because his best friend was a Spurs fan. Maybe it was a touch far to go to watch Liverpool. Whatever the reason, he was converted, and I did nothing to convince him; he found his way all on his own.

From Bill Nicholson to Harry Redknapp, I have got to know all the managers, owners, chairmen, and players better than most fans ever could and I feel privileged to have done so.

They are quite a mixed bag – some great, some not so good, and some just no good at all. You probably know who is who as well as I do, but perhaps now you may have a slightly different view on certain individuals.

Spurs fans might not have had it so good in recent years, but there is every reason to feel optimistic.

The plans for a new super stadium are well under way and Harry Redknapp has the backing of the players, media and the fans.

Supporting Spurs has been like a roller-coaster ride. The ups and downs have given me a lifetime of drama. It's been lovely to look back, but I am now looking forward to the good times ahead. Let's hope it's sooner rather than later, and I live long enough to see it!

In my formative years, it was always Liverpool who won the league and Spurs who won the FA Cup. A great cup team, but never able to punch their weight in the league. My greatest wish is to see Spurs win the title for the first time since I started to support them in 1960 and then to make a good fist of trying to lift the European Cup. Dream on you might say, but that's what this game is all about.